COGNITIVE GRIEF THERAPY

A Norton Professional Book

COGNITIVE GRIEF THERAPY

Constructing a Rational Meaning to Life Following Loss

RUTH MALKINSON

W. W. Norton & Company

New York • London

For information about permission to reproduce
selections from this book, write to
Permissions, W. W. Norton & Company, Inc.,
500 Fifth Avenue, New York, NY 10110

Production Manager: Leeann Graham
Manufacturing by Haddon Craftsmen

Library of Congress Cataloging-in-Publication Data

Malkinson, Ruth, 1938-
    Cognitive grief therapy: constructing a rational meaning to
life following loss / Ruth Malkinson. — 1st ed.
        p.; cm.
    "A Norton professional book."
    Includes bibliographical references and index.
    ISBN-13: 978-0-393-70439-6 (hardcover)
    ISBN-10: 0-393-70439-4 (hardcover)
    1. Grief therapy. 2. Cognitive therapy. I. Title.
    [DNLM: 1. Cognitive Therapy—methods. 2. Grief. WM 425.5.C6
M251c 2007]
RC455.4.L67.M35 2007
616.89'14—dc22   2006030935

W. W. Norton & Company, Inc., 500 Fifth Avenue, New York, N.Y. 10110
www.wwnorton.com

W. W. Norton & Company Ltd., Castle House, 75/76 Wells St., London W1T 3QT

1   3   5   7   9   0   8   6   4   2

This book is dedicated to
Dr. Albert Ellis, an inspiring teacher.

Table of Contents

Acknowledgments

Writing a book is a challenge which is compounded when the subject is grief and cognitive grief therapy. Writing is a lonely experience, the success of which depends on the availability of supportive surroundings. I was most fortunate in being surrounded by encouraging people who provided me with the most inspiring support.

Writing this book was a special journey of reading and researching the literature on grief and bereavement and cognitive therapy, while discussing with my colleagues and clients how best to convey the experience of the loss of a loved one and how to describe the process of therapy so that it will make sense to the reader. The challenge is particularly great when trying to balance the general knowledge on grief and bereavement and the fact that it is an idiosyncratic process always occurring within a socio-religious-cultural context. Throughout writing I was aware that as an Israeli, my personal and professional experience might differ from that of my American peers. I asked myself time and again if it is possible to capture the wide range of human experiences regardless of its geographical location. I consulted with my colleagues and my clients who reassured me that although cultural differences do exist, grief is human and universal and knows no boundaries.

There are many people who provided nurturing support. A book about grief therapy involves individuals who have experienced a loss of a loved one and have sought professional help, and without whom writing would not have been possible. In addition to thanking all my clients who trusted me, in particular I would like to thank those clients who gave their permission to share their experience in grief therapy with the readers of this book. Together we searched to find the "secret" of continuing life after such a loss. Although I have disguised their identities so as to respect their privacy, I respect their courage in believing that sharing their stories will benefit others.

My friends provided support in encouraging me to take on the project of writing and in doing so contributed many ideas. Simon Rubin and Eliezer Witztum I mention in particular, as they co-authored two important chapters. I am indebted to each of them and to many other colleagues who added their comments and ideas. In particular, I wish to thank Haim Be'er who determined the source of the final quotation.

While clients provided the major content of this book, I would like to say a special thanks to my husband Mertyn, who assisted me with the task not only by reading the manuscript but also by being patient when my writing kept me away from home. His unconditional support has been a most meaningful resource.

My cousins Rivka and Zvi invited me to stay in their house and write in a very inspiring part of Israel, the town of Arad, situated in the southern part of Israel, in the middle of the desert. Rivka lost her brother Amos during the Six Days War, and almost forty years later, she wrote him a letter which she shared with me. Reading this letter has convinced me once more that a relationship with the deceased loved one never ends, but continues to be transformed throughout one's life.

Throughout the course of writing my children and grandchildren waited patiently for the book's completion so that the family gatherings can be resumed with no restrictions on time. Hopefully, this situation will be corrected soon.

Special thanks to Michael McGandy, my former editor at W. W. Norton, who started it all by inviting me to write a book on cognitive grief therapy. His belief that such a book will be a contribution to professionals inspired me to take on this challenge.

Ruth Malkinson, Rehovot, Israel
November 2006

Introduction

"For everything there is a season and a time for every matter under heaven:
A time to plant and a time to pluck up what is planted
A time to be born and a time to die. . . .
A time to weep and a time to laugh
A time to mourn and a time to dance. . . .
A time for war and a time for peace."—Ecclesiastes 3:1–9

We grieve for a variety of losses throughout our lives, so the death of some-one close reflects an attack on every aspect of our being, because it is our relationships that signify what it means to be human. From birth and throughout our lives, relationships with significant others are being formed and transformed, at times being modified or dissolved. But only with the death of a loved one is the relationship organized by the survivor alone, with the person who died as a silent inner partner. The experience of loss is over-whelming, at times traumatic, and changes us forever. Personal identity, the nature of our interpersonal fabric, and the quality of our relationships undergo change, and transform personal history and memory.

The process of organizing one's relationship with the deceased is com-plex and involves a variety of responses on both the outer and inner levels of functioning. The grief process thus entails reorganizing the bereaved's functioning, behavior, thinking, and feeling in order to find a way of shap-ing the life that has changed, while the painful process of reworking the relationship with the deceased continues. In this book we will view the inner relationship with the deceased as a lifelong process of a continuing bond.

Reworking or reorganizing life without the lost person is a multidimen-sional process that touches upon every aspect of the bereaved's life. The search to discover a meaning for the loss, and for the bereaved's reconstituted life without the deceased, is central to this endeavor. Cognitive construction of a meaning to life without the lost person is a process, the individual course, tempo, and length of which vary in response to the bereaved's per-sonality and social and cultural factors, and equally to the circumstances of the death.

Many of the bereaved find within themselves and in their surroundings the requisite support and resources to reorganize their lives following the death of a loved one. However, there are others who may benefit from professional assistance. Psychotherapy for the bereaved has been linked to theoretical frameworks of grief, its aims and outcome. Approaching grief as a process of adaptation to life without the deceased, which includes both overt and covert components, is central to the cognitive model of grief therapy which is the focus of this book.

The book is organized around three axes: Continuing bonds with the deceased, the Two Track Model of Bereavement (Rubin, 1981, 1999), and grief therapy from the Rational Emotive Behavior Therapy (REBT) cognitive–constructivist perspective. Both empirical and clinical issues will be reviewed to highlight critical cornerstones within the discipline of thanatology; more specifically, the focus is on the concept of continuing bonds with the deceased, the adaptive consequences, and maladaptive ones in the form of complicated grief. Cognitive grief therapy as outlined in this book will follow a framework of continuing bonds with the deceased, to facilitate an adaptive grief process by applying strategies to reconstruct and re-create meaning in life after loss. This psychobiological process will be assessed as occurring on two parallel tracks that emphasize overt and covert manifestations of functioning and the relationship with the deceased. The focus is on assisting the bereaved person in reorganizing his or her life and inner relationship with the deceased using cognitive–constructivist strategies.

There are three parts to the book: Part I (chapters 1–4) addresses the theoretical foundations of cognitive grief therapy; Part II (chapters 5–10) deals with the practice of cognitive grief therapy. Part III (chapter 11) is devoted to the difficulties and challenges encountered by therapists who work with the bereaved, and use a cognitive framework as a resource for potential growth.

The Continuing Bond Perspective

A loss through death is recognized as most painful because of its finality. It is followed by a psychological and physiological process of adaptation to the new reality without the deceased. Numerous variables affect the nature of grief, and influence its intensity and duration: the nature of the relationship, type of death, past experiences with loss, demographic and personality components, availability of a support system, and the sociocultural context within which bereavement is experienced.

Definition of Terms

First, some definitions of terms that occur frequently in the literature: *mourning, grief,* and *bereavement.* Although they are at times used interchangeably, there is now a growing agreement that there are conceptual differences between them. They are used widely in various disciplines to explain the multifaceted consequences of death. Their meanings and implications reflect the many levels of the process (personal, social, and situational) that follow the loss of a loved one.

Death and the grief that follows it is an individual event that takes place within a specific context for which society and religion have developed a set of rules and norms (Malkinson, Rubin, & Witztum, 2000; Stroebe & Stroebe, 1987). In other words, though grief following death is a universal phenomenon, there are diverse ways to define what is normal and complicated within a specific cultural context (Rubin, Malkinson, & Witztum, 2005). A culturally sensitive approach to grief is clearly essential.

The term *mourning,* as it is applied today, refers to a set of practices and acts that are defined in cultural, social, and religious terms. It provides a framework of guidelines for the bereaved and the community to which the bereaved belongs. In Old English, to mourn means to be anxious and careful, but the word has come to mean "to feel sorrow." Anthropologists often understand mourning to be an expressive act or display that is distinct from what a person is feeling (Kauffman, 2001, p. 313). The term *bereavement* is understood to describe an objective situation for an individual who has recently experienced the loss of someone significant through death; this emphasizes the social or external component of the process. This is in contrast to *grief* which represents the internal emotional response to loss (Stroebe & Stroebe, 1987, p. 7).

Although the tendency is to use each term to denote a specific aspect (sociocultural, interrelational, and intrapsychical), as noted above, they are frequently used interchangeably. The term *grief,* more than *bereavement* and *mourning* is most often linked with a therapeutic intervention, commonly referred to as grief counseling and grief therapy. The term *grief* represents the emotional response to loss frequently associated with individuals who experience a loss through death and have sought therapy. The person who has experienced a loss is a *bereaved person,* and the term indicates his or her social position. Here, *grief* will be associated with the emotional response to loss, and *bereavement* will be used to emphasize the objective components of the process.

In describing the phenomenology of grief it is important to take into account the diversity in responses, and their varying intensity among bereaved persons. For these reasons, different models should be regarded as guiding frameworks rather than a predetermined set of stages to explain the phenomenology of normal grief and to understand how the individual reacts to loss through the death of a significant other.

JOHN BOWLBY: ATTACHMENT AND LOSS

The centrality of the relationship with the deceased in bereavement has never been questioned. However, the bereavement process aimed at continuing or severing ties with the deceased has been a key issue in determining its outcome as adaptive or maladaptive. One of the major works that had a great impact on conceptualizing bereavement, its process, and outcome was that of the British child psychiatrist, John Bowlby. The centrality of relationships and the evolution of attachment in children were the foci of Bowlby's work.

It was Freud's conceptualization of normal grief as distinct from clinical depression that inspired other theorists to study further the centrality of attachment toward significant persons in one's life, and the process that follows when loss occurs. Grief, according to these theories, is the experience of detachment from the loved person, and as such is a natural, human, and normal response to a lost relationship. It is a painful experience both mentally and physically, but it is one that the majority of the bereaved find ways to overcome and come to terms with.

Among those researching attachment, it was John Bowlby who most significantly and systematically advanced understanding in the field of loss. Bowlby set forth an attachment theory as a frame of reference for conceptualizing the making and breaking of relationships across the life cycle. According to Bowlby, who derived his ideas from psychoanalysis and ethology, attachment behavior has a survival aspect. He postulated that human beings are born with an innate psychobiological attachment system which is activated as a way to protect them when experiencing threat or when they are under stress. His observations of the hospitalized child's responses to separation from the mother led him to describe a sequence of protest-despair responses. Protest-despair later became the initial phase in his stage model of grief, preceding those of disorganization and reorganization.

In describing the importance of the mother–child bond in the child's development, Bowlby developed a comprehensive theory that emphasized both intrapsychic and interpersonal relationships. He proposed that people have an innate need, which is most apparent at times of danger or stress, to be close to an important attachment figure who provides a secure base and reduces the distress. Bowlby suggested that in the same way that relationships are central to the physical and psychological well-being of an individual, so too is the threat to significant relationships. In childhood, a threat to closeness, such as an actual separation of some duration from a caretaker, is a source of anxiety. This is generally referred to as separation anxiety or separation distress. The individual will try to reduce this by rejoining or getting closer to the attachment figure. Bowlby described differences in how individuals form and retain attachments, which are related to perceived availability of the significant figures. When attachment figures are perceived as available when needed there is a sense of attachment security. On the other hand, when attachment figures are perceived as unavailable and unhelpful, the sense of security is threatened and affects the individual's way of searching for and maintaining relationships with meaningful others. Avoidance and anxiety are attachment-related strategies. Avoidance "reflects the extent to which the person distrusts relationship partners' goodwill and strives to maintain behavioral independence and emotional distance from partners. . . . Attachment-related anxiety, reflects the degree to which a person worries that a partner will not be available in times of need" (Mikulincer & Shaver, in press, p. 3). In its original formulation, the identified attachment styles were related to children in situations of temporary separation from a primary caregiver, and eventually they were expanded to describe different relationships throughout life whenever a potential or actual threat occurred. When the attachment figure disappears there is no longer a secure base, hence the increase of distress, which Bowlby saw as a universal reaction to separation. As people mature, usually the same attachment function is performed by connecting to an inner representation of the significant others. The need for attachment is central (Bowlby, 1969, 1973, 1980, 1988; Rubin, Malkinson, & Witztum, 2000; Stroebe & Stroebe, 1987) and integral to the development and function of an individual throughout life.

The tendency to retain closeness to the significant or attachment figures of childhood remains throughout the life cycle. Attachment primarily functions intrapsychically, with only a small part emerging as interpersonal behavior and interaction (Archer, 1999; Rubin, Malkinson, & Witztum, 2000).

From an attachment perspective, loss through death is an event that shatters attachment resources and necessitates working through the loss while at the same time searching for alternative support. Under such circumstances attachment-related strategies are activated in efforts to regain the lost relationship. There coexists the wish to retrieve the lost person and to be physically close to him or her, and the wish to become close to the mental representations associated with the deceased. A set of responses that include shock, yearning, protest, a search for the lost figure, disorganization and reorganization, are experienced as a way to bring about a physical reunion with the other.

Based on his observations on how children react to separation from a care-giving figure, Bowlby (1980) conceptualized the response as a set of phases which later on were adopted to loss following the death of a close person. Together with Collin Murray Parkes (1970, 1975, 1985), Bowlby conceptual-ized the response to loss as a set of three recognizable phases (Bowlby, 1980), which later included a fourth phase: (1) numbness and disbelief, a phase that characteristically can include outbursts of distress and sometimes anger; (2) yearning and searching for reunion with the deceased and reminders of him or her, often accompanied by anxiety; (3) disorganization and despair expressed in depression and apathy and the collapse of previous ways of being with the self and the other; and (4) a reorganization expressed in the evolution of new ways of dealing with the changed reality, or in other words, recovery.

These phases represent heuristic constructions which reflect aspects of the response to loss. There is a great deal of overlap and fluctuation in how the bereaved responds to loss, and yet the phase theory sets forth important ele-ments of the progressive nature of the adaptive response to loss and how its dis-tribution evolves over time. The importance of recognizing a wide variation among individuals in their response to loss, together with attention to the approximate nature of any stage theory of human behavior, is a necessary parameter for theoreticians and clinicians alike (Rubin, Malkinson, & Witztum, 2000). "The phases are not clear cut, and any one individual may oscillate for a time back and forth between any two of them" (Bowlby, 1980, p. 85).

Only when it becomes clear to the bereaved that there is no way to change the situation, is the loss appreciated. According to Bowlby, a reorgan-ization of life after this great loss is only possible once the loss has been accepted as irreversible. Bowlby (1980) described healthy mourning as the acceptance by the bereaved that a change had occurred in the external world, and that corresponding changes needed to be made in the inner, representational world, and these in turn required reorganization of the attachment behavior. "During the months and years that follow, he [the bereaved] will probably be able to organize life afresh, fortified perhaps by an abiding sense of the lost person's continuing and benevolent presence" (1980, p. 243). The idea of continuing attachment as representing successful adaptation to the loss is described by Bowlby as follows: "For many widows and widowers it is pre-cisely because they are willing for their feelings of attachment to the dead spouse to persist that their sense of identity is preserved and they become able to reorganize their lives along lines they find meaningful" (Bowlby, 1980, p. 98).

In other words, grief is a process of reorganizing the mental schema of the attachment to the deceased that is no longer part of the new reality (Field, Gao, & Paderna, 2005). Reorganization of inner representation of the relationship with the deceased is central to the process of accommodating to life without him or her. We can postulate that Bowlby's conceptualization of maladaptive grief outcome will refer to the bereaved's failure to distinguish between the reality that excludes the deceased and the inner continuing attachments to him or her, and acceptance of the irreversibility of the separation. We will return to this issue when discussing complicated grief.

It is difficult to draw definitive conclusions as to whether or not Bowlby, like Freud, advocated the detachment idea or that of continuing bonds, but it is not surprising that his ideas continue to inspire attachment theorists, and more recently, bereavement theorists as well. Clearly, Bowlby saw grief as a sequential process of the individual response to the realization of a lost attachment, and a process of reorganizing its inner representations, probably in line with what was accepted in his day as being preceded by detachment; perhaps the particular derivation of a term is also related to the zeitgeist.

In contrast to the idea of continuing bonds as it is practiced today, bereavement as a process of detachment from the deceased was dominant for many years as related to Freud's conceptualization of normal grief as distinct from clinical depression.

The Abandonment of Relationship Perspective: A Historical Review

The works of Sigmund Freud, Eric Lindemann, and John Bowlby have provided us with the underlying patterns for how the discipline has evolved its current thinking on loss and bereavement.

Sigmund Freud: Loss and Abandoning the Bonds

The foundation in modern psychology as to what constitutes normal and complicated grief was set by Freud in his seminal paper, "Mourning and Melancholia" (1917/1957). When Freud distinguished between *grief* and *depression*, it was the beginning of the clinical literature of modern psychology on loss. He did so in order to learn about clinical depression, which interested him most, rather than to understand grief. As an observer of the human condition, Freud focused attention on the profound mourning that arises from the loss of a beloved person, bringing with it feelings of painful depression, a loss of interest in the outside world, a loss of the ability to love, and a turning away from all that does not recall the deceased. Bereaved persons are totally immersed in mourning their loss. Freud made the assumption that more important than a mere description of the clinical condition was the indication that this process had a clearly defined goal, namely, to allow the bereaved to abandon his or her commitment to the relationship with the deceased. The psychological processes of grief and mourning were presented as part of the healing process following loss, a process that Freud called "the work of mourning." In accomplishing this goal, the bereaved would complete the mourning process and be free to invest anew in relationships with others. Melancholia, as Freud suggested, was a deviation from the normal course of grief, and was the result of ambivalence toward the deceased, accompanied by feelings of guilt and reduced self-esteem.

According to Freud, the recognition of the finality of the relationship with the deceased, combined with the fact that the deceased could no longer function as a source of concrete satisfaction, would eventually have an impact. Moreover, successful completion of the process would free the bereaved from bonds with the deceased and signify a letting go of the relationship. At its completion, the bereaved would reinvest the emotional energy in new relationships (Malkinson, Rubin, & Witztum, 2000; Rubin, 2000). The distinction between normal grief and clinical depression, according to Freud, was the absence of guilt feelings in normal grief.

Much has been learned since the article's publication in 1917, but there is an enduring validity to the idea that depression as a response to the experiences surrounding loss can have major health implications on later functioning (Rubin, Malkinson, & Witztum, 2000; Schafer, 1992; Spence, 1982). From a more theoretical perspective, what we have learned from Freud is that grief is a universal human response to a significant loss and an absolutely normal response and working through is understood to occur within the bereaved person where recognition and acceptance of the finality of loss constitute the primary goal of the loss process.

COMPROMISING IMPLICATIONS TO FREUD'S VIEW
Freud's contribution to the study of loss is unquestionably important, yet the extent of his influence was such that it also had compromising implications for the theory and practice that form the treatment of normal and pathological grief. Because the goal of the grief process is, according to Freud, to free the bereaved from emotional bonds with the deceased, and to fully accept

the irreversibility of the loss, the absence of detachment led some theorists to consider the continuing involvement with loss as a maladaptive response (Rubin, Malkinson, & Witztum, 2000). The medical model of viewing the progression of overcoming an illness as a linear course from the moment when symptoms are diagnosed, to the point when recovery is complete, was to inspire Freud's concept of decathexis. The bereaved was anticipated to follow through a process of identifiable phases so that healing could be achieved. Any deviation, such as prolonged intensity of grief that was extended beyond what was then considered as a normal period of mourning, blocked healing and was regarded as pathological. An ambivalent relationship with the deceased was considered as a criterion that predicted a maladaptive outcome.

Interestingly, Freud's own personal life suggests the limitations of his conceptualization of grief. He experienced several losses that affected him profoundly, although we know relatively little about his own grief work. For example, Freud described the death of his father in 1896 as the most single significant event in his life, one that led to continuous self-analysis in order to understand his response to the death. Freud's personal letters following the death of his daughter Sophie depict the changes shortly after her death and years later as portraying his personal feelings of substantial grief, which stand in contrast to his theoretical conceptualization. The ideas expressed in his letters about the purpose and outcome of grief work include a much wider view than that described in "Mourning and Melancholia." As a psychoanalyst, Freud saw the function of grief as a process aimed at freeing the bereaved from attachments to the deceased. His personal encounters with loss, however, suggest that he refrained from completing the painful process of grief. The following is a letter he wrote soon after the death of his daughter Sophie in 1920:

> Since I am profoundly irreligious there is no one I can accuse, and I know there is nowhere to which any complaint can be addressed. "The varying circle of a soldier's duties" and the "sweet habit of existence" will see to it that things go on as before. Quite deep down I can trace the feeling of a deep narcissistic hurt that is not to be healed. My wife and Annerl are terribly shaken in a more human way. (quoted in Jones, 1957, p. 20)

Freud understood the continuous attachment of the bereaved to memories of the deceased as a natural and even desirable feature that existed along with and even after the mourning process. This attitude is sensitively expressed in his letter to Binswanger soon after the latter's child had died:

April 12, 1929

My daughter who died would have been thirty-six years old today. . . .
Although we know that after such a loss the acute state of mourning will
subside, we also know we shall remain inconsolable and will never find a
substitute. No matter what may fill the gap, even if it be filled completely,
it nevertheless remains something else. And actually this is how it should
be. It is the only way of perpetuating that love which we do not want to
relinquish.(Freud, 1929/1961, p. 386)

In contrast to his theoretical conceptualization of the function of grief as a
process of undoing the relationship with the deceased, in Freud's letters we
can trace the idea of their continuation as a desirable outcome.

Lindemann: The Symptomatology of Grief

Freud's view of grief following loss as a process leading to withdrawal from
investing emotional energy in the now-deceased person, and redirecting
that energy to other love objects, was the basis for other works that followed. Eric Lindemann, a prominent therapist in the Freudian tradition,
identified some common features and components characteristic of the normal course of grief. Lindemann described one of the most prominent features of the grieving process as the initial reaction to loss, or as he referred to
it, "acute grief." A German psychiatrist who emigrated to the United States,
Lindemann was probably best known for his empirical study of grief and
the course of both normal and pathological processes. Lindemann sub-
scribed to the psychodynamic understanding that for grief to be resolved
grief work is essential.

This grief work has to do with the effort of reliving and working through
in small quantities events which involved the now-deceased person and the
survivor. Grief work is focused on internal struggles occurring deep within
the psyche. Like Freud, Lindemann saw grief as a process aimed at "emanci-
pation from the bondage to the deceased" (1979, p. 234). His classic article,
"Symptomatology and Management of Acute Grief" (1944), the result of
work with many individuals who suffered the loss through death of a loved
one, addressed the symptoms accompanying acute grief and proposed clinical intervention following loss. He described the experiences and
responses of a group of 101 bereaved individuals (many of whom were traumatically bereaved in the Boston Coconut Grove fire) to provide a more
concrete account of grief. Based on his observations, diagnosis, and clinical

experience, Lindemann described a syndrome of responses that accompany the initial response to loss.

There were serious methodological limitations to this study, such as a heterogeneous sample of individuals suffering from different types of losses. But because he worked with a relatively large group of people who had experienced a variety of losses, and because he based his work on empirical phenomena, the study is both accessible to and utilized by a range of disciplines and theoretical approaches. Lindemann's description of the normative response to loss, especially the stage he called *acute grief*, is most detailed when referring to interpersonal, somatic difficulties, preoccupation with the deceased, and following the death, a general loss of functioning in the areas that characterized the individual (Rubin, Malkinson, & Witztum, 2000). Among some of the bereaved in his study, Lindemann observed that these responses were extreme and overwhelming. Lindemann saw grief as an active process carried out by the bereaved alone, each of whom was involved in the isolated "work" of grief. This included the need to become liberated from an overly strong link to the deceased, new adaptation to the environment surrounding the bereaved, and the establishment of new interpersonal relationships. Morbid grief was the result of failing to do the grief work necessary in order to detach from the deceased. Lindemann observed other types of difficulties in postloss adjustment that arose from difficulties among bereaved persons who had problems in experiencing the pain involved in the process. Lindemann referred to what these people underwent as symptoms of "distorted" grief.

Despite criticism of his empirical study, Lindemann's contribution to the field is important. In addition to describing the syndrome of grief he also developed an understanding that a short-term intervention of 8 to 10 sessions was sufficient to address the client's needs in the acute grief period. The acute grief period itself was defined as lasting from four to six weeks. This temporal definition is in line with the periodization of the grief process presented by what became known as *crisis theory* (Malkinson, Rubin, & Witztum, 2000; Parad, 1966; Rubin, 2000). Crisis theory, as postulated by Lindemann (1944) and Caplan (1964), assumed that a breakdown in human functioning is not necessarily a disease to be medically treated but a temporary state whereby the individual's coping capacities are insufficient or inadequate, resulting in a psychological disequilibrium. According to crisis theory, regaining equilibrium did not always require professional help. The concept was further developed to include crisis interventions provided by professionals as well as laypeople whose support and empathy were central in overcoming the crisis

(Malkinson, 1987; Silverman, 2004). The idea of the availability of a helping hand was central in crisis intervention.

The Application of Decathexis in Contemporary Models

The decathexis framework created an expectation that the bereaved should move through and experience each stage. A failure to "let go" of the deceased was viewed as an obstacle to positive outcomes of the grief process. Those models derived their concepts from Freud's work, and although in years to come they were not empirically supported (Neimeyer & Hogan, 2001; Wortman & Silver, 1989, 1993) their principles remained as the foundation for most theories and practices of bereavement and grief. An example of a model that was based on viewing bereavement as a process toward breaking the bonds with the deceased is that of Kübler-Ross, which was very popular during the 1970s and 1980s.

C. M. Sanders: The Grief Process as Multifaceted Phases

Catherine M. Sanders was a psychologist, herself a bereaved mother, whose experiences with the loss of her son, son-in-law, her mother, and her husband, increased her interest in studying psychology and specializing in grief. She developed (Sanders, Mauger, & Strong (1985/1991), the Grief Experience Inventory consisting of 135 true or false items covering feelings, symptoms, and behaviors as an attempt to assess empirically the complexity of the grief experience and provide a standardized measure to evaluate the grief process more objectively. Based on her extended Tampa Research Project, Sanders (1980, 1989, 1993) delineated five distinct phases which individuals pass through in the bereavement process. The phases are: shock, awareness of loss, conservation withdrawal, healing, and renewal. The symptoms that accompany each phase are psychological, physical, and social in nature. Aware of the limitations of a phase model, and the fact that there is an overlap among the phases, Sanders emphasized that the model should be viewed as a guideline and not as a necessary or linear sequence. Not all people go through these phases in a linear progression, nor do all bereaved people experience all the symptoms. Also, the length of time required to grieve varies from one individual to another.

Sanders's contribution was her detailed and sensitive description of each component within each phase. This descriptive power possibly reflected her own experience of loss. By normalizing the various forms of experiences in moving among and within the phases, she stressed the diversity of reactions among bereaved persons without necessarily evaluating outcomes as maladaptive. In her model Sanders had begun to shift away from the linear progression of the grief process so popular throughout the 20th century, but she nevertheless remained within that framework.

J. W. Worden: The Model of Tasks of Grief

J. W. Worden's model of grief in his book, *Grief Counseling and Grief Therapy* (1982, 1991, 2003) as a four-task process, has undergone remarkable adaptations throughout the years. These adaptations parallel the changes that have taken place in the field of bereavement in conceptualizing its process and outcomes. In his original conception of the model, Worden (1982, 1991, 2003) viewed grief as a process to be completed in order for the bereaved person to be considered normal. The four tasks, which were listed derived from Freud's idea of seeing grief as a process leading to the abandonment of a relationship with the deceased and included accepting the reality of the loss, working through pain and grief, adjusting to an environment that excluded the deceased, and fourth, "to emotionally relocate the deceased and move on with life" (1991, p. 18). The expectation that one might accomplish the tasks of grief, leading to an abandonment of the relationship with the deceased, shifted in the revised edition (1982/2003) to a process aimed at adapting to the loss in one's life by continuing the bonds with the deceased. Worden (1982/2003) explained the rationale for the shift:

> I suggest that the fourth task of mourning is to find a place for the deceased that will enable the mourner to be connected with the deceased but in a way that will not preclude him or her from going on with life. We need to find ways to memorialize, that is to remember, the dead loved ones, keeping them with us but still going on with life. (p. 35)

Worden's adaptations of his tasks model provided a summation of the changes and development throughout the years in approaching the process and outcome of bereavement, and signified a conceptual shift from breaking bonds to continuing bonds with the deceased.

Bereavement as a Multifaceted Process

As noted, the field of grief and bereavement has undergone a transformation in how the grief process is viewed, its aims and outcomes, from abandoning bonds with the beloved person to continuing those bonds.

Assessing and evaluating the earlier models discussed above, challenged the linear sequential stage progression. Furthermore, accumulated empirical data (Neimeyer & Hogan, 2001) found no support for Freud's ideas of grief work as a process with preset stages leading to the breaking of the bonds with the deceased.

It became obvious that it is not the orderly, sequential, stage-based course that determines the level of adaptation, but rather the intensity of the responses and the oscillation taking place between them along the phases (Kleber & Brom, 1992) or a process resembling a spiral (Landau, 1987) within which emotions move in a more circular form.

Wortman and Silver (1989) presented a comprehensive review of research studies that questioned the validity of the traditional stage models which had been applied by most theorists and clinicians at that point. Their review became a landmark when they proposed that bereavement and its outcome be revised and reformulated. Their findings led to the following conclusions: (1) There is variability among individuals in the response and adaptation to loss; this is contrary to the expectation that the bereaved progress in an orderly manner from one stage (or phase) to another, leading toward letting go of the now deceased person. (2) While some bereaved people experienced intense distress immediately following the loss, others did not. (3) Some individuals did not respond negatively to the loss, but expressed positive emotions. (4) Bereaved individuals varied in the way they attached meaning to the loss and their lives following it. (5) Grief is an idiosyncratic process of assimilating the loss event into one's life (Wortman & Silver, 1989,1993).

Wortman and Silver also challenged what had come to be known as the grief work hypothesis. Specifically, they looked at a number of assumptions considered to be crucial for working through the grief process; the assumption that depression is a necessary experience for completing the grief process and that its absence indicates pathological grief; the belief that "time heals," and, most importantly, the assumption that grief work is essential for recovery. More studies that included nonclinical bereaved populations were carried out (Bonanno, 2004; Bonanno, Wortman, et al., 2002; Rubin, 1999; Stroebe & Stroebe, 1987). These studies revealed that individual responses fall within a much wider range of what is regarded as normal grief. As a result, many of the studies concluded that, in important respects, normal or complicated grief is also culturally defined.

Integrated Models of Bereavement

Studies carried out by Bonanno (2000) and Bonanno, Wortman, et al. (2002) point to some aspects that affect treatment and research trends:

1. Not everyone has to experience grief work.
2. There is no indication that complications or pathology necessarily affect those not undergoing grief work. On the contrary, when compared with mourners who had done grief work and experienced deep depression, there were others who coped better following bereavement. In contrast, the group suffering from deep depression at the outset of mourning was more likely to have complicated grieving experiences.
3. In the high risk group, into which between 10 and 20% of mourners fall, according to reports (Bonanno, Wortman, et al., 2002; Bonanno, Wortman & Nesse, 2004), it seemed that most of them have a combination of factors (e.g., the cause and circumstances of the death, closeness to the deceased, availability of support, personality and social-demographic factors) which affect the assumptive world and predict the outcome of the process. Under- or overreaction to the response in itself does not determine the outcome of the process. The appraisal given by the mourner in rating the event is what determines and molds the process and its outcome.

As data have accumulated, a combination of several theoretical approaches was proposed by a number of researchers in the field of bereavement (Rubin, 1981, 1999; Stroebe & Schut, 1999). The most salient was the combination of stress models and attachment models that provide an integrated model of bereavement. In these integrated models the relationship component is central, along with an emphasis on cognitive processes of accommodating to the loss: Grief is a process of searching for the lost attachment figure (Bowlby, 1980), which eventually leads to the realization that the lost person cannot return.

The Social-Functional Perspective of Bereavement: Bonanno and Kaltman

Bonanno and Kaltman (2001) proposed an integrative perspective that provided researchers and clinicians with better operationally defined hypotheses to be investigated and empirically challenged, or supporting the validity and exclusivity of the grief work perspective (Stroebe & Stroebe, 1987; Wortman & Silver, 1989). In this integrative framework they laid out a number of theoretical perspectives as alternatives: Cognitive stress, attachment, trauma, and a social-functional approach to emotions. All are combined to offer a more systematic framework to examine bereavement and the many patterns it may take. In addition, four aspects of the grief process are discussed: The context of the loss (circumstances, sudden-ness of the loss, gender, age, and social support); the continuum of subjective meaning attributed to the loss (appraisal and reappraisal of a stressful event such as loss); the changing representation of the lost relationship (the continuum that runs from relinquishing bonds to continuing bonds with the deceased); and coping strategies and emotional regulation processes in adapting to the loss. These per-spectives, combined with various aspects of the grief process, have provided a wider spectrum for the study of bereavement. For example, in one such study of conjugal loss, reported by Bonanno and colleagues (2002), five core bereavement patterns were identified: common grief, chronic grief, chronic depression, improvement during bereavement, and resilience. Based on the results obtained in a series of studies, Bonanno, Wortman and others (2002) applied the social-func-tional perspective to grief and emotions and proposed a shift from a hypothesis that emphasizes the necessity of expression of negative emotions as an indication of recovery following a loss through death, to one that emphasizes recovery when grief-related distress is minimized and positive emotions are activated or facilitated (Bonanno, 2001, p. 493). The importance of these results is that they emphasize variability among bereaved persons in how they appraise adverse events, such as the loss of a spouse, and move away from viewing grief as "a one size fits all suits" as cautioned by Neimeyer (1999), by placing cognitive aspects and meaning con-struction as central elements in the process.

The Dual Process Model of Bereavement (DPM)

The idea that grief is at times confronted and at times avoided is basic to the Dual Process Model of Bereavement (DPM) developed by Stroebe and Schut (1999, 2001), two researchers from a group studying bereavement, its process and outcome.

The dual process model views bereavement as a combination of two orien-tations: loss and restoration. The loss-orientation refers to the processing of the loss experience itself (grief work, breaking the bonds/ties, denial, or avoidance of restoration changes); the restoration-orientation refers to sec-ondary sources of stress (attending to life changes, doing new things, distrac-tion from grief, new roles and identities). As the name of the model implies, bereavement is seen as a process that entails broad types of stressors, which can be classified into those focusing on the loss itself, and those focusing on stressors related to organizing life after the loss. "Loss-orientation," according to

Stroebe and Schut (2001), is consistent with attachment theory in that it focuses on the lost relationship and the grief that is involved in working through the loss. Cognitive stress theory is relevant to restoration-orientation because it refers to the stressors involved in working through life without the deceased. There are times when the bereaved person is distracted or forgets the loss, while at other times he or she can be immersed in it. Loss-orientation involves confrontation and emotional reactions to the loss even with some resistance to change, and restoration orientation focuses on coping with the changes in daily life, the search for new roles, learning, and adaptation. Integrating attachment and stress theories suggests that coping is a dynamic process of oscillation between the two orientations:

> At times the bereaved will confront aspects of loss, at other times avoid them, and the same applies to the tasks of restoration. Sometimes, too, there will be "time out" when grief is left alone . . . DPM postulates that oscillation between the two types of stressors is necessary for adaptive coping. (p. 395)

Oscillation is presented as a multidimensional process between loss and restoration-orientations, as well as oscillation between positive and negative reappraisal of each orientation as an important part of coping and coming to terms with the loss. The model presents an integrated perspective of cognitive-affective processes as dynamic, and provides a framework for evaluation of various components within each orientation as they change over time. Although not explicitly specified from the DPM perspective, adaptive coping is gained by weakening the ties with the deceased and reinvesting in new roles and relationships.

The Two-Track Model of Bereavement

The Two-Track Model of Bereavement (TTMoB); (Rubin, 1981, 1999), views intrapersonal and interpersonal aspects of loss as part of the process. The model combines stress and attachment theories somewhat differently from the DPM proposed by Stroebe and Schut (2001). According to the TTMoB, the process of grief comprises two parallel tracks; that of functioning and that of the relationship with the deceased (see chapter 1).

Common to these models is their view of the bereavement process as one that includes coping with the stress evoked by the death event on the one hand, and ongoing relationships with the deceased on the other (Rubin, 1993; Stroebe & Schut, 1999); they emphasize that there is no single predictable pathway through grief and regard it as an idiosyncratic process (Neimeyer, 1999, 2005a).

Conclusion

A number of conclusions can be drawn from studies on accommodation to loss through death:

1. The idea of accommodation to loss through death as a time-limited process, which involves a set of sequential linear phases toward reorganization of one's life without the deceased, have given way to the "continuing bonds" view that sees the loss as a lifelong developmental process. In that sense, Bowlby's work has remained significant in that it has viewed grief following death as an experience of separation from an attachment figure and a process of reorganizing life without the deceased, while maintaining his or her internal representation.

2. The bereavement that follows the death event is a multifaceted process, and so are the ways to explain and understand it. The integrative perspective has combined stress theories of appraisal of the event, attachment theory focusing on attachment styles, and an understanding of the impact of the traumatic circumstances of the death.

   According to these integrated approaches, grief is viewed as a process of constructing a meaning to life following loss through death, an event that changes one's life forever. The loss event is devastating and the process of grief that follows is a multidimensional one that involves both psychological and physiological reactions. Additionally, the integrated models postulate that it is a process which has no "ending point," and the relationship with the deceased continues throughout the bereaved's life.

3. Integrated models such as the DPM of bereavement and the TTMoB view bereavement as a double-axis process accounting for the multiplicity of factors. The interaction and the oscillation between them allows us to evaluate the degree of adjustment along the time axis.

4. The inclusion in studies of nonclinical populations of different groups of bereaved (e.g., widows, widowers, parents) resulted in the recognition of the great variability among the bereaved in their patterns of adaptation to the death event, which resulted in a reevaluation of the adaptive and maladaptive outcomes.

One final remark about the value of the phase model, which, although not empirically validated, has not lost its value from a developmental perspective: changes in occurrence and intensity of symptoms are important markers in evaluating the course and direction of the process of adaptation to life without the deceased.

To sum up, although many of Freud's ideas have remained, the idea of abandoning the relationship with the deceased has been challenged (Klass, Silverman, & Nickman, 1996), and instead it has been suggested that bereavement involves reorganizing one's life and worldview without the deceased, but with bonds remaining intact and unbroken. Also, grief is viewed as a dynamic process throughout the bereaved's life where each phase introduces another opportunity to examine and reevaluate the bonds with the deceased blended with life tasks specific to the stage of life of the individual.

In Table I.1 we compare and summarize the abandoning and continuing bonds perspectives discussed above.

TABLE I.1
Abandoning Bonds and Continuing Bonds: A Comparison

ABANDONING BONDS	CONTINUING BONDS
Provides a framework for understanding the phenomenology of grief and its course (stages, phases).	The phenomenology of grief is understood to be subjective and idiosyncratic incorporating the "objective" framework as a guideline
Describes the individual's emotional experience (anger, depression, guilt, shame, ambivalent feelings).	Views grief as a negative, painful experience with a distinction between functional negative (sadness) and dysfunctional negative reactions (depression)
Prescribes the individual grief experience and defines its expected outcomes of relinquishing bonds with the deceased: grief work, letting go, resolution (normal vs. pathological)	Views grief as a continuous, never ending process of meaning construction regarding the loss and life without the deceased
Views grief as a psychobiological process with a focus on observed overt behaviors as indicators of grief outcomes (somatic and functioning)	Views grief as a psychobiological process wherein the cognitive component is central to reorganizing one's shattered assumptions (scheme) about self, others, and the world
Adopts a medical orientation (i.e., grief is an illness) with its sequential stages, and views grief as mostly an intrapersonal process	Existential, phenomenological models. Grief is an interpersonal process viewed within its sociocultural context.

Part I

The Theoretical Foundations
of Cognitive Grief Therapy

Chapter 1

The Two-Track Model of Bereavement: A Balanced Model

Coauthored with Simon S. Rubin, Ph.D.

The Development of the Two-Track Model of Bereavement

The two track model was first reported in 1981, when Simon Shimshon Rubin described the effects on young mothers living in the Chicago area of a sudden and unexpected child loss. The study was an in-depth assessment of 30 mothers who had lost an infant through sudden infant death syndrome (SIDS). Half of the bereaved mothers had experienced the loss seven months earlier on average, and the other half had lost their child 4.5 years earlier. These groups were compared to a control group of 15 mothers who had not lost a child or a spouse. The study was based on the hypothesis that a sudden and unexpected loss would "leave a notable and permanent residue in its wake" for young mothers (Rubin 1999, p. 687). On applying measures of general functioning, (i.e., what would become Track I), this was shown to have deteriorated markedly among the recently bereaved mothers, but not among non-recently bereaved mothers, nor among mothers who had not lost a child. There were no significant differences, however, between the bereaved groups (recent and nonrecent) as measured by a pronounced ongoing preoccupation

---

The Two-Track Model of Bereavement (1981, 1999), was developed by Simon Shimshon Rubin, an American-Israeli researcher, with the objective of capturing more fully the experience of the response to interpersonal loss. His approach is well-suited for viewing the response to loss as a multidimensional process that may persist across the life cycle.

with the deceased (i.e., what would become Track II), despite the passage of time. These findings lent support to the notion of ongoing involvement with the deceased and a persistent impact of loss on personality. In its conception and execution, this research relied on an integration of two disparate bodies of literature that led to a new conceptual approach to the assessment and understanding of loss.

In the two-track model of bereavement (TTMoB), the union of the two approaches forms the basis for the overarching schema. On the one hand, the model derived some of its ideas from a psychodynamic/relational perspective. From this perspective, loss and grief constitute a process involving "mourning" and aspects of separation from the deceased. This meant that the focus and rearrangement of the psychological involvement with the deceased (diluting, as it were, the intensity of the ties with the deceased) were central to the process. Some of the follow-up on the response to loss reflected the intensity of the mourning process. For example, the bereaved's intense focus on the internal psychological experience of grief and accepting the reality of death did not necessarily leave sufficient emotional energy to devote to many of life's other requirements or opportunities. Viewed from this vantage point, depression was potentially a mixture of sadness regarding the person who was lost, the psychological concentration on the work of mourning, and a lack of energy for other investments in life. As long as the individual was intensively engaged in psychological mourning (and particularly when the process went awry and the bereaved was "stuck" in this mode), one could conclude that there were ongoing difficulties in separation from the deceased. Hence, those who were mourning actively were characterized by difficulties in returning to earlier pre-loss levels of functioning, and this element continued to characterize others who were unable to "conclude" the mourning progress satisfactorily.

Moreover, the TTMoB also integrated a second conceptual–empirical approach based on literature relating to the response to stress and trauma. These perspectives viewed the response to, and later the outcome of, interpersonal bereavement as products of the biological–cognitive–emotional processes that occur when individuals respond to stress and trauma. These data were minimally concerned with the centrality of the emotional bonds linking the deceased to the bereaved. In their place, the manner, significance, and magnitude of coping with the change process were central. Evaluations of the changes in functioning following the loss were measured, as were changes in function following any number of stressful life events. Hence, the symptomatic responses, as well as the degree of involvement with the bereaved in various life activities, were considered as valid measures of "recovery" from the loss process (Rubin, 1999).

In their initial formulation, Rubin's ideas were congruent with an approach that saw the purpose of the grief process as leading to the weakening of ties with the deceased. Failure to rearrange the ties resulted in the bereaved's ongoing focus on the intense thoughts, memories, and feelings about the deceased being conceptualized as negative outcomes. By the same token, however, behavioral and psychological difficulties following loss that were not resolved were also conceptualized as problematic outcomes. Thus Rubin argued for a bifocal approach to the assessment of response to and outcome of loss. He advocated placing the ongoing relationship of the psychological memories and experiences vis-à-vis the deceased as a central axis in understanding and assessing loss. These were seen to exist alongside the axis concerned with evaluation of biopsychosocial well-being. In a paper titled, "Mourning Distinct from Melancholia," the examination of the relationship (mourning) from dysfunction (melancholia) was considered separately (1984a). This was in contrast to Freud's work (1917/1957) in which the two themes are treated as interdependent. Other studies that focus on the significance of the relationship in conceptualizing, assessing, and intervening in bereavement have further developed these themes (e.g., Rubin, 1985).

Together with the conceptual developments and theoretical papers, Rubin set out to test these ideas in a second round of research studies. The specific focus on the functional and relational tracks was sharpened. The researchers worked with bereaved parents (who epitomized the notion of a continuing relationship with the deceased), and with a model employing groups that were subdivided according to the time that had elapsed since the loss. A series of studies were published on parents who had lost young adult sons in combat during Israeli military service. It was possible to examine questions relating to parental role and gender, age both of the deceased and the bereaved, the time that had elapsed since the death, the expression of features unique to the individual, and the special nature of the bereavement circumstances. In one such study (1986), cohorts of bereaved parents from the 1973 Yom Kippur war and the 1982 Lebanese war were recruited for participation. A control group of nonbereaved parents was included. A broad battery of objective, narrative, and semistructured interviewing measures were utilized.

The results revealed significant differences on some of the functional indices (Track I) and sharply distinguished between bereaved and nonbereaved parents (Rubin, 1992). A marked trend in the differences between bereaved and nonbereaved parents was also found based on measurements of relationship (Track II). As a group, bereaved parents described their relationship with the deceased son with a greater degree of interpersonal closeness when compared with nonbereaved parents who described their living sons with greater distance, conflict, and separation. A comparison of the cohorts of bereaved parents found pronounced differences for bereaved fathers (but not mothers) using measurements of functioning (Track I). No differences were found using measurements assessing the relationship to the deceased (Track II).

Thus in a second cultural setting, when examining both parents regarding a different type of parental loss, the dramatic and salient nature of the ongoing relationship to the deceased was pronounced. Direct contact with the population of bereaved parents yielded an unequivocal impression that the relationship to the deceased was not only ongoing and involved strong elements of psychological attention, but was also normative. These findings were congruent with emerging work that advocated continuing bonds with the deceased as an adaptive rather than a maladaptive outcome. Perhaps not surprisingly, a number of these investigators were studying loss involving parent–child relationships. Silverman was studying children who had lost parents, Klass was following parents who had lost children, and Nickman was working with adopted individuals preoccupied with a search for their lost parents (Klass, Silverman, & Nickman, 1996). These studies of loss within the parent–child relationship portrayed a group having unique grief responses and were valuable in themselves. Even more important, they provided an opportunity to compare various groups of bereaved and types of losses. As noted earlier, for many decades, widows and widowers were the most frequently studied group on which observations were made and recommendations offered (e.g., Lund, 1989; Lund, Castera & Dimond, 1993; Moss, Moss, & Hanssow, 2001; Stroebe & Stroebe, 1987). Saunder's (1989) study was among the first to compare the mourning process among different groups of bereaved, alongside studies that focused on the parent–child relationship (such as those carried out by Klass et al., 1996; Rubin, 1981, 1984a). The ongoing relationship with the deceased child was a central recurrent theme.

Based on the theoretical and research data, Rubin (1996) pointed to the paradox of the assessment of the process of mourning: On the one hand, the relationship to the deceased was considered central to initiating the process of adapting to the loss, which sought to facilitate the reorganization of the relationship to the deceased. On the other hand, the field applied the general functional yardstick and measures of behavioral, emotional, and psychiatric symptoms to evaluate successful or problematic outcomes in terms of the ability or inability to return to the preloss functioning levels that were regarded as a measure of adaptation. Rubin (1984) noted:

"Does the absence of psychopathological symptomatology mean that mourning has been successfully worked through? If the survivor has been able to return and fill a productive role in society, has the loss been resolved? When protest, searching, despair and reorganization have been traversed (Bowlby, 1980), is mourning finally complete? The prevalent premise that mourning is incomplete in the presence of psychopathological reactions is characteristic of an emphasis on overt behavior and affect in the assessment of reaction to loss (Freud, 1917/1957; Lindemann, 1944; Bowlby, 1980, p. 339).

Ultimately, external markers are equated with internal psychological processes. As an alternative, Rubin (1996) has consistently proposed a multidimensional view of bereavement, its process, and outcomes that balances sensitivity to covert and overt processes. This approach places the issues that initiate the experience of loss; that is, the challenge to the relationship with another, as the heart of conceptualizing what adjustment to bereavement is ultimately all about.

The Lay and Professional Views of the Bereavement Process

In order to clarify the degree to which the two-track model of bereavement's underlying premises were reflected in lay and professional thinking, a series of studies were conducted by Rubin's group at the University of Haifa. The aim was to measure the degree to which people are attentive to issues arising out of problems in the bereaved's functioning or in his or her ongoing relationship to the deceased. On the basis of the research conducted to date, some support emerged for the conceptual distinctions advanced by the model, as well as evidence that the two tracks are approached differently by many people. As we shall see, when it comes to identifying problems following loss, the impact of difficulties in functioning (Track I) are considered much more significant than problems in the ongoing relationship to the deceased (Track II). Whether assessing the degree of psychological difficulties, suffering, or the need for psychological intervention, what the bereaved is able to *do* outweighs what he or she *thinks* and *feels*. The deemphasizing of the relationship to the deceased runs counter to research findings that demonstrate a significant link between relationship to the deceased and bereavement outcome assessed on measures of functioning. What can be confirmed is that the studies gave support to the outlines of the two-track model of bereavement by showing that participants tended to evaluate issues of general functioning differently from how they evaluated the nature of the ongoing relationship to the deceased's memory. Although both were seen as relevant to loss, there was clearly an uneven weighting of the two tracks when it came to determining the significance of problems along each track.

Lay Views of the Bereavement Process

The initial series of studies focused on what individuals in society think about the impact of loss, how long it takes to recover, and the nature of the bereaved's needs. As indicated above, culture is an important variable when considering what to expect following loss. It is important to note that Israeli culture is one that stresses the importance of memory and memorialization. As a result, one might predict that society would regard the relationship to the deceased as a matter of great significance given the emphasis on remembrance. While there is some support for this idea, its overall significance is less than what might be expected.

The first study addressed the question of lay perceptions of loss and how these perceptions varied according to characteristics of the deceased's identity. What do people see as the impact of the loss of an adult child and to what extent did it differ from spousal loss? In one such study, middle-aged men's ability to cope with various losses was assessed. One hundred lay participants (some of whom had experienced bereavement) rated a series of vignettes describing response to these losses 18 months after the death. They were given stories in which the bereaved were portrayed as responding to loss with either no difficulty, difficulty on items related to functioning in the workplace, difficulty in relationship to the memories of the deceased, or difficulties in both areas. They also completed measurements that allowed the researchers to construct a map of what forms the response to loss across a five-year period. Finally, their ratings of preferred means of offering various types of support to the bereaved were requested (Rubin & Shechter, 1997).

The results were quite instructive. The participants perceived the impact of loss as very disruptive for middle-aged bereaved men. Furthermore, factor analysis of the raters' responses found that they tended to group the list of responses to loss into a two-factor structure consistent with the two tracks of the model. This lent support to the conceptual validity of the two components identified within the model. Raters tended to see bereavement as continuing to affect the lives of bereaved men for five years following loss (the maximum period examined in this study). However, while features associated with functioning as conceptualized on Track I were seen to subside more quickly and completely, those of ongoing relationship to the deceased were seen to diminish more slowly and to remain somewhat elevated as long as five years after the loss.

Comparison of the types of loss indicated that an adult child loss was seen as more powerful and disruptive than that of a spouse. When the relative impact of the difficulties of adjusting to the loss was examined, however, the impact on the various dimensions of loss weighed very differently. Asked to rate the severity of response, participants rated features associated with Track I problems in functioning as most significant. When the ability to function adequately at work was described as impaired, the participants rated it as a serious difficulty. On the other hand, if the bereaved father or spouse was able to function at work, but was tormented by guilt regarding the relationship to the deceased, the raters tended to downplay its significance. The fact that difficulties in the relationship to the deceased were not seen as particularly significant is at odds with the native understanding of the same laypeople who believed that relationship features continue for five years after loss. Thus, while relationship to the representation of the deceased is seen to continue, the importance of difficulties in the nature of the relationship is not intuitively available to the lay raters.

On the basis of this information, a replication and extension of research was developed that examined the nature of the understanding of the relationship to the deceased. In a second study, the responses of 196 Jews and Arabs to descriptions of parental loss of children were examined. The gender of the deceased and the bereaved were systematically varied to examine the impact of gender variables on the way loss was approached. The results indicated that there were no group differences according to religion, subculture, or gender among college-educated respondents. Their assessment of the impact of loss was similar regardless of whether mothers or fathers were bereaved of sons or daughters. All respondents saw the impact of child loss as very powerful and disruptive. When it came to considering the relative significance of difficulties on features of Track I as contrasted to those on Track II, the results repeated and confirmed those of our earlier study. Again, the relationship to the deceased and accompanying feelings were seen to continue five years after the loss, and difficulties in the relationship to the deceased were considered as less significant than problems at work or difficulties in interpersonal relationships within the family (Asmar-Kawar, 2000).

A third study sought to understand lay conceptualizations of children's loss of parents. This extended our examination from the parent side to the child side of the parent–child relationship from the vantage point of the model. The impact of father loss on 8-year-old children was examined using a series of questionnaires and vignettes (Aviad, 2001). The features of Track I were represented by examining two variables: the relative contribution of general function (school, peer relationships), and importantly, a feature of family function/the relationship to the surviving parent. As before, Track II was represented by descriptions of the relationship to the deceased father. The raters were randomly given descriptions of children that contained no difficulties, or difficulties on one or more of the variables described. The results of this research study were interesting. When behavioral difficulties in functioning or the relationship to the surviving parent (in this case, the mother) were present, the ratings of the bereaved child indicated greater difficulty and problems. These features were the primary factors that influenced the degree to which the children were identified as currently suffering from the loss and showing psychological difficulties. Problems manifested in the relationship with the deceased father, however, were not considered particularly important.

In other words, the pattern repeated in all the studies described so far is that laypeople intuitively understand that bereavement is the result of the loss of a significant life relationship. Furthermore, they believed that these internal psychological relationships after a death continue together with accompanying affects. Despite these facts, the nature and valence of the psychological experience of the relationships are not intuitively perceived as significant in the recognition of difficulties following a loss. Laypersons considering response to loss do not behave as though the cognitive–affective difficulties that arise in the nature of the ongoing relationship to the bereaved are highly relevant to the question of how adjustment to loss is proceeding.

Professional Views of Bereavement

Having established that Track II, the relationship to the deceased, is both recognized and yet undervalued by laypeople, the next question addressed by the Haifa University group was to determine whether professionals held similar views. Accordingly, in a new study, a group of 138 clinical psychologists, physicians, and laypeople were presented with a series of measures and vignettes designed to survey their evaluation of loss in adults (Wiener-Kaufman, 2001). As before, items tapping the familiar domains of functioning and difficulties in the specific relationship to the deceased, which are associated with the model, were included. As before, functioning was addressed by focusing on two variables: general functioning at work and the bereaved's experience of self. This selection highlighted the self-perception and comfort level following interpersonal loss of a spouse 18 months before.

The self-experience variable was added to consider its utility in the identification of problems following loss.

The results of the study support the awareness that the death of a loved one, and the relationship to the deceased spouse, is understood as the precipitating cause of the loss experience. However, this understanding did not progress to a nuanced appreciation, for all of the importance of the quality of the relationship to the deceased following loss. For the study participants, the weakest of the factors associated with the identification of difficulties following loss was the nature and quality of the relationship with the deceased. Analyzing the responses by participants showed that medical professionals and laypeople tended to view loss in a similar fashion. The mental health professionals, however, tended to see the relationship with the deceased as a more significant factor than the other groups. They also gave it more weight than the other groups as a factor that influenced their evaluation of how well the bereaved was doing. Clinical psychologists (many of whom have a psychodynamic orientation consistent with mapping the internal psychological world of individuals) tended to incorporate the relationship in their assessment of difficulty following loss. The focus was on the individual's narrative of whom he or she had lost, and how that loss was recollected and remembered. Such an approach goes to the heart of the reorganization following interpersonal loss that is associated with the relational track in loss. From an assessment perspective, the evaluation of these psychologists reflected a greater appreciation of relationships than either physicians or laypeople.

To summarize: The research offers support for the identification of the two domains contained in TTMoB. One set of items was primarily associated with the biopsychosocial functioning domain, and the second set with the domain of the relationship with the deceased. The participants tended to see a response to bereavement as a long-term phenomenon, and that items associated with relationships to the deceased tend to diminish more slowly than behaviors and responses associated with the Track I function domain. Overall, when there are difficulties associated with the bereaved's responses along Track I, the general tendency is to see this as problematic. In contrast, emotional difficulties and distress associated with the nature of the relationship to the memories of the deceased were less likely to be identified as problematic or potential responses that might signal difficulty in the nature of the response to loss. There is evidence to suggest that mental health professionals are more attuned to variables in the relationship to the deceased and thus attribute greater weight to the nature of those responses in the assessment of how bereavement proceeds and outcome indications of difficulty.

Loss as Experienced by the Bereaved

To what extent do the domains of functioning and relationship to the deceased influence each other within the bereaved themselves? Here we find that the manner in which the relationship to the deceased is recollected has a strong connection to how bereavement unfolds over time. This concluding set of research studies draws on quantitative, qualitative, and narrative work as a means of capturing some of the unique expressions of individual differences. By taking into consideration a longitudinal perspective extending beyond indicators of behavioral or emotional dysfunction, a broader view of loss is adopted. In these studies, Rubin's group examined the impact of adult child loss over time via the reported narrative and related experiences of bereaved parents. First the researchers set out to quantify and analyze the taped interviews of 30 war-bereaved parents who had participated in the earlier studies on the trajectory of loss (Ariel-Henig, 1998). The in-depth interviews of these parents, who were seen from 4 to 13 years after the loss, were analyzed and coded. The results of the coding were then compared with the quantitative results of the parents who had completed a series of measures earlier (Rubin, 1992). For our purposes, the relevant question is the issue of whether the nature of the recollected and experienced relationship with the deceased's son is related to greater or lesser difficulties over the years. The results were unequivocal. For bereaved parents, the domains of life satisfaction, health, and personal satisfaction were linked to how the relationship to the son was organized. In general, higher levels of organization and complexity were linked to higher levels of general function and fewer somatic problems. This means that those bereaved parents who were able to think of their sons in a coherent manner, whose stories and vignettes conveyed a robust view of the son, and who gave more details, did better on life tasks and functioning that those who had a less well-developed picture. In addition, in situations where bereaved parents' interviews were rated as manifesting high levels of disorganization in what they related about their son, or in cases where significant conflict in the relationship with the son was present, the results in the other domains of functioning were apparent. These markers of difficulty were linked to lower levels of resolution or comfort in the relationship with the deceased. The more disorganized the narrative about the deceased son, the greater the likelihood that elements of despair, guilt, and social isolation characterized the bereaved. In other words, where elements of problematic relationships with the deceased were present, a wider net of difficulties was also present.

To apply these results directly to the experiences of bereaved parents, a focus on specific individuals rather than on group data trends is valuable.

Accordingly, in a follow-up study by Ariel-Henig (1998) the responses of eight parents using the insights and approach of narrative research methodology were investigated in depth (Shechory, 2003). These were bereaved parents who had scored significantly better or significantly worse than their cohort of similarly bereaved parents (Rubin, 1992). The parental levels of functioning and relationships to the deceased were assessed in 1986 and again in 1996 (Reuveni, 1999). By comparing the data records of those who had improved with those who had not, it was possible to show through individual life narratives that the nature of the relationship to the deceased son was a significant factor in the reorganization of the postloss parental world. This was true for those who had improved and for those who had not.

The parents who improved described their son in very favorable terms. They tended to convey a strong and positive evaluation of their son and the way he lived. These parents could describe in detail his character, worldview, values, relationships with friends and family, and his lifestyle. The description was full, complete, and rich with examples. The parental explanations allow one to see in one's imagination a complete person who is both complex and understandable. The descriptions are believable and convincing. For example (Shechory, 2003):

> And he was always the quiet leader of the group. He knew how to lead, to pull the strings quietly where it was necessary. Whether in grade 5 or 6, with a teacher whom everyone hated and they [the students] did not know how to deal with, he decided that he would do his thing. They [the students] had decided that they would put glue on her chair. But when she came in, he decided that something amiss might happen, so he warned her, and said, "Teacher, we decided to 'teach you a lesson' but beware, don't sit on the chair because it is full of glue." This is him again; it is education, behavior, and it is a way of life a little different from your average home, but that is the way we behaved. (p. 42)
>
> Another example is when they went to war, and he did not smoke. The army gave out cigarettes, he filled his backpack with cigarettes, and his friends asked, "'Why are you taking them?' Don't worry, and when they did not have any left, he began to distribute his ration. You understand, not everyone is like that." (p. 44)

In contrast, the parents whose conditions had deteriorated described their sons in a more constricted manner. Their stories were less detailed, somewhat superficial, and contained less positive descriptions. They used positive "titles/headlines" which tended to repeat themselves and did not yield details that would convey a description of a believable and real human being. It was difficult to understand the personality of the son. "He was like any kid, he was not a genius, he was a kid, a good kid, he was a good kid, he was, I think, also a good father, and I think also a good husband, he was a normal child, who finished high school, went to the army, and studied afterwards very well" (Shechory, 2003, p. 44).

The thrust of the research with bereaved parents points to the significance of the description and relationship to the deceased in positive and negative outcomes to bereavement. We interpret this research as lending support to the significance of the relationship to the deceased in the response to loss (Malkinson, Rubin, & Witztum, 2005; Rubin, Malkinson, & Witztum, 2003). Furthermore, to assess outcome to loss without recourse to the nature of this dimension is to deprive the bereaved, as well as those who conceptualize the needs and manner of intervention, of one of the most succinct and direct lines into the genesis and maintenance of the entire bereavement experience.

A 70-item self-report Two Track Bereavement Questionnaire (TTBQ) has been developed for use (Rubin, Malkinson, Bar Nadav, & Koren, 2004). The TTBQ is based on the two-track model of bereavement. The 70 items in the measure are grouped into four clusters, each of which shows good internal consistency: *general functioning* (Track I), including items bearing on self-esteem, meaning in life, depression, anxiety, and functioning in social roles; *relationship to the deceased* (Track II), with items focusing on imagining, missing, searching for, and memorializing the lost other; *relationship prior to loss* (Track II), assessing the relationship to the loved one during his or her life; and *traumatic features* (Track I), highlighting the assessment of trauma, broadly defined (Rubin, Malkinson, & Witztum, 2003). Items are phrased as statements (e.g., "My relationship with——had many and ups and downs"; "The loss was traumatic for me"), on which the respondent expresses agreement on a five-point scale. Psychometeric evaluation of the measure has been completed and the scales derived from the factor structure allow for evaluation for research and clinical purposes (Gofer-Shnartch, 2006).

The Model in Clinical Practice

As can be seen in Table 1.1, bereavement is viewed as a response occurring along two main axes, each one multidimensional. The first axis or track is how people function naturally, and how this functioning is affected by the devastating life experience that loss may entail. The second is how people maintain and change their relationships with the memories and mental representations of the deceased. Even though the bereaved may not always be aware of the nature of this relationship or of its consequences, this component is nonetheless critical for what the bereavement response involves throughout the life cycle.

TABLE 1.1
Two-track Model of Bereavement

TRACK I: GENERAL FUNCTIONING

Anxiety	To what extent is the bereaved experiencing anxiety, restlessness, and nervousness? When and what provides a sense of relative calm? What provokes the experience of more upset? To what extent are these similar to what was encountered in the past? The greater the overlap with the past, the greater the ability to incorporate information about previous responses and salutary factors following loss.
Depressive affect and cognitions	To what extent does the bereaved seem to experience thoughts and feelings with components of extreme sadness, hopelessness, lack of energy, and truncation of future perspective? The extent of these depressive responses can range from minimal to extremely disruptive to the ability to function.
Somatic concerns	The physical pathway is sensitive to the disruption of loss. For some individuals with a limited ability to conceptualize, think about, and talk about their inner experience, the somatic complaints may reflect their difficulty better than "emotional" or "insightful" discourse. Appetite (loss of appetite or overeating), sleep, and illness are often involved.
PTSD/general symptoms/ responses of a psychiatric nature	Those familiar with the medical model will be attuned to exploring for psychological difficulties. In particular, features associated with PTSD or with lesser variations of this response syndrome.
Familial relationships	The domain in which much interpersonal support takes place is often within the context of close familial relationships. These may be a source of comfort and solace, as well as a source of disappointment and miscommunication. What is the nature of the family support available to the bereaved? Keep in mind that the family members may also be responding as individuals and as a family system to the loss.
Interpersonal relationships	Does the bereaved manifest changes/difficulties in his or her ability to interact with friends and colleagues? What kind of use is being made of the interpersonal network?

(continued)

Self-system	The experiences of self-worth, of a sense of efficacy (the ability to be in some control over things or over oneself), and of a sense of inner coherence are important to explore. For some persons, significant interpersonal loss can be stressful without shaking their self-system to the core. For others, loss and trauma can be wrenching and fragmenting experiences. Restoring a sense of cohesion may be required in some cases.
Meaning structure	The importance of examining the extent to which the overarching structure of the individual as well as the individualized personal meaning structure of the bereaved have changed, as a result of loss is implied. Religion and secular meaning structures are important to explore.
Work	Is the bereaved able to fulfill the requirements of his or her job, including the duties and roles that are sensitive to age and status? How does the bereaved approach issues of work? Some may resume a job; others may quit.
Investment in life tasks	Being involved and invested in things in life is important for the well-being of all individuals. When the bereaved are able to find the energy and the direction to which they wish to apply themselves, the features associated with living life are squarely in the focus of inquiry. Some persons incorporate the loss experience into their life investments in constructive and creative ways.
TRACK II: RELATIONSHIP TO THE DECEASED	
Imagery and memories	To what extent do the descriptions of the deceased or relationship convey completeness or constriction? The fuller the imagery and the more accessible the memories, the easier it is to estimate the nature of the relationship. Constriction reflects a story that is not elaborated. It may be a constriction on top of a full story, or it may be a constriction that operates as a valid indicator of the paucity of a story about the deceased and the bereaved.
Emotional closeness or distance from relationship	It is possible to describe the deceased but to maintain an aloofness and distance from that description. Conversely, it is possible to be unable to maintain structure and any sort of the perspective on the loss and the deceased. What is the nature of the emotional bond as expressed?

Positive effect regarding the bereaved	Is the information about the bereaved and the relationship associated with good feelings? When do they arise and in what contexts? What words are used to convey these feelings?
Negative affect regarding the bereaved	Is the information about the bereaved and the associated relationship with negative feelings? When do they arise and in what context? Are they related to the relationship with the deceased or are they more rooted in the circumstances of the death? How are these described?
Idealization	To what extent is the story about the deceased one of a person much larger than life? Although an idealized description of the deceased may be normative, analyzing what is idealized and what it says about the person doing the idealization is also relevant.
Conflict	What are the areas of conflict that emerge when the bereaved is able to communicate about the nature and quality of the deceased and the relationship?
Features of loss (shock, searching, disorganization and reorganization)	Although the notion of fixed stage theories of loss as applied to the Bowlby–Parkes model have lost favor, the characteristics associated with the loss process remain. In this inquiry, we are interested in the extent to which "shock" is conveyed in the narrative of the loss experience, to what extent do the phenomena associated with "searching," and how much disorganization and sense of devastation is communicated. Many of these features continue on indefinitely following bereavement to one degree or another. The "stage," reorganization, includes both perspective and elements of coming to terms and accepting that life has to be lived in the shadow of the loss. It coexists with the other elements but is important in its own right.
Self-perception	When the bereaved thinks about the deceased, is the process set in motion one of essentially positive support or one that functions to attack or weaken the sense of self of the bereaved. Remembering feelings of being loved can strengthen the sense of self. Thinking about disagreements and failures can serve to weaken and upset the sense of self.

(continued)

Preloss relationship	Here the nature of the relationship prior to loss is explored. What patterns characterized the interactions? To what degree were elements of a secure attachment present? What aspects of dependency, mutuality, and conflict were present in the evolving relationship?
Memorialization and transformation	Many times, the bereaved evolve toward setting up a series of memorials. Gravestones, memorial corners at home or elsewhere, being involved in self-help groups, are just a few of the ways that people become involved in reworking the relationship to the deceased and their status as bereaved persons. At times, investment in life can include elements relevant to the memorialization. Exploring the personal relationship to the deceased can shed light on the relative distribution of the multiple meanings of how one lives life following loss.

Track I of General Functioning

In considering the features that comprise the response to loss, we examined the bereaved's life from a variety of vantage points. Track I, general functioning, reflected the individual's adaptive or maladaptive reaction to life across a number of domains. The Track I formulation included the individual's functioning across affective, interpersonal, somatic, and classical psychiatric indicators, which are often cited as characterizing the response to bereavement (Bowlby, 1980; Rubin, Malkinson, & Witztum, 2000; Stroebe & Stroebe, 1987). Family and other relationships were additional information resources for evaluating the bereaved's responses. In evaluating the extent and quality of these interpersonal interactions, the emotional strength of the bereaved and the emotional support these interactions may provide were measured. The bereaved's religious and other worldviews were also important because they can indicate the degree of connection with fundamental beliefs necessary for inner emotional support and organization. For example, a parent may feel that the loss of a child is a failure of God, his or her own failure, the physician's, or in cases of war or terror attacks, the failure of the political leadership. If, however, this failing or immersion seriously distances him or her from the previous positively experienced relationship with a spouse, faith, community, or God, the consequences can be debilitating. The person may be cast adrift from the matrix of much of what was familiar and supportive. Finally, the investment in life tasks manifests the ability or inability of the bereaved to be absorbed by something other than his or her own grief and mourning. The ability to invest in life tasks distinguishes those who are obstructed by their loss from those who have reentered the stream of life and will be borne along by it (Wikan, 1988). As is true for the bereaved's ability to manage interpersonal relationships and work, the ability to invest in life tasks in a balanced fashion is a benchmark for understanding the response to loss.

Track II: Relationship with the Deceased

Track II, the relationship to the deceased, captures the salient features of the memories that the bereaved experiences and sets the stage for understanding the current relationship with the deceased. The degree to which the bereaved person seeks emotional distance from or immersion in these representations of the deceased can be associated with difficulties in the response to loss. A bereaved individual who for an extended period of time, constantly avoids or is constantly involved with the overt or covert stimuli of the deceased, is having difficulties in maintaining an adaptive balance to dealing with the reorganization of loss. Likewise, the positive and negative affects associated with memories of the deceased; the extent of preoccupation with the loss, and the indications of idealization of and conflict with the deceased, provide a picture of the bereaved's cognitive and emotional view of the deceased. The bereaved's response to loss can be filtered through part or all the features, of what was once seen as the classic stage theory of Bowlby and Parkes (Bowlby, 1980; Parkes, 1985). It is most likely that disorganization and reorganization can be identified in the bereaved's description of the loss and the deceased along with elements of shock. The predominance of each of these features, and their complex interplay, reflects the dynamic ways by which the deceased and the loss are currently integrated by the bereaved. Proceeding further, we considered the extent to which thinking about the deceased leads to a negative self-view (e.g., "I feel guilty whenever I think of the deceased") (Horowitz, Weiss et al., 1984; Horowitz, Wilner, Maramar, & Krupnick, 1980). These helped us understand the many ways in which bereaved persons construct the relationship with and vis-à-vis, the deceased (Rubin, 1996). Finally, the memorialization process provided important information about the way in which the bereaved had transformed the relationship with the deceased into something more.

Memorialization can take many forms: for example, identification with the deceased, or formal or informal memorials which reflect the ways in which the loss of a person has been transformed into something beyond grief and mourning and shades into the life fabric (Malkinson & Witztum, 2000; Rubin, Malkinson, & Witztum, 2005).

Assessment Based on the Model

The implications of the two-track model of bereavement are relevant for both theory and research and clinical and counseling interventions. One can always examine how far the bereaved's response on each of the tracks is consistent with expectations along any particular dimension of functioning and relationship. The balanced model enables us to assess the bereaved's response according to the various components within each track and the interaction between the two through time. Thus, the model is not limited to a specific phase in the process but can be used clinically to reassess the bereaved's response during therapy or counseling. Given the variation and fluctuation that characterize the process of response to loss, discrepancies will be interpreted differently by different people.

The clinical implications of the model derive directly from the focus on both the functional and relational aspects of the response to loss. Interventions may deal directly with one or both domains of this response. There is clearly some mutual interaction between the tracks of function and relationship to the deceased (see Table 1.1 for a tabular representation of the model in clinical use).

Case Studies

We now include brief case descriptions to illustrate how the two tracks or two axes perspective can be applied in the initial stages of clinical assessment:

The Story of Mrs. Pain

Mrs. Pain, an Israeli in her 50s lost her husband under very violent circumstances. After visiting friends in the territories, he was driving home to Israel at night. On the way he was attacked by Palestinian gunmen. Mr. Pain died at once and his body was burned in the remains of the car. A few months later Mrs. Pain arrived for therapy and told her story in a very quiet, somewhat remote, way:

> The evening prior to the attack I had an argument with my husband whether or not it was safe to travel through the area after dark. I was very worried about the risks and didn't want to travel at all, and wanted to stay at home, but he wanted to meet with his friends and thought that it wasn't so dangerous, so he decided we would make the trip and insisted I join him. I refused as I had many times previously. He promised not to come back too late. During the evening I waited patiently for him and felt as if

something was wrong. I stayed awake waiting for him and must have fallen asleep when I heard early in the morning a knock on the door. There were two policemen asking me for my name and at that moment I knew something terrible had happened. I was told that my husband was brutally attacked on the way home. Mrs. Pain described her initial reaction:

I was in a shock, as if I was stabbed, I felt pain in the chest, and although I wanted to cry I was unable to do so, I felt frozen. Since then I am unable to either sleep or eat. I gave up my work and stay at home. I don't do much and I feel very restless and irritated, and I can't concentrate. I don't go out of the house because I am afraid something will happen to me. I have pains in my chest and my breathing is heavy. I have flashbacks during which I experience the night of the attack and as much as I try to push these memories away they keep returning.

I think over and over again of my last moments with him and immediately I recall what had happened, which saddens me greatly but also frightens me. My life is worthless and I really don't want to go on living, life has lost its meaning.

Mrs. Pain said she felt depressed most of the day. Her heavy sense of grief expressed itself in her feeling of guilt and self-directed anger for not agreeing to join him that night to visit his friends. She felt that had she insisted that he stayed at home, he might still be living. These feelings are blended with yearning for her husband to whom she was married for over 30 years, she has two grown-up daughters.

The Story of Mrs. Hope

Mrs. Hope's husband was killed in an airplane disaster. The airplane was shot down by a missile, killing crew members and passengers. There were no survivors.

Mrs. Hope told her story sobbing and in a very quiet voice, as if talking to herself:

When I was notified of my husband's death in the airplane disaster, the first thing I wanted to do was to join him. My life has lost its taste and meaning and I don't want to live. I feel that my world has been shattered. My husband was all I had, he was my friend, lover, a dedicated father to our daughter, my support, and now I have lost him. I am not a healthy person, in the past I suffered from health problems which improved tremendously after we were married. We waited for a long time before I became pregnant. Frustration and agony were part of our experience and it took many efforts before our little girl was born. She was the present I gave my husband. My husband adored our little girl and he was the one who helped me to care for her, and now that he is dead, life for me has lost its meaning. And now that he is dead the only thing I want to do is to go to the place where the airplane was shot down and join my husband. They conducted a memorial service at the place of the disaster. I didn't go because it was too much for me. I was devastated and couldn't comprehend the idea that he died. My brother went instead. Had I been there I would have jumped into the sea to join my husband.

Mrs. Hope went on to explain that she feels committed to her daughter but she fears the emotional and financial burdens are too much for her to cope with. A few weeks after his death, Mrs. Hope hadn't yet told the little girl, who she said is used to her father's absence as part of his work. She dreads the moment of breaking the news to her daughter.

We can see that both cases involved the loss of a spouse under traumatic circumstances without personal exposure to the event and an interpersonal loss. Addressing these traumatic losses from the perspective of the model reveals that the two narratives have elements of both the functioning track (anxiety, depression) and the relationship track (despair, yearning). Clearly, both issues would need to be addressed during therapy. However, there seem to be differences in the stories in the magnitude of the elements representing each axis. Whereas the elements of the trauma (functioning in Track I) are more pronounced in the former, the dominant features in the latter are focused on the relationship to the deceased (Track II). The differences in the foci of the stories are critical in trying to determine what intervention to apply. In our method of working, we would postulate that in Mrs. Pain's story the trauma elements should receive priority in the initial phase of therapy, while Mrs. Hope's story is predominantly Track II and therefore should receive priority in the initial stage of intervention. The reasons for this are as follows. Research studies quoted earlier have clearly demonstrated that functioning and relationship to the deceased are important domains in the bereavement process, while emphasizing the latter's centrality. Although clinically, both domains need to be assessed and addressed, the decision as to what would be the focus of the initial phase of the intervention depends on the narrative told by the bereaved. At times, the traumatic event has an overwhelming effect and delays the moment when the bereaved approaches the relationship to the deceased. Sometimes, talking about the deceased seems to be avoided or blocked and may indicate some difficulties, while at other times the "channel" to this axis is more accessible and can be discussed. Avoidance of the relationship axis at an early stage needs to be assessed as well and included as part of the intervention plan, as in the case of Mrs. Pain's story. This stresses the importance of attentive listening to what is told as well as what is omitted or missing from the initial story when determining how to initiate the therapy, in contrast to the recommendation that therapy should begin by attending to the trauma (Kubany & Menke, 1995).

These two cases demonstrate that not only a multidimensional perspective is essential for assessment but that assessment should also refer to the magnitude of the elements and their relative primacy in the case presentation. Furthermore, the conceptualization of how to balance and utilize both tracks of the model allows one to maximize the use of this framework in a flexible and effective manner.

Conclusion

The two-track model of bereavement derived its ideas from two main approaches and integrated them into a unified conceptual framework: The first is based on stress and trauma ideas (Track I of general functioning) and the second on a relational-attachment perspective (Track II relationship with the deceased).

The findings from the quoted studies have repeatedly illustrated that, (1) the relationship with the deceased is central in the process of bereavement; and (2) the internal relationship with the deceased is not abandoned but is one that continues throughout the bereaved's life.

Each track consists of 10 components that include those elements identified to be part of the process of reorganizing one's life following the loss of a loved one; these elements can be assessed each within both tracks in addition to its empirical application, the model can be employed clinically:

1. The components comprising the two domains can each be examined and assessed to provide information on the progression in therapy or counseling.
2. In assessing and reassessing the bereaved's response according to the various components within each track and the interaction between the two with time.
3. In assessing the magnitude and primacy of each track during therapy.

Chapter 2

Grief and Bereavement: Cognitive-Behavioral Psychotherapy

"If you can't bring my child back, how can you help me?"—A bereaved mother referred to therapy

For the therapist, grief therapy is a very special encounter involving pain and sorrow, human emotions that evoke many thoughts and feelings related to issues of life and death, and the client's special needs. A client whose child died in a road accident three months prior to requesting therapy, a client who feels guilty for not being a careful parent, or a client who feels depressed as the first anniversary of her brother's tragic death is approaching: How could they best be helped in therapy? Is bereavement in itself something that requires intervention? Do all bereaved people need help? What is their perception with regard to being helped, and is help always helpful?

Clinical and Empirical Issues in Grief Therapy: From Saying Goodbye to Life in the Heart

Theoretical changes occurring within the field of bereavement have an impact on psychotherapy as well. In general, grief psychotherapy is a focused short-term type of therapy, and cognitive-behavioral therapy is regarded as being very effective for bereavement issues.

As noted earlier, a review of the literature on grief therapy reveals that treatment with bereaved persons has undergone significant changes, and the development of psychotherapy has been strongly linked with theoretical conceptualizations and definitions pertaining to the various forms of bereavement outcomes. From a time-limited process with the individual resuming "normal life" on its completion, grief is now recognized as a much more complex process that is experienced in multiple ways and at multiple levels, and is in many ways a lifelong process of adapting to loss (Malkinson, 2001; Malkinson, Rubin, & Witztum, 2000; Rubin & Malkinson, 2001). One of the consequences of this change is that normal grief work is no longer expected to be completed within 12 months, once regarded as the expected time frame. By the same token, the notion that grief is a linear process that ends with the bereaved's acceptance of the loss has received little empirical support (Artlet Thyer, 1998).

The link between applied interventions and the theoretical models from which they were derived has always been strong. For decades treatment interventions aimed at grief resolution and "letting go" were applied, and grief therapy was a tool to facilitate this restoration (Malkinson, 2001; Van der Hart, 1986; Worden, 1982/2003). The idea of breaking the bonds with the deceased was deeply embedded theoretically and clinically, and terms such as "letting go" and "saying goodbye" indicated that therapy's major goal was to assist the bereaved with "moving on."

Interestingly, interventions applied then and now are in many ways similar, but they represent different goals. Whereas letter writing then (Van der Hart, 1985) was applied to assisting the bereaved in saying goodbye and disconnecting from the deceased, letter writing as applied within the continuing bond perspective would encourage the bereaved to search for connectedness with the deceased (Neimeyer, 2000). (In chapter 7 we will elaborate on letter writing as a cognitive intervention of meaning construction.)

Worden's conceptualization of the task model reflects the changes in the goals of interventions that took place within the field of thanatology. A comparison between Worden's initial version of the four tasks of the grieving process, as appeared in the first edition of his book *Grief Counseling and Grief Therapy* (1982), captures the changes within the discipline: from the task of "healthy emotional withdrawal from the deceased" (1982/2003, p. 36) to "finding a way to remember the deceased while feeling comfortable reinvesting in life" (1982/2003, p. 52), which emphasizes the idea of continuing bonds.

Based on Worden's original Task 4, a therapist would say the following to a client: "Look at the photo again, tell him how much pain and misery his death has caused you, tell him how difficult it has been for you because of his death, he deserted you. . . . say farewell to him." This quote is from Ramsay (1979, pp. 241–243), who developed a *behavior therapy* for pathological grief and was one of the first to apply the flooding technique in such cases. He emphasized that "The mourner has to relinquish the lost person, object or role before new ways of life can be found in which the lost object does not play a major part" (1979, p. 241).

In applying the revised Worden's Task 4, the therapist would phrase the intervention as follows: "Look at the picture and tell me what Ron would be saying if he could have said something to you?"

Ron's mother: He would have said to me, "Don't cry I know how much you loved me and how much you miss me. I know how painful it is."

Therapist (continuing to probe): What else would he have said about the pain?

Ron's mother: I don't know what he would have said but I know that remembering him is so painful.

Therapist: Yes. Memories bring pain. Is it possible that the two (memories and pain) live together?

Ron's mother: It's not easy but I guess this is how it has to be.

Though both forms of intervention focus on the deceased, the former is based on the therapist leading the client toward a predetermined path of relinquishing his or her relationship with the deceased; whereas in the latter, the mother is the one who tells the therapist what thoughts and feelings comprise her painful experience, and provides the lead to the therapist. Listening attentively to her choice of words as well as nonverbal cues, the therapist then leads the mother via paraphrasing to view her experience in a way that has meaning for her.

Over the last few decades a number of studies have been conducted to empirically evaluate clinical issues of the bereavement process and its outcomes to assess the effects and affectivity of grief interventions. The outcome of this reassessment has been the reconsideration and at times redefinition of what constitutes "normal" and complicated bereavement, the variables affecting its outcome, and the most effective interventions to assist mourners in need of help. In other words, interventions applied now are more carefully planned, are evidenced-based, and are client-needs based.

All in all, the literature on grief therapy is in agreement that caring, availability of support, and a genuinely empathic relationship between the therapist and the bereaved, are central ingredients that go above and beyond a specific mode of intervention (Raphael, Middelton, Martinek, & Misso, 1993). Also, most forms of intervention focus on the loss, and to a greater or lesser degree on the relationship to the deceased. Interventions are typically structured and time-limited and deal with grief-specific themes.

The introduction of formulations such as the dual process model (Stroebe & Schut, 1999), and the two-track model of bereavement (Rubin, 1999) described in chapter 1, greatly contributed to viewing grief as a process of fluctuation between orientation of loss to orientation of restoration (DPM), and moving along parallel axes of functioning and relationship with the deceased (TTMoB).

Does Grief Therapy Work?

One of the most salient trends within the field of bereavement has been the development of a variety of intervention programs to assist the bereaved in adapting to loss. Grief counseling, grief therapy, self-help groups (Worden, 1992, 2003), and the widow-to-widow program (Silverman, 1981, 2004) indicate the importance attributed to the different kinds of "helping hands" available at times of crisis, such as the death of a significant person. Availability of support was considered to be of prime importance as a preventive measure, which led to the development of intervention programs. These programs were offered to the bereaved population at large. A key element in the provision of help was prevention of future complications among the bereaved, and efforts to identify those at risk of developing "pathological" grief, those having difficulties in "letting go" (chronic), or those who do not show any grief symptoms (delayed or absent grief).

Outcome studies undertaken in the 1970s and 1980s were in line with the following. Though normal and universal grief following a loss through death is a crisis (Caplan, 1964), and, being an interpersonal experience, cannot be carried alone, so the "helping hand" should be available and activated (Polak, Egan, Vandenbergh, & Williams, 1975). Intervention programs were aimed at preventing "pathological grief," which was assessed with measurement of general symptoms (depression, anxiety) and not grief-specific ones (Horowitz, Marmar, Weiss, DeWitt, & Rosenbaum, 1984; Marmar, Horowitz, Weiss, Wilner, & Kaltreider, 1988). Interventions applied were in line with the theoretical framework of breaking the bonds with the deceased (Gauthier & Marshall, 1977; Mawson, Marks, Ramm, & Stern, 1981).

An example from my clinical work with a bereaved person, as applied within the perspective of abandoning the bonds, will illustrate some of the points mentioned.

Miriam, in her 30s, came to therapy a year after her husband was killed in military action. She was left with a one-year old baby daughter. Miriam, a delicate-looking woman with a very sad face and a quiet voice, described the moment she was told about the death of her husband, the circumstances of his death, and the life that was shattered. She had lost interest in life but realized that as the mother of their daughter she didn't have what she called "the privilege" to even think about such a possibility. The baby cried a lot, hardly slept at night, and Miriam said that having to look after the baby had become a burden for her.

Following an assessment in line with what was then considered an adaptive process, Miriam's was assessed as suffering from a prolonged grief and the intervention of good-bye letter writing was formulated. The purpose of the therapy, to say "farewell" to her husband, was explained to Miriam and she agreed to it. After a number of sessions Miriam said she couldn't bring herself to say goodbye to her beloved husband and asked to end therapy. It was decided that she could return whenever she felt it was right for her. Miriam, however, never returned.

For me as a therapist there was a feeling of failure as well as disappointment with Miriam for "giving up" what I assumed would help her to continue with life and resume her role as a mother. In retrospect Miriam was one of my "teachers" as I came to learn about the bereaved's continuing relationship with the deceased, and most importantly, that interventions should be applied to fit the client's idiosyncratic needs and not the other way around.

Indeed, studies reveal that there is great variation among the bereaved and many paths to accommodating to life without the lost person. In contrast to what was assumed in the past, lack of emotional distress is not necessarily an indication of denial or complication in the process but needs to be assessed based on the individual's idiosyncratic expression of the loss (Bonanno, Wortman, & Nesse, 2004; Exline, Dority, & Wortman, 1996).

Similarly, evidence-based outcome studies of grief therapy have examined the efficacy of interventions for the bereaved as compared to therapeutic interventions for other psychological problems. These studies provide a wealth of information on issues such as the typical and most frequent responses to loss through death; the circumstances necessitating intervention; which bereaved individuals are at risk; what would constitute an effective intervention; and the relationship between theories of bereavement and outcome studies (Jacobs & Prigerson, 2000; Kato & Mann 1999; Litterer Allumbough,1999; Malkinson, 2001; Neimeyer & Hogan, 2001; Potocky, 1993; Sabatiani, 1988).

One overview study by Litterer, Allumbough, and Hoyt (1999) concluded that no-treatment control groups improved less than treatment groups, and that the factor contributing to the effect size was related to whether participants were self-referred or recruited by investigators. These findings suggest that on encountering difficulties, bereaved people who actually seek help benefit from it most. But the viability of comparing treatment efficacy in these studies by Schut, Stroebe, Van den Bout, & Terheggen (2001) in their review was questioned.

An interesting categorization in line with Caplan's (1964) crisis theory was proposed by Schut and colleagues (2001) in their review of efficacy studies, which included three types of preventive interventions: (1) Primary preventive interventions were offered to anyone who experienced a loss through death to prevent complications in the grief process (historically, in a majority of cases widows were the target population of these interventions); (2) Secondary preventive interventions for those bereaved who are at high risk for complication related to the circumstances of the loss, such as loss through suicide, homicide, or mass killing (as in a terrorist attack); (3) Tertiary preventive interventions for treatment of those who experience complicated grief due to multiple losses or the circumstances of the loss.

Several observations were made from the analysis of outcome studies with regard to benefits of interventions following loss through death, and in the course of bereavement that led in many cases to reconsidering timing, type, and target population. Contrary to what had been assumed, there appeared to be very little empirical support for primary prevention interventions for bereaved adults who experienced uncomplicated grief (Hansson & Stroebe, 2003, p. 519), which questioned the prevalent assumption that the state of bereavement and being bereaved require help. A greater efficacy of intervention is found in cases of bereaved individuals, couples, and families who solicit help as opposed to nondiscriminatory provision of such help. This applies particularly to secondary and tertiary preventive interventions. It was observed that at times interventions were modestly effective when compared to no-intervention control groups, while at other times the help provided did not produce a reduction in symptomatology, nor was immediacy of intervention proved to reduce symptomatology. To put it in terms of effect size (which refers to the percentage of people who benefit from the intervention), the results revealed a smaller effect size when compared with general psychological problems. Moreover, interventions can be ineffective and even harmful. In contrast, the effect size was higher in the five studies reported where patients were selected for treatment of complicated grief or included participants who were assessed as being at high risk (Jacobs & Prigerson, 2000; Neimeyer, 2003). This finding has led researchers and clinicians alike to review the assumption concerning bereavement intervention being essential as was understood up to that point, and the affectivity of the intervention

(Neimeyer & Hogan (2001); Neimeyer, 2000 & 2004). As for tertiary preventive intervention, it was repeatedly demonstrated in outcome studies to be efficacious with bereaved people who are experiencing complicated grief. In the words of Schut and associates (2001), "the more complicated the grief process appears to be or become, the better are the chances of interventions leading to positive results" (p. 731).

To summarize, accumulated empirical and clinical data suggest that (1) not all bereaved need help, particularly during the initial phase; (2) intervention in bereavement can be effective but can also be harmful; (3) intervention is more likely to be effective in cases of self-referral; (4) therapy in cases of complicated grief has the potential of being efficacious; (5) interventions by professional caregivers have yielded better outcomes; (6) interventions applied were in line with the theoretical framework of breaking the bonds with the deceased; (7) women tend to solicit help more often than do men.

The consequence of review and empirical studies has led to greater attention being given to evaluation prior to intervention, rather than providing help undifferentially at all times. By the same token, identifying bereaved who are at risk and reaching out is recommended, and developing measures to assess accurately cases of complicated grief, has become an essential part in planning an intervention. It is necessary to reach out to those bereaved who may be unaware of the possibility of getting help and support (Prigerson, 2004).

Importantly, findings about separation anxiety (Prigerson & Jacobs, 2001) indicated that the relationship with the bereaved is the central issue to be addressed in therapy. In accordance with these findings, the following is a description of an evidenced-based study aimed at evaluating interventions for bereaved individuals who were assessed with complicated grief. Interpersonal psychotherapy was the mode chosen, along with medication and a control group.

Reynolds et al. (1999) studied a sample of 80 bereaved adults, most of whom had lost a spouse, and the majority of whom were self-referred; eligibility was based on grief-specific measures such as Prigerson and associates' (1995) *Inventory of Complicated Grief (ICG)* and Faschingbauer's (1981) *Grief Inventory and Texas Revised Inventory of Grief Manual*. Participants were randomly assigned to one of four treatment conditions: Nortriptyline and interpersonal psychotherapy; nortriptyline alone in a medication clinic; placebo and interpersonal psychotherapy and placebo alone in a medication clinic. The results showed that the combination of nortriptyline and interpersonal psychotherapy yielded the highest rate of treatment completion. From a psychotherapeutic perspective, of interest are the findings with regard to the application of interpersonal psychotherapy (IPT) which showed no differential effect. The authors suggested the following explanation:"

> Why the symptoms of grief apparently do not resolve with the same clarity of depression is, we believe, an issue of considerable conceptual and theoretical, as well as clinical, importance. There are at least two possible explanations for this phenomenon. The first is that depressive symptoms may represent biological dysregulation amenable to pharmacologic intervention, while (e.g., sleep) persisting grief may represent unresolved problems of loss, and difficulty in performing the role transition tasks. A second possibility, however, is that persistence of grief is not necessarily abnormal or pathological. Preoccupation with the memory of the lost spouse might be the normal or necessary sequela of genuine attachment and part of a necessary sustenance of life. (1998, p. 207)

Interpersonal psychotherapy as developed by Klerman, Weissman, Rounsaville, and Chevron (1984) is a short-term intervention (16–20 weeks)* which focuses on current psychosocial functioning related to an identified interpersonal problem area: grief, interpersonal disputes, interpersonal deficits, and role transitions. Two issues are specifically assessed as related to the current distress: recent changes in the client's life and ongoing difficulties in interpersonal relations. It is assumed that both are related to the occurrence of emotional and physical symptoms. Intervention is aimed at reducing symptoms and improving current social functioning (Blanco, Lipsitz, & Caligor, 2001; Cutler, Goldyne, et al., 2004). We can see that grief is one of the identified interpersonal problem areas. However, focusing on symptom reduction and current interpersonal problems associated with the onset of grief complication (which is important in itself) without addressing an inner continuing relationship and preoccupation with the deceased, explains its limited outcome efficacy.

Indeed this explanation for the findings in the cited study was offered by Shear et al. (2001; 2005) pertaining to the fact that the standard treatment of interpersonal psychotherapy does not account for specific features of complicated grief, that explain its infectivity, suggesting that interpersonal psychotherapy for complicated grief needs to be modified to include cognitive-behavioral

---

*Unlike in the United States, where short term therapy consists of 16 to 20 sessions, in Israel therapy for the bereaved extends for a longer period (sometimes up to 30 sessions). In Israel, individuals and families who lost someone due to military service or in terror attacks are eligible for therapy subsidized by the government.

therapy. In their 2005 study, Shear et al. reported the application of complicated grief therapy (CGT) with a higher improved rate over interpersonal psychotherapy.

A case example will illustrate the differences:

A woman in her late 30s, who had lost her husband under traumatic circumstances in a road accident a few months prior to requesting therapy, said she felt depressed and had difficulties in daily functioning (work and social).

These are her words: "I don't feel like going to work. For me going to work to earn money is disgusting. It's against my values. A person has to do what he likes and what satisfies him and if not—leave it. And I go to work and loath it. In the not so distant past my husband was my back. Whenever I needed to stay extra hours to finish a project he encouraged me to stay, and I was only too happy to complete it. Now my back is no longer there and I don't feel like going to work, and least of all to stay extra hours."

From the IPT perspective, intervention would include reviewing the symptoms and exploring current difficulties in light of her loss, as well as explaining how the loss may affect current difficulties in going to work. Following provision of information, intervention would aim at reducing her depressive symptoms, and search for ways to reduce her work-related difficulties.

It is likely that the goals would be attained with regard to her present work context; it is also likely that the depressive symptoms that undoubtedly relate to the tragic loss of her husband would be reduced.

A cognitive-constructivist framework will explore both thinking errors and difficulties in accommodating to the demands of the new reality from which her husband is missing. The following is a dialogue between the client and the therapist about the difficulties she has encountered in terms of going to work:

Client: Every morning when I wake up I feel depressed at the thought of having to go to work.

Therapist: Is it possible to consider quitting?

Client: No way, I have to work to earn money and support the family.

Therapist: In that case is it possible that what increases your distress now is the discrepancy between the values you believed in while your husband was alive that "one needs to do only what one loves doing," and the present one that "one needs to go to work to earn money"?

Client: Exactly. That is what is so distressing, and I hate myself for that. I know that this is what I have to do since my husband died and I force myself to go to work. But every morning I feel the pain of his loss.

Therapist: There is self-criticism and pain. Are they related? You are very critical with yourself, aren't you?

Client: Oh, yes, indeed I am.

Therapist: What are you telling yourself?

Client: I hate myself for having to do something that I dislike.

Therapist: Is going to work under the present circumstances a choice or choiceless?

Client: Of course it is choiceless.

Therapist: Or maybe it is a choice under choiceless circumstances? Perhaps it is worth examining the difference between something that you have no choice over, its occurrence, and the choice to decide what to do under such circumstances? Is your decision to go to work the right one?

Client: Very much so.

Therapist: Is it possible that you made the right decision but a difficult one?

Client: Yes, a right and a sad one.

Therapist: Yes, a right and a sad one. How does it compare to decisions you took in the past?

Client: All my decisions all my life were right and satisfying ones. It felt good to discuss the pro and cons with my husband and to reach the "right" one.

Therapist: So perhaps this explains the difference between then and now. Now you took a very courageous decision in that it is the right sad one, and not one that you reached together with your husband; one that was right and brought a feeling of satisfaction.

Client: Yes, that is what has changed. My life has changed for ever and thinking about it is so painful and unbearable.

Therapist: Yes, your life has changed for ever and with it the need to take some sad and painful decisions.

Client: Every morning there is a reminder of that. And I am forcing myself and telling myself to get up and go to work because I have no choice. This is something that I often tell myself.

Therapist: I can see how difficult it is for you to think of it as the right but sad decision.

Client: Yes, because if I accept it, then it means that I accept my husband's death, something that I can't say yet, it is a reminder of the pain of the loss. It is yet another reminder of what was lost forever; a reminder of what he will never be able to experience and this is painful.

Therapist: Indeed it is a reminder of the lost future. You seem to think that you need more time to accept the loss and that seems to be in conflict with the decision not to quit work. Is that what you think?

Client: It is clearer to me now that the need to go to work is "a forced choice" and looking at it in such a way makes more sense to me.

Therapist: And when you think of it that way how do you feel? More, less, or the same intensity of distress?

Client: (thinking and smiling) It feels less. It is sad but there's less distress.

Therapist: That is an important change. During the next few days pay attention to how you wake up in the morning and we will further explore it in the next session.

In the next session the client discussed current issues and when asked about her "homework" of paying attention to what she had experienced in the mornings, this is what she said:

> Oh, yes, I thought about it for two days and realized that if I can't quit work I can still enroll at the university and study something, and because as of now I can't choose something for fun I will take some work-related courses. Once I took that decision the view of work changed and it is much less of a burden. I still yearn for my husband but somewhat differently, although it is still painful.

The issue of pain was threaded throughout therapy as she oscillated between avoidance of experiencing it or accepting the loss with the pain that it elicited. As can be seen, values that were valid prior to the loss (going to work for fun) were shattered after the husband died. The focus on changing her values has related not only to staying or quitting work, it has also represented the traumatic loss of her husband and the difficulties in accepting his death. Thus, both the issue of functioning and the relationship to the deceased need to be addressed in therapy.

Moreover, grief-specific therapy must focus on the relationship with the deceased, the pain and the yearning elicited by the loss, preoccupation with the deceased, and who the deceased represented for the bereaved.

The Development of Behavioral and Cognitive-Behavioral Therapy for Grief

The application of various forms of behavioral and cognitive-behavioral interventions for treating depression, anxiety, and other psychiatric conditions was introduced during the 1960s with the pioneering work of Ellis (1962) and A. Beck (1963, 1964). In comparison to its application in such situations, cognitive-behavioral treatment was limited in cases of loss following death but nonetheless was reported to be effective, especially in cases of "pathological" grief. Behavioral interventions for "pathological" grief included desensitization, flooding, and gradual exposure in order to overcome avoidance of perceived difficult "stuck" situations in the process of mourning. One such example (quoted earlier) is Ramsay's work with difficulties in bereavement.

In a way Ramsay's work is a link between the "old" and "new" traditions of grief therapy. Although it originated within the psychodynamic framework, Ramsay's behavioral model was one of the first reported to be applied effectively in individual therapy with maladaptive (pathological) forms of grief. Grief therapy from a psychodynamic perspective views the relationship that develops between the client and the therapist as central in the treatment process and aims at reworking the relationship with the deceased. Unlike psychodynamic grief therapy, Ramsay (1979), like many other behavior therapists, did not regard as centrally essential the relationship between therapist and client. The focal point of intervention, according to Ramsay, is "to help the client give structure to the process of feeling and expression, to relearn how to feel, to code it correctly, and to express it in an appropriate way since most people are emotionally inhibited and have learnt to suppress their emotions" (p. 217). Thus, the treatment of bereavement from a behavior therapy perspective includes "flooding, repeated confrontation, with prolonged exposure and response prevention where the client tries to escape or avoid" (p. 217). The aim of employment of flooding techniques is to enable expression of avoided painful feelings. Ramsay outlined a scheme wherein he combined phases and components for purposes of identifying and assessing difficulties in the process of bereavement. The scheme included the following phases: shock, disorganization, searching behavior, emotional components (desolate pining, despair, guilt, anxiety, jealousy, shame, protest, and aggression), resolution and acceptance, and reintegration. According to Ramsay's scheme, denial is a component that ebbs and returns throughout the process. Ramsay suggested viewing denial as a defense mechanism to protect from too much pain all at once, a form of avoidance which paradoxically prolongs it, to be followed by additional efforts to refrain from the pain. It is denial of the occurrence of the loss and the related emotions. The emphasis is on a learned dysfunctional behavior signifying complications, which will require intervention and emotional training to stimulate experiencing avoided feelings. According to Ramsay, missing uncontrollable bursts of crying in the phase of desolation is yet another example of "pathological grief reactions" indicating a delayed or distorted process; or continued searching behavior that signifies that the process has not yet been worked through. Underlying this approach is the idea that grief has to be worked through and resolved, reflecting the common view that failing to do so was considered "pathological"; that is, grief is distorted, exaggerated, prolonged, inhibited, or delayed. As a behavioral therapist, Ramsay proposed a link between grief and phobias characterized by anxiety and avoidance. Because the loss of a person involves situations that evoke pain, the bereaved who avoid its confrontations tend to get "stuck" in the grief process, and any extinction that was considered essential for resolution of grief is delayed. Avoidance reinforces depression, and the cycle of further avoidance is then followed by increased depression. The purpose of applying flooding and prolonged exposure is to evoke the various emotions by identifying related stimuli ,which can be an avoided picture or place. Once emotions are evoked and expressed, time is allowed for these emotions "to extinguish" (p. 242).

Ramsay's therapy with "pathological" grief focused on avoided behaviors; flooding techniques using pictures of the deceased were applied so as to encourage the client to overcome avoided behavior. Therapy was completed when the client was able with the help of the therapist to confront the heretofore avoided behavior. A leave-taking ritual marked the completion of the process.

Ramsay's behavior therapy model is an example of carefully assessing and planning a gradual live in-session exposure, assisting the client in confronting avoided situations or other cues, and with homework between sessions, "so that there is a resolution of the process and an acceptance that the calamity has occurred; it is taking leave of the dead and an acceptance that life must goes on in a changed form where the departed has no central place" (Ramsay, 1979, p. 225). Seemingly, grief work can be done that leads to reintegration and resolution.

In line with the idea of overcoming avoided behavior, Gauthier and Marshall (1977), Mawson, Marks, Ramm, and Stern (1981), and Sireling, Cohen, and Marks (1988), carried out three separate studies, each of which combined guided mourning and systematic desensitization for patients with "morbid grief." Gauthier and Marshall's assumption was that maladaptive (pathological) grief is maintained largely through social reinforcement of the bereaved's repeated pattern of behavior. They proposed the use of flooding procedures and rescheduling of social reinforcement as a treatment strategy to reduce the emotional distress: "If grief responses are encouraged by social reinforcement, or if social reinforcement is not consistently given for alternative behavior, then grief will be maintained" (p. 42). The notion of completion of grief and breaking the bonds with the lost person was grounded so strongly in grief therapy that "[A]t no time was sympathy shown by the therapist for [a] display of distress on the part of the patient" (p. 43). They report successful treatment with four women patients suffering from "pathological" grief. Treatment included six sessions: three sessions for assessment of the problem and making arrangements for behavioral desensitization, and three sessions when exposure techniques were employed, resulting in marked changes of behavior.

Another form of intervention was applied by Mawson and his group (1981) in an outcome study on the behavioral "guided mourning," the term used for exposure therapy to assist the bereaved with relinquishing ties with the lost person, which involved reliving avoided painful memories and feelings related to bereavement, and the use of homework. Sireling and associates (1988) repeated the exposure procedures. The reported results showed improvement on measures of grief (Texas Inventory of Grief) in reducing avoidance symptoms, which were maintained through a follow-up as compared to the control group.

In all three studies the treatment with forced prolonged exposure was aimed at "curing" patients with morbid grief. A difference exists in the application of the exposure treatment procedures as used by Ramsay and those used in the other three studies. Ramsay's flooding techniques appeared to be more confrontational and forceful during the session compared to what appeared to be more instructive and less confrontational approaches in the remaining three studies.

Interestingly, exposure therapy or guided mourning, as first applied to cases of grief, actually originated from behavior therapy and focused on changes in observed behavior, with less attention being given to cognitive components of the grief process. It was Eysenck (1967) who suggested that the development of phobic behavior can be considered in many ways to be the learning of maladaptive behavior. As a behavior researcher, Eysenck emphasized the relationship between stimulus and response. From that perspective the occurrence of a traumatic event is the stimulus that produces unconditional, strong emotional responses. There is the traumatic event, and as stimuli become associated with the emotional response of fear or anxiety (conditional stimuli and conditioned response), the cycle of its avoidance is perpetuated. The result is a generalization of the response rather than its extinction. We can see that avoidance of the pain of grief, as well as reminders of objects or situations relating to the deceased, were assumed to resemble phobic responses and were treated similarly (i.e. applying flooding or gradual exposure to extinguish a maladaptive response). Behavior therapists have proposed a relationship between the traumatic event (loss through death) as the stimulus, and the avoidance of the pain of grief as a response, but from a cognitive stance (as will be elaborated later) there can be additional reasons or interpretations of avoidance. A frequent interpretation given by bereaved individuals is that they fear forgetting the deceased, and avoidance of stimuli such as reminders of the deceased is their way not to think of him or her as dead. Clearly, assessing the cognition related to avoidance is paramount. (Also, guided mourning can be focused on reliving painful memories in order to extinguish undesired behaviors.)

Similar to approaching "pathological grief" as a phobic reaction of anxiety and avoidance, chronic grief was assessed in cases where patients continued to be preoccupied with the deceased for a longer period than the regarded norm of 12 months (Gauthier & Marshall, 1977; Mawson et al., 1981; Ramsay, 1979; Sireling et al., 1988). It was assumed then that in both cases a stimulus or a cue was provoking the distress, followed by avoidance. By the same token, a prolonged preoccupation with the deceased was assessed as a form of "morbid grief" (Mawson et al., 1981). Desensitization and prolonged exposure to avoided stimuli were effective interventions in diminishing avoided behaviors as a way to sever bonds with the deceased, a therapeutic goal which has been altered into assisting him or her in making sense of the loss and life without the deceased.

Prolonged Exposure: From a Behavioral to a Cognitive-Behavioral Intervention

In general the employment of "guided mourning" incorporating mostly behavior strategies was reported to yield a positive outcome in most studies, but not in all. In some studies improvement in reduction of anxiety and depression was reported in both treatment and control groups (Walls & Meyers, 1985), lending support to the notion that interventions in and by themselves are not always efficacious, while their effect increases in cases of complicated grief.

Several trends within the field of bereavement have led to better understanding of the process and its outcome, and what grief therapy should include if it is to be efficacious both in terms of "ingredients" and timing of its application. The study of stressful life events such as death has expanded to include man-made and natural disasters, violence, and terrorism, which has served to enhance professional understanding of coping processes and distinguish between the adaptive and maladaptive reactions, while comparing the outcome of a number of interventions (Kleber, Brom, & Defares 1992; Schut et al., 1996). One such compartive study of a review of evidence for psychotherapeutic treatments was carried out by Jacobs and Prigerson (2001), and focused specifically on complicated grief.

A study, which was inspired by the development of the Inventory of Complicated Grief (Prigerson, Frank et al., 1995) and the proposed diagnostic criteria for complicated grief by Prigerson and Jacobs (2001a), was carried out by a group working in collaboration with them. The study of Shear, Frank, Foa et al. (2001) involved the development of a systematic treatment modality for complicated grief which was reported as effective. In this pilot study of grief treatment for bereaved individuals who scored above 25 (the original cut-off point between uncomplicated and complicated grief which in a later study was changed to 30), on the complicated grief inventory (CGI) experienced intense preoccupation with the deceased, yearning, disbelief, and inability to accept the loss, anger about the death, and avoidance of reminders of the loss, all responses associated with traumatic grief. The treatment modality was the first in a reported series of studies (Shear, Frank, Honck et al., 2005) to combine strategies from interpersonal therapy for depression (Klerman et al., 1984), and cognitive behavior therapy for posttraumatic stress disorder (PTSD), a treatment protocol developed by Foa and Rothbaum (1997). The treatment protocol adopted by Shear, Frank, Foa et al. for complicated grief included imaginal reliving of the death, in vivo exposure to avoided activities and situations applying interpersonal therapy. The results indicated a significant improvement in grief symptoms, associated anxiety, and depression for both groups.

Posttraumatic stress disorder (PTSD) was one area where CBT has been increasingly applied and reported as effective. Several outcome reviews reported the application of cognitive-behavioral interventions among which were exposure, cognitive restructuring, guided imagery, and a variety of psychoeducational tools. Foa and Rothbaum (1997) were among the researchers who developed cognitively-oriented treatment modalities in PTSD, which later became part of Shear and colleagues' model of cognitive therapy for complicated grief. Other studies applying CBT in individuals suffering from

PTSD, depression, and anxiety were reportedly effective (Black, Newman, Harris-Hendriks, & Mezey, 1997; Clark, 1986; Kavanagh, 1990; Kubany & Manke, 1995; Resick & Schnicke, 1995; Richards & Lovell, 1997). Similar to behavioral prolonged exposure, cognitive-behavioral imaginal, or in vivo exposure, CBT involves confrontation with the feared and often avoided trauma-related situations, with a focus on cognitive and behavioral components as change targets. Foa and Rothbaum's (1998) prolonged exposure, evidence-based model for treatment of PTSD is a structured protocol consisting of 12 to 15 sessions aimed at reducing PTSD symptoms such as nightmares, flashbacks, and hypervigilance, which stem from a distorted evaluation of the response to situations that resemble the traumatic event, that are anxiety provoking, and are avoided. It is based on the observation that there is a continuous pattern of intense fear prevailing over time, which thereby prevents normal functioning. The distorted cognitions of increasing anxiety include an exaggerated evaluation of emotional, physiological, and behavioral consequences that a person might experience if exposed to threat-related stimuli, while estimating that avoidance of the anxiety-provoking stimuli is a way to overcome it. Thus, prolonged exposure is applied toward assisting the individual to overcome the avoided and feared stimuli by way of confronting it using psychoeducational elements, guided and in vivo exposure, and homework assignments. Consequently, the individual is able to reconnect to memories of the trauma, retell the traumatic story in a more organized and controlled manner, and correct distorted cognitions related to the trauma. Prolonged exposure was reported to reduce PTSD symptoms among 52% of participants compared to 31% of those receiving stress inoculation treatment (Foa et al., 1999).

Cognitive therapies that focus on the client's belief system and related consequences (emotions and behaviors) were found to be suitable and effective (Kleber, Brom, & Defares, 1992). Cognitive therapy and cognitive-behavioral therapy are based on the premise that emotional disturbance and behavioral symptomatology are maintained as a result of distorted thinking, which can be modified using a variety of cognitive, emotional, and behavioral techniques during the sessions, and also between sessions in the form of homework assignments. Both these therapies are also increasingly applied in cases of acute and prolonged grief following death, combining guided imagery, exposure techniques, thought stopping, cognitive restructuring, breathing exercises, and skill acquisition, all aimed at assisting clients to cope with loss, to reorganize one's relationship with the living and the dead, and the search for a new meaning to a changed life (Beck et al., 1993; Ellis, 1995; Mahony,1991; Neimeyer et al., 2000; Rubin & Malkinson, 2001).

Conclusion

As can be seen, the efficacy of cognitive-behavioral interventions, in particular exposure, guided imagery, and desensitization has not diminished through the years. What has changed is the framework within which they are applied, thus changing the purpose of the intervention from extinction of bonds with the deceased to assisting the bereaved in reconstructing a new meaning to the ever-changing reality.

Within CBT and CB modalities (which nowadays are used synonymously, reflecting their resemblance rather than differences) such treatment that uses prolonged exposure, stress reduction inoculation, cognitive restructuring (Foa & Othbaum, 1998), and cognitive processing therapy (Resick & Schnicke, 1993) were reported to be effective in the treatment of PTSD.

Although the literature approached avoidance in grief as similar to a phobic behavior and to avoidance in PTSD (Jacobs & Prigerson, 2000; Kavanagh, 1990; Matthews & Marwit, 2004; Ramsay, 1979), from a cognitive perspective, the differences among the three need to be considered in planning an intervention in cases of avoidance. The key element in the treatment of avoidance is the idea that the bereaved has to confront the avoided stimuli, and exposure is a strategy applied to overcome it (Kavanagh, 1990). Apparently, preoccupation with the deceased is dissimilar to the avoidance of stimuli that is characteristic of phobic reactions; therefore, extinction is not pertinent. In complicated grief, what might be observed as avoidance behavior is more likely to be withdrawal, frequently reported by bereaved persons (Kavanagh, 1990). Similar to the observed differences between depression where the focus is on the self, and complicated grief where the focus is on the deceased, as suggested by Prigerson, Frank et al. (1995), avoidance in grief can be viewed as a way to deal with the pain involved in experiencing the loss which is similar to that in cases of anxiety and PTSD. But unlike phobic behavior and PTSD, where efforts are made to avoid the pain as well as memories of the traumatic event, in grief, the purpose of avoiding objects (abstract or real), which are reminders of the deceased, is to reduce pain but not to eliminate memories of the deceased. At other times, mourners report their efforts to maintain the pain as a way "not to forget the deceased," many times a source of worry. Another form of complicated grief that resembles phobic reactions is avoidance of thinking "painful" thoughts of the loved one as one who died, and refraining from any reminder of the loss or deceased as a way to cherish "as if alive" memories ("I know he or she is dead but I don't want to think of him or her as such").

By the same token, from a cognitive perspective, continuing bonds with the deceased are not in themselves a form of complicated grief. Rather, persistence over time of distorted, irrational beliefs maintains dysfunctional emotional and behavioral consequences. Exposure intervention, therefore, is aimed at confronting and challenging distorted beliefs which lead to "excessive" emotions.

Undoubtedly, a detailed and thorough cognitive assessment is necessary to determine the function, frequency, and intensity of avoiding pain, maintaining it, or persistently holding distorted beliefs concerning a life following the loss.

Chapter 3

The Cognitive Model of Bereavement

"Thinking about him is too painful."—A widow

"The pain of thinking about my son is the only way to ensure my memories of him."—A bereaved parent

"Man as a Scientist": Grief from a Cognitive Perspective

From the cognitive perspective, a loss through death is an adverse external event over which there is no control, but which nevertheless changes one's belief system and its related emotions and behaviors. Grief is a cognitive, emotional, behavioral, and physiological experience in which cognitions have an important mediatory function, integrating them into the process of adaptation following a loss. Yet, the role of cognitions has typically been viewed as less central than that of emotions, perhaps due to the latter's overt nature as opposed to the covert nature of cognition. Also, emotions often have a flooding effect during the acute crisis following death. When the cause of death is more sudden, stressful, or traumatic (i.e., homicide, suicide, accidents, or natural or man-made disasters), emotions seem to dominate over cognitions, especially during this acute phase.

In traditional therapies, the emotional dimension of the grief process is the focus of intervention. The presence or absence of anger, depression, shame, and guilt reactions have customarily been crucial indicators to our understanding and evaluating short- and long-term bereavement outcomes, and also normal and complicated forms of bereavement (Rando, 1993). According to traditional models, the absence or avoidance of exaggerated emotional responses is assessed as an indicator of complicated grief (Worden, 1991; Hogan, Worden & Schmidt, 2004). For this reason, most traditional interventions apply cathartic techniques to help the bereaved alleviate the intensity of these emotions (Volkan, 1981; Worden, 1991), and cognitions are seen only as byproducts of emotional disturbance. The therapists' tendency to emphasize emotions as central to the process of grieving has led them to undervalue its cognitive aspects (Rando, 1984).

In contrast, the cognitive perspective emphasizes the centrality of cognitions as a key element in the process of grief on the one hand, and the relationship between emotions, behaviors, and cognitive evaluations on the other hand.

The view of "man-as-a-scientist whose ultimate aim is to predict and to control," as posited by G. A. Kelly (1963, pp. 4, 5), emphasizes the notion that humans think in a constructivist manner and form theories about themselves, the world, relationships, and events as they occur. These theories (or schemas), are reevaluated and reconstructed when experiencing events such as loss through death by shaping and guiding the person's way of coping with life events (DiGiuseppe, 1991). DiGiuseppe, using Kuhn's (1970) philosophical model, argued that like scientists, people generally tend to hold onto their theories. They change them for one of several reasons:

> first, there are logical inconsistencies in the theory; second, substantial empirical evidence is accumulated that is inconsistent with the theory; third, the theory cannot solve important problems and loses its practical or heuristic value; and finally, there is an alternative theory that is better (1991, p.177).

Death is an event that provides a reason, or may even force an individual to change his or her theory about the self, others, and the world. A similar idea was conceptualized by Janoff-Bulman (1992) in what she termed "world assumptions" and "shattered assumptions." Accordingly, "world assumptions" signify the way humans perceive the organization of the world around them. These perceptions stem from several basic assumptions that are sources of meaning attributed by the individual to the world and the events that take place in it. According to Janoff-Bulman, "traumatic events shatter these world assumptions, and change them." Three main theories underlie world assumptions: "Benevolence of the world," "meaningfulness of the world," and "self-worth." Sudden and unexpected death is considered as a traumatic event and is assumed to have a profound impact on a person's most fundamental assumptions (Janoff-Bulman, 1992; Kauffmann, 2002), or assumptive world. Parkes (1975, 1988, 1993) has proposed that the internal world must change when an individual experiences a psychosocial transition. This is a process of giving up assumptions and expectations that need to be revised as a result of dangerous life-changes. The metaphor of an earthquake best depicts the collapse within moments of one's world assumptions, to be followed by efforts to pick up the shattered pieces and reconnect them to yet another meaningful belief system. Although these conceptualizations use different terms (*theories, schemas, assumptions*), they all focus on the significance of cognitive processes in human experience.

Thus, from a cognitive-constructivist perspective, a loss due to death is the struggle between retaining a worldview that was, and the one that has yet to be searched for and constructed. Based on Marris's (1974) observations, every loss entails a change and every change involves a loss.

A Schema and its Role in Psychotherapy Following Loss

The conceptualization of construction and reconstruction of one's worldview has also been defined as a schema. In cognitive therapy in particular, schemas are central in the understanding of dysfunctional thinking. What are schemas? How are they formed? Can a schema be modified? Cognitive theory deals with these and related issues in an effort to understand better the role they play in therapy.

The term *schema* refers to a person's representations of past experiences with people or events upon which similar potential events or experiences are constructed or interpreted. The word *schema* is defined as "a diagram, plan or scheme; an underlying pattern or structure; conceptual framework, or (in Kantian epistemology) a concept similar to a universal but limited to phenomenal knowledge, by which an object of knowledge or an idea of pure reason may be apprehended" (*Random House Dictionary*, 1987, p.1713). Thus a schema is a mental structure that enables the processing of information. It has a biological basis, and it develops and changes with time (Stein, 1992). Importantly, there is a link between mental and physical, sensational and behavioral schemas.

Three basic assumptions are common to most definitions of a schema: It is a way to organize types of experiences with people and situations into a more global concept; the way a schema is formed is "bottom-up," based on repeated past experiences which are examples of the concept they represent; its function is to guide the organization of new information (Thorendyke & Hays-Rose, 1979, cited in Goldfried, 1995, p. 56).

Piaget (1950, 1952) made an important contribution to our understanding of how schemas develop while studying thinking processes among children. He described how the child develops "knowledge" about the world. Initially, the object is real only when the child sees and gets a sense of its realness through seeing and touching it. Gradually, the child develops a concept of

the object, even if it is not within reach or visible, while the actual development of the abstraction of the object is what Piaget termed a *schema*. A mental
schema develops through assimilation and accommodation, where the former
is the process of incorporating new information into an existing one, and the
latter refers to revising the schema to fit new information. In other words,
adaptation consists of two complementary processes, integrating new information with the existing one, and modifying the schema to the new information. Thus, new information can be assimilated or blended with existing
beliefs, or beliefs and ideas need to be changed as new information is being
introduced. Piaget demonstrated that a schema simultaneously both modifies
and becomes modified by experience. This perspective widens the interpretation of the complexity of the experience of loss as a process of reorganizing a
schema that has changed as a result of the death event. Grief can be considered as involving both assimilation and accommodation processes. Loss is a
negative event that often involves sudden and traumatic information. As
such, it implies having to deal with adaptation of the existing information to
the new one (accommodation), which will be partly processed, by incorporating it into preexisting constructs (assimilation). For example, the loss of a
loved one necessitates accommodation to the reality of everyday life that
excludes this person, and at the time it involves the incorporation of the
event into the individual's existing mental structure of relationships and
attachment patterns with the deceased and survivors. Adaptation can be
viewed as a process of oscillation between accommodation and assimilation. This pattern can also be found in the two-track model of bereavement
(see chapter 1).

A death event deconstructs a person's existing views about life and relationships, and requires a painful internal process of cognitively reorganizing what has been shattered following the external event. It also involves
modifying one's knowledge, thoughts, and feelings, of giving up old meanings to life, and forming new ones (Fleming & Robinson, 2001; Gluhosky,
1995; Horowitz, Bonano, & Holen, 1993; Kavanagh, 1990; Moorey, 1996
Neimeyer, 1999).

Whether primarily cognitively processed or emotionally experienced,
the cognitive perspective asserts that the more traumatic the event is, the
greater is its impact on one's belief system and other cognitions. Thus, the
cognitive approach upholds that for the grieving process to take an ade-
quate and adaptive course toward functional and satisfying outcomes,
grief-related cognitions should be identified, then included and treated as
an equal part of intrapsychic process (Gluhosky, 1995; Kavanagh, 1990;
Rando, 1988).

Cognitive Models:
Contributions by A.T. Beck and M.J. Horowitz

A characteristic shared by cognitive-behavioral therapy and cognitive therapy is a focus on the client, with the aim of relieving symptoms or resolving a problem. This is unlike more traditional therapies that tend to view the person as the problem and as the focus of an intervention that aims to produce a personality change. Cognitive-behavior therapy has evolved from what was mostly an extension of behavior therapy, central to which was to change the observed maladaptive behavior (stimulus response connection), with less attention given to the person's thoughts and beliefs. From the outset, cognitive therapy (CT) viewed the person's beliefs to be the source of emotional distress or disturbance with behavioral consequences. Nowadays, the terms CBT and CT are used interchangeably; the former specifically incorporates more typical behavioral types of intervention (i.e., practicing social skills), while the latter focuses more on the cognitive constructivist part of the therapeutic process by employing interventions that are typically more cognitively oriented (i.e., cognitive restructuring). These differences have narrowed and cognitive, emotional, and behavior interventions are now an integral part of the various cognitive formulations of psychotherapy.

Characteristically, all models of CBT and CT are short-term types of therapy. They focus on the here-and-now, and the therapist is active-directive in teaching and guiding the client who always actively participates in the course of treatment. Following the formation of a therapeutic alliance and assessment (general and cognitive), both parties engage in defining the problem and determining the goals of therapy, in defining each one's responsibility and commitment to therapy. A basic principle of CT implies the centrality of cognitions in emotional distress and the interplay between cognitions, emotions, behaviors, and physiological responses in maintaining the distress. Additionally, focusing on the here-and-now in therapy is an important element, while past events and relationships, as well as one's inborn predisposition and vulnerability to stressful situations, are assessed and considered as a source of the present distress.

The centrality of cognitions as mediators between adverse life events and emotional distress, and the option which characterizes CBT and CT, of adapting cognitive alternatives to alleviate the distress, make them efficient therapeutic models for grief. Cognitive therapy and its development is linked with a number of professionals who have sought alternative models for explaining emotional distress and also, more efficient interventions to help people suffering from it.

Among the founders of cognitive therapy, two psychiatrists, Beck and Horowitz, each of whom developed a cognitive model of therapy, have contributed to our understanding of grief as a cognitive process following a negative event. Beck and Horowitz are both linked to the psychodynamic school of thought, they trained as psychoanalysts, and each developed the concept that was to become a cognitive model of therapy.

A. T. Beck's Cognitive Model of Depression

A. T. Beck's contributions (1976, 2006) to cognitive therapy in depression are landmarks. Beck formulated his cognitive model for the treatment of depression during the 1960s, observing that depression is the result of a pervasive negative thinking about self, the world, and the future (what he termed the *cognitive triad* of depression), rather than anger directed inwardly that turns into depression, as was assumed by the psychoanalytic view of depression. According to Beck, an emotional disturbance is related to automatic thoughts derived from a person's schema about himself, his past, and future. Thus the interventions applied are aimed at identifying and changing distorted thinking. In Beck's words:

> As I have indicated previously, my own development of the cognitive model of psychopathology and of cognitive therapy began when I was practicing psychoanalysis. I intended initially to subject certain psychoanalytic concepts, such as the dammed-up aggression theory of depression to experimental validation. I found to my surprise that the studies of dreams, projective tests, verbal conditioning experiments, and success-failure experiments did not support the psychoanalytical hypothesis. However, they did fit into simple explanations provided by a cognitive model. (Beck, 1976, p. 334)

The studies and observations that led to the development of Beck's cognitive model involved a comparison between depressed and normal participants. In one study, Beck assessed the impact of task failure and success on self-esteem. He expected depressed people to react negatively to success. Much to his surprise he found that success was followed by improved self-esteem, which impacted positively on subsequent tasks, especially among depressed people. He concluded, contrary to existing notions, that depressed people do not have a wish to fail, but adjust their views of themselves to conform to their experience. Beck was critical of both psychoanalytic and behavioral models in that they undermined people's reports and the meaning they attribute to their internal and external experiences. In his view, minimizing the importance of reports and meaning is neglecting a critical psychological process for understanding emotions and emotional distress: "Meaning provides the richness of life; it transforms a simple event into an experience. Yet, contemporary systems of psychology and psychiatry either completely disregard meanings or go to extremes in seeking esoteric ones" (Beck, 1976, p. 47).

Beck (1996) first applied the concept of negative schemas to explain the "Thinking disorder" in depression, which he borrowed from Kelly's (1955) cognitive constructs. Kelly proposed that the activation of certain idiosyncratic cognitive schemas represented the core problem in depression and could be assigned a primary role in the production of various cognitive, affective, and behavioral symptoms.

Like Ellis (1962) and R.S. Lazarus (1966), Beck emphasized the importance of appraisal in understanding emotions. Beck's (1976) delineation of specific appraisals that lead to specific emotions of depression, though psychoanalytically oriented, is innovative in viewing the cognitive processes of meaning and appraisal as key elements in producing emotions. His analysis of the relationship between loss and sadness is pertinent to the theme of loss and grief, and will be discussed in the section on core beliefs and automatic thoughts.

Beck's efforts to validate psychoanalytical formulations empirically resulted in the cognitive model for explaining and treating emotional distress. His views of dreams are therefore no surprise; he concluded that dreams are reflections of everyday life rather than expressions of unconscious desires or motivation (Salkovskis, 1996). During his detailed exploration of the relationship between cognition and affect among depressed patients Beck (1963, 2006) could demonstrate that this existed among his interviewees. The proposed relationship between cognitions and affect was contrary to the psychoanalytic model that he practiced. This assumed that depression was caused by hostility turned against the self, and that internalized anger was at the core of depression. Based on his studies, Beck (1963) concluded that,

> distorted ideas of depressed patients appeared immediately before the arousal or intensification of the typical depressive affect, it was suggested that the affective disturbance may be secondary to the thinking disorder. The possibility of a reciprocal interaction between cognition and effect was also raised. (p. 232)

The negative interpretations that Beck observed were of the self, the world, and the future, which were formed in early childhood. These interpretations later became known as "core assumptions" upon which the schema is organized. According to Beck (1967), a schema is an organized (cognitive) structure of

> elements constructed of past experience that form a relatively cohesive and persistent body of knowledge capable of guiding subsequent perceptions and appraisals. (p. 147)

Based on the matrix of schemas, the individual is able to orient himself in relation to time, space and to categorize and interpret experiences in a meaningful way. (Beck, 1967, p. 283)

Since its first formulation as a model for treating depression, clinical and empirical experience has expanded its application to anxiety (Beck, Emery, & Greenberg, 1985), personality, and compulsive disorders such as substance abuse and dependency (Liese & Franz, 1996). Beck also proposed interventions "aiming at moderating or modifying the dysfunctional interpretation and predictions as well as underlying dysfunctional beliefs (incorporated into the dysfunctional schemas) could ameliorate the clinical disorder" (p.1).

The Formulation of Schema, Core Beliefs, and Automatic Thoughts in Beck's Cognitive Model

In cognitive therapy the concept of information processing is central. Information processing is filtered through schemas or core beliefs defined by Beck as the person's representations of past experiences with people or events upon which they construct or interpret similar potential events or experiences. As was mentioned earlier, Beck's initial model of the psychotherapy of depression was a psychoanalytic one, and his observations of the patients' verbal responses to his request to say anything that entered their mind without selection (which is a basic rule of free association), led him to explore these thoughts (pp. 29, 32). Beck noticed that unreported thoughts that preceded emotions were typically self-evaluative and included anticipation of the therapist's response. For example: "I am not expressing myself clearly. . . . He is bored with me. . . . He will probably try to get rid of me" (p. 32). So embedded in one's thinking were these unreported thoughts that Beck termed them *automatic thoughts.*

Beck observed that automatic thoughts had common characteristics. They were specific and discrete, expressed in a "shorthand" manner.

Moreover, these thoughts . . . , did not arise or result from deliberation or reasoning, or reflection about an event or a topic. There was no logical sequence of steps as in goal-oriented thinking or problem-solving. These thoughts "just happened," as if a reflex (1976, p. 36).

Automatic thoughts are a moment-to-moment stream of consciousness made up of ideas, beliefs, or images.

David Burns (1989) collaborated clinically with Beck in conducting research elaborated on automatic thoughts. Together they identified 10 common forms of these thoughts that are thinking or distorted errors that lead to negative moods. They include: all or nothing thinking ("If she doesn't say hello to me then she doesn't love me"); overgeneralization ("I always do it"); mental filter ("It's my fault that she died, why did I let her go?"); discounting the positive ("I know I did good things but I was a bad parent"); jumping to conclusions ("I will never get over it"); magnification ("It's awful to be criticized"); emotional reasoning ("I feel I am a failure"); "should" statements ("I shouldn't have made so many mistakes with her"); labeling ("I am a jerk"); and personalization ("If she left me I must be a rotten person"). Automatic thoughts are derivatives of schemas which are the person's basic beliefs about the self, others, and the world. Schemas are believed to be less flexible and are thought to be learned and shaped in early life (Dattilio & Padesky, 1990).

Departing from a psychoanalytic perspective, Beck searched for an alternative framework for understanding depression, and based on his studies developed the cognitive model of depression. He noticed that individuals who tend to be depressed construe a particular cluster of cognitions, which they repeatedly apply to life situations, and thereby form a continuous vicious circle. Beck observed that cognitions were all related to the theme of loss; past, present, and future, real and imagined. The tendency is to interpret adverse events in a very pessimistic way and draw extreme conclusions about oneself. Beck assumed that traumatic life experiences predisposed individuals to appraise subsequent life events in a more extreme manner, leading to extreme conclusions that are perpetuated by their tendency to overgeneralize. Real losses may then be interpreted as total losses. Beck's interpretation of depression among bereaved individuals focused on their negative evaluations of the self, unlike Freud's idea that depression among bereaved individuals was an unconscious expression of hostility, which could not be directed toward the deceased and instead was directed at themselves.

Characteristic of cognitive models, Beck's included interventions to treatment of emotional distress such as depression and anxiety, include training individuals to identify and evaluate their "thinking errors," and learn ways to challenge them through active procedures (including homework), and to explore alternative thinking. Cognitive and behavioral interventions applied so as to change them into more functional ones, lead to a relief from their depression (Beck, Rush, Shaw, & Emery, 1979). Similar to cognitive therapists, Beck approached cognitive therapy as a collaborative process between the therapist and the client, focusing on the here-and-now and time-limited type of therapy. The Beck Depression Inventory (BDI) is a validated, reliable measure of depression and is used worldwide.

Studies conducted in recent years (Dunmore, Clark, & Ehlers, 2001) support Beck's and Ellis's conclusions on the connection between cognitions and emotionality as sources of emotional distress. Likewise, studies on bereavement demonstrate that a cognitive centrality exists in the bereavement process. These and other studies show important differences between distorted cognitions appearing during depression and during complicated grief.

Mardi J. Horowitz's Model of Treatment of the Stress Response Syndrome

Psychiatrist Mardi J. Horowitz has written about PTSD, coping with stress and grief, and psychotherapy. Horowitz has developed a psychodynamic theoretical perspective combined with stress theory, cognitive elements of information processing to studying PTSD, and complicated grief, as well as a brief psychotherapy for bereavement (Horowitz, 1976/1986, 1979, 2001, 2003).

Horowitz developed his model of stress response syndromes based on Breuer and Freud's observations, (1883–1895/1955) in their work on hysteria, of the tendency of individuals experiencing a traumatic event to repeat compulsively their memories and perception of the event. Freud (1955b/1920) explained compulsive repetition as the ego's attempt to master the overwhelming effect of a traumatic experience and assimilate it through repeatedly reviewing the event. Elaborating on Freud's idea of compulsive repetition, Horowitz explained it as the individual's attempt to reduce the discrepancy between new information elicited by the traumatic event and a preexisting schema, and referred to it as "completion tendency." He compared the efforts to reduce discrepancy arising from a traumatic event to the process of assimilation and accommodation, and the oscillation between the two as proposed by Piaget (1950, 1952).

Horowitz further observed that the subjective response to stressful life events (loss through death, for example), comprises two independent forms of the experience: intrusion and avoidance, and the oscillation between them.

Whereas "intrusion involves the involuntary entry into awareness of ideas, memories and emotions associated with the event," avoidance "is the conscious attempt to divert attention from cognitions and feelings related to the life event" (Horwitz, Field & Classen, 1993, p. 761). The Impact of Events scale (IES) was developed to measure both forms.

Together with his associates Wilner and Alvarez (Horowitz, Wilner & Alvarez, 1979), Horowitz developed the IES to measure subjective distress that can be used in different kinds of stress-inducing life events, and can be repeatedly used to remeasure over time for both research and psychotherapeutic purposes. In one study the IES was applied to a group of outpatients who sought psychotherapy after experiencing the loss of a parent (Zilberg, Weiss, & Horowitz, 1982). They were compared to a group of volunteers who also experienced the loss of a parent. Two conclusions were drawn from the results: One is that there is a similar pattern of stress response between patient and nonpatient groups, and the other conclusion is that, "it is more useful to think of normal and pathological levels of stress as differing in degree rather than kind . . ." (Horowitz, Field & Classen, 1993, p. 763).

Schema, Appraisal, and Reschematization in Coping with Trauma

Central to Horowitz's model of coping with stressful life events is the notion of information processing in relation to preexisting schemas. The schema is an inner structure of expectations, assumptions, and notions about self and relationships with others that is developed in early childhood. This guides the person's appraisal in an almost automatic fashion through various life events and also includes assumptions about one's future plans. A traumatic experience such as loss through death is new information that is evaluated according to existing cognitive structures and undergoes a process of reschematization. In this process parts of the new information will be assimilated in the preexisting schema, while parts of the preexisting schema will change to accommodate the new information. When information cannot be assimilated within a preexisting schema or cannot be accommodated it will act to increase stress. According to Horowitz, stress events "are defined as a notable discrepancy between the implications of the event and the person's schema for understanding and reacting to events" (Horowitz et al., 1993, p. 768). In his analysis of the process of grief, Horowitz (2001) uses the terms *working model* and *enduring schemas* to describe the way the bereaved individual tries to reorganize the perception of the new reality with enduring schemas. If the working role relationship and the enduring schemas do not match, "intense emotions may arise, serving to motivate either plans for correcting the mismatch or defensive avoidance to reduce its recognition" (p. 164). For example, a traumatic event such as loss of a spouse affects one's enduring schema about the self (from a wife or a husband to a widow or widower) and the enduring schema of role relationship (from sharing life together with a partner to cherishing memories of him or her). The incongruence between inner representation of the other as part of one's life and the reality of the other missing from daily life needs to be assimilated into one's schema. It is a process of working through the new information in relation to inner models in ways of repeating and experiencing the event, so that the reality of the event and the inner model are congruent with one another.

The way that Horowitz (2001) conceptualizes the coping process is in terms of active and passive memory. A nontraumatic event is perceived, processed, and stored in passive memory. In contrast, a traumatic event is experienced time and again until it is part of the schema and there is a balance between what was and no longer exists and what is experienced as a result of the traumatic event.

Reschematization involves control processes that are the individual's way of selecting a specific schema to regulate emotions (Horowitz, 2001). Complicated grief can take two forms: Too much control by avoidance of processing the information and avoidance of its accommodation to the schema, or revising it, prevents completion of the process. In other words, too much control prevents the repeated memory from becoming what is characteristic of active memory. On the other hand, too little control results in a continual experiencing of the traumatic event in active memory leading to an emotional flooding which also prevents its processing and storage in passive memory. An optimal control includes alternation between denial and intrusion in a more balanced way, which in turn results in the new information being congruent with the person's schema (assimilation), and the schema that has changed to accommodate the new information. Horowitz's cognitive model of coping with stress is psychodynamically oriented and as such is typically an intrapersonal process, where cognitions and emotions are linked and activated consciously and unconsciously.

Coping with Stress as a Working Through Process and Psychotherapy

Horowitz (1976/1986) identified and formulated a phasic pattern in the process of working through a traumatic life event. What distinguishes between a normal and a complicated course of working through the loss event is not the composition of the phases but rather the level of intensity of the responses. In a traumatic event, such as a loss through death, the event initiates a pattern of responses. Schematically described, the normal course of responses includes outcry (fear, sadness, rage), followed by denial (refusing to face memory of disaster), and intrusion (unbidden thoughts of the event). These responses are followed by the phase of working through (facing the reality of what has happened) and rounded off by completion (going on with life). The maladaptive pattern of response is an intensification of the normal one. The response to the loss is overwhelmed and the outcry is experienced as panic or exhaustion. Denial is experienced as extreme avoidance, and intrusion takes the form of flooded states. These lead to psychosomatic responses which then develop into character distortion, whereas working through and completion are absent.

In cases of complicated grief, Horowitz has developed a time-limited psychodynamic grief therapy to assist the individual in overcoming difficulties in the coping process. In line with his theoretical framework of coping with stress, Horowitz's intervention model is a combination of psychodynamic theory and one processing cognitive information. Through facilitation of ego growth the traumatic experience can be assimilated and accommodated into preexisting cognitive schemas. Therapy is viewed as a learning process of reappraisal of the loss event, the meaning attached to it, and a way of identifying the emotions associated with the deceased.

The working relationship between the therapist and client is central to achieving this aim. It is noteworthy that within the therapeutic relationship the therapist is also a role model. Thus, a major component is the establishment of a working alliance with the client; while a trusting relationship is central and continues throughout the course of therapy. A working alliance is formed through the client's account, in as much detail as possible, of the traumatic experience and its circumstances. Once a working alliance has been formed, therapy proceeds to reevaluating and changing the client's control pattern of either too much control or its lack (denial and intrusion) toward a more balanced control pattern with oscillation between the two. Working through involves reconstructing the event or the schema through exploration and reexamination of the meaning attached to them.

Accurate empathy, flexibility, and encouraging the client to take an active role in therapy are important ingredients in the therapeutic process. Horowitz is aware of the implications of the final phase in this short-term treatment model of traumatic life events, and the possibility of the client feeling abandoned, feelings similar to those experienced as a result of the traumatic event. According to Horowitz, termination is anticipated and needs to be addressed as such in the initial phase, not as a way of preventing it but rather as an expected step in therapy. Thus, the client's feelings of anger and anxiety are discussed early in therapy so as to allow the client to gradually face the upcoming termination. In this model the therapist is more active, compared to a long-term psychodynamic therapy, transference is applied differently, and a useful technique for the therapist to apply is reconstructive interpretation.

Cognitive-Constructivist Perspective: Grief as a Process of the Search for Meaning

Constructivism is a theory of knowledge that refers to the way individuals construe reality. Among constructivists, the work of Michael Mahoney (1991, 1993, 2004, 2004a), on constructivism is noteworthy in being different from the mainstream cognitive therapies. Mahoney has clearly stated that in contrast to cognitive psychotherapies, originally developed to focus on information processing, constructivism saw the processes of meaning making as more central. It proposed a perspective wherein knowledge processes are intrinsic self-organizing activities, in part unconscious, in contrast to the more passive perspective of knowledge processes adhered to by models of information processing.

Constructivist approaches had a number of differences between them and the more traditional cognitive therapies in terms of how each explained and approached psychopathology, in how each viewed cognitions and emotions, and how each approached the focus of psychotherapy. According to Mahoney (1993) there are three assumptions characteristic of the rationalist (more traditional) approach: "(1) that irrationality is the primary source of neurotic psychopathology; (2) that explicit beliefs and logical reasoning can easily overpower and guide emotions and behavioral actions; and (3) that the core process in effective psychotherapy is the substitution of rational thinking for irrational patterns." (p. 189)

Constructivists object to the rationalists' view that emotions are the expression of problems and as such need to be "corrected." Rather, they hold that cognition and emotion are "dynamic expressions of the same (dis)organization processes that characterize the development of the self-system" (Mahoney, 1993, p. 191). Constructivists, according to Mahoney "share a view of human beings as active, complex and connected lifelong learners" (2004, p. 4) implying activity in shaping life. Mahoney maintains that emotions play a central role in organizing the pattern of being. Motivation and emotions, mind and body are inseparable and form the individual's identity, which is always in a relationship, even if it is a symbolic one.

Mahoney's conceptualization of human change processes is a dialectical one in which change and stability are two parts of the same system. Although humans tend to resist change, they continuously change from the moment of birth until the moment of death. The motivation to change is challenged by the will to keep things unchanged. Loss of a loved one is an event that forces a change requiring a psychological rebalancing.

Throughout the years both traditional cognitive therapies and constructivist ones have tended to emphasize the experiential dimension of psychotherapy, even though traditional approaches such as REBT maintain the reciprocal relationship between the adverse event, the belief one holds about it, and the emotional consequences (the A-B-C model of emotional disturbance as developed by Ellis).

A fundamental tenet in the constructivist approach is that humans construct their worldview of themselves, others, and the world. Events in one's life are much more than mere happenings or occurrences; they are perceived and interpreted by the individual and form a unique reality to which he or she responds. Experiencing stressful life events such as a loss through death threatens and sometimes shatters one's belief system; its reconstruction forms a process of sorting out and deconstructing old beliefs that no longer hold "true" and constructing new ones that make sense of the new reality. It entails a search for an accepted meaning of the event so it can be an integral part of the reconstructed belief system. Constructivism holds that a story that was shattered at the moment of death, and can no longer be told in its former form, will eventually be replaced by another one that has yet to be sought and constructed. The personal "theory" that held valid up until the moment of the loss event has been invalidated, and because of the circumstances is "forced" to undergo changes.

Furthermore, a loss through death is a loss of a relationship, which is one of the most fundamental experiences encountered by human beings. A loss of a significant other is painful and sad, an end of an era, but at the same time it is a beginning that entails an adaptation process that with varying degrees of intensity can last for a lifetime. Following loss many events will be perceived as reminders of the person who died; not only anniversaries such as birthdays and holidays, but also places, voices, smells, and other objects associated with the deceased. Thus, remembering is not only in the inner world of the bereaved but is also encountered in everyday life; thinking of how she or he would have responded, reacted, behaved in certain situations, and at other times how he or she would expect the bereaved to act, respond or behave.

From a constructivist perspective, grief is a process of reconstructing a new meaning to life without the deceased. Grief therapy and grief counseling interventions are seen more as a guided journey to searching for a new meaning to life without the deceased, rather than one with an end.

R. A. Neimeyer

If Mahoney has been noted for his general contribution to constructivism, Neimeyer's contribution has been noted for being grief-specific. His writings on the meaning of loss from a constructivist perspective have had an impact on both the theory and practice of grief and bereavement. Neimeyer's (2000, 2002) teaching of meaning reconstruction following loss has provided a broad view of theoretical aspects of the constructivist approach and its application to psychotherapy with the bereaved. In his numerous writings he has outlined what he considers to be the basic assumptions reflecting a constructivist perspective of human mortality and bereavement in general, and the implications of when and how to intervene with bereaved individuals in particular.

Accordingly: (1) Death as an event can validate or invalidate the construction of the basis on which we live, or it may stand as a novel experience for which we have no construction. (2) Grief is a personal process, one that is idiosyncratic, intimate, and inextricable from our sense of who we are. (3) Grieving is something we do, not something that is done to us. (4) Grieving is an act of affirming or constructing a world of meaning that has been challenged by the loss. (5) Feelings have functions, and should be understood as signals of the state of our meaning-making efforts in the wake of challenges to the adequacy of our constructions. (6) We construct and reconstruct our identities as survivors of loss in negotiation with others (Neimeyer, Keese, & Fantner, 2000, pp. 202–210).

Neimeyer (2000) viewed the process experienced by the bereaved individual as both a search for the meaning of life without the deceased and a search for the meaning of the death of the loved one. It is a continuous process of searching and sometimes finding a meaning, and sometimes not, adding new beliefs and subtracting old ones from one's existing worldviews of self and others. It is a dynamic process of constructing, deconstructing, and integrating meaning to the current frame of meaning. Thus, a meaning that is accepted by one individual is not necessarily accepted by others. At the same time, a specific meaning can turn into a less meaningful one as the bereaved continues to search for a meaning that makes "sense." Making sense following a traumatic loss is in many ways the individual's effort to rebuild a narrative that has lost coherence and continuity, to retell a story that in part is no longer applicable and needs to be replaced (Neimeyer, 2005a; Rynearson, 2001).

In his conceptualization of the process of grief as a narrative of meaning construction, Neimeyer asserts that both intrapersonal and interpersonal dimensions comprise it and occur within a sociocultural context, an important element in shaping the constructions. Bereaved individuals are part of a family that belongs to a community and a society. All these systems represent religious, cultural, and social traditions that play a role in the process of meaning constructions.

The constructivist approach to therapy has shifted away from the more "traditional" forms of CBT and their "simplistic" approach to viewing cognitions as an explicit linguistic form of thinking with intervention aimed at changing the "wrong" cognitions. Furthermore, CBT theorists like Beck and Ellis were criticized for focusing on the "rationality or irrationality" of thinking while ignoring the complexity of the link between language and its deeper "texture," which is implicit and inexpressible and therefore can neither be formulated as "beliefs" nor be changed by ways of challenging them. "A common shortcoming of cognitive accounts of meaning making is their simplistic assumption that the construction of significance is (or should be) [a] logical, verbalizable process." Rather "our construction of reality is in principle (sic) tacit, inexpressible in any complete sense in public speech" (Neimeyer, 2000, p.201). A constructivist narrative approach in psychotherapy, grief psychotherapy included, is less cognitive specific, but has a more holistic focus on the disrupted story, which is being reconstructed through a search for meaning of the loss and meaning to life following the loss (Neimeyer, 2005a). Narrative strategies are used, through writing (one's autobiography, and metaphorical stories), as well as oral narrative interventions to assist clients in verbalizing their "untold" story and creating a "dialogue" with the distressing parts of their disorganized narrative. Another method is psychodrama, using psychotherapeutic enactment to facilitate more adaptive ways to life following loss of a loved one (Neimeyer, 2005b). This vantage is essential if psychotherapy with the bereaved is thought to be a creative construction rather than a corrective one. The emphasis is on the therapist as a cocreator or coauthor of the process of reconstruction.

Chapter 4

Albert Ellis and the Model of REBT: The ABC Model of Psychotherapy

"What upsets people are not things in themselves but their judgments about things. For example, death is nothing dreadful (or else it would have appeared so to Socrates), but instead the judgment about death is dreadful—that is what is dreadful."—Epictetus, p. 326

From the Psychodynamic to the Philosophical Perspective: The Development of the Model

Rational Emotive Behavioral Therapy (REBT) is a cognitive-behavioral model developed by Albert Ellis during the mid-20th century. Ellis, a clinical psychologist, trained in psychoanalysis, part of the training process for a psychotherapist at that time. Ellis completed his training in 1947 and started his supervisionary training, employing traditional psychoanalytic methods with his clients. To his dismay, he realized their inefficiency as a mode of therapy. He questioned the number of sessions, the length of therapy, the passivity of the therapists, and the role of transference in resolving the clients' past parental conflicts. The insights that he observed were important but insufficient in inducing a change in the client's disturbance. Like A.T. Beck, Ellis noted clients' self-talk as a source of their disturbance. He termed what Beck referred to as "automatic thoughts" as "self-statements" and "irrational beliefs," while agreeing with Beck's observation of the tendency of depressed and anxious individuals to think automatically about themselves as failures. Ellis went on to say:

"I knew from my first year of using REBT with scores of clients that behind their "automatic" unrealistic thoughts were often unconscious, deeper evaluations that "really" led to their disturbances and even helped them create their disturbed thoughts. For example, "if I fail at this valuable relationship, and if people despise me for failing that will mean I am a rotten failure and an incompetent person." And "if I fail at this task, I'll be no good at anything important, and because being successful is beneficial, I'll be an inept individual." (Ellis, 1994a, p. xvi)

Ellis decided to terminate his psychoanalytic training and later published his seminal paper, "Rational Psychotherapy," presented in 1956 at the American Psychological Association's Annual Convention in Chicago. The first edition of his book *Reason and Emotion in Psychotherapy* appeared in 1962; in it he outlined his ideas about human nature and psychotherapy. In the 1950s Ellis was interested in Pavlovian ideas about dogs that responded to signaling (presenting food with or without noxious stimuli), which resulted in approaching or avoiding the meat presented to them. He soon realized, however, that unlike dogs, human approach or avoidance processes involved evaluations of "self-consciousness or thinking about thinking" (1994a, p. 11).

Ellis observed that humans can define, create, and evaluate "real" life (pleasant or stressful) situations as well as imagined ones. This was to become a central tenet in his REBT model of explaining human disturbance or distress. The introduction of the distinction between preferences, wishes, and desires (rational thinking) as functional forms of thinking, and absolutist needs and "must" (irrational thinking) as stress-increasing ones, laid the foundation of Ellis's ABC model of psychotherapy. These two alternative forms of thinking represent two contradictory yet innate human tendencies. One is the innate human tendency to interpret in an absolutist manner the occurrence of adverse situations ("It shouldn't have happened and if it did, it's awful"), while the other is the strong biological human motivation to change or improve things for the better (including changing one's defeatist thoughts and feelings).

In the ABC model Ellis included also the G (Goal) component that represents the human motivation to change and achieve one's goals. The D (Disputation) and the E (new Effect) represent the importance of disputing irrational thoughts that block the individual's motivation. Both tendencies are apparent in this model. Next to the wishes and desires to achieve goals, humans have a tendency to construct musts and demands that block them from actualizing themselves. When disputation (D) has successfully been applied, the result is a new Effect (E). The emphasis is on the choice one has to construct preference-focused beliefs (rational beliefs) or demand-focused beliefs (irrational beliefs). While the former increase the likelihood of more satisfying life activities, the latter are more likely to increase emotional distress.

Ellis postulated that the innate tendency to think irrationally is universal, and is assumed to have had survival reasons which nowadays are no longer functional. Human personality disturbances are thus a combination of biological predisposition and cultural-environmental factors. Adopting these views can explain Ellis's departure from the psychoanalytic approach of viewing human disturbance as related to unresolved conflicts with parental figures in early childhood (which in psychoanalytic therapy can be overcome with an insight about it). Rather, he came to view the past as a given event which cannot be changed, although the meaning that one attributes to it can (according to REBT, attributed meanings about one's past are changeable).

Right from its inception the cognitive model focused on the centrality of cognitions as a source in understanding emotional disturbance, but emphasized the circularity between thoughts and feelings. Related to the centrality of cognitions are two kinds of anxieties that Ellis refers to, ego anxiety that is identified in most CT psychotherapy, and discomfort anxiety, which he identified as a source of emotional disturbance. While ego anxiety is the client's total self-downing of themselves, discomfort anxiety deals with the client's low frustration tolerance. "Discomfort anxiety is emotional hypertension that arises when people feel (1) that their life or comfort is threatened, (2) that they must not feel uncomfortable and have to feel at ease, and (3) that it is awful or catastrophic (rather than merely inconvenient or disadvantageous) when they don't get what they supposedly must get" (1994a, p. 253).

Another important concept relates to secondary symptoms of disturbance. This concept stemmed from Ellis's observation that people tend to make evaluations about their thinking. The following quotation from the first edition of *Reason and Emotion in Psychotherapy* (1962) describes the construction of the thinking about thinking error:

> If you strongly construct negative feelings (C^1) such as panic and severe depression about unfortunate Activating Experiences (A^1) you then may create a set of rational beliefs (rB^2) about your (C^1) such as "I don't like feeling panicked. I wish I were not." But also often create a set of irrational Beliefs (iB^2) about your (C^1), such as "I must not be panicked! It's awful to feel this way. I can't stand it! I am no good for making myself panicked!" You then have pronounced secondary symptoms (C^2) about your primary ones (C^1)". (p. 19)

Again, it is not the negative event and the construing of negative feelings about it that produces distress, but evaluating the negative feelings experienced as ones that "ought," "should," and "must" not occur, is what is likely to increase emotional distress and therefore is considered as a disturbance about

disturbance (Ellis, 1962, 1994a). In REBT in particular, secondary (or even tertiary) symptoms of disturbance are identified, assessed, and followed by showing
the clients how to minimize their effect.

REBT stresses that the link between the A (Activating event) the B (Belief),
and the C (Consequence) is cyclical; also thinking, emoting, and acting are
interactional; though thinking is a major source for creating distress, it can be
changed into a more functional one. In other words the way we think influences the way we feel and behave as much as the way we feel and behave
affects our thinking. Secondary symptoms are the evaluation of how we
might feel under certain negative circumstances (thinking about the fear I will
experience if I enter the elevator increases the panic I experience).

Core Philosophy and the Belief-Consequence Connection: Functional and Dysfunctional Emotions

When first formulating his cognitive model, Ellis (1962, 1994a) assumed that
emotional problems resulted from people talking to themselves in a self-
defeating manner, but realized that self-talk only partially explained it. People's core philosophy underlying self-talk was the reason for disturbance. A
core philosophy (schema according to Beck) is the person's construction of
past experiences with people or events with which they evaluate or interpret
similar potential events or experiences. These processes are formed in early
childhood and continue to be repeated in self-talk both consciously and
unconsciously ("below-the-surface irrational belief," Ellis, 1994a, p. 28) and
are activated under what is perceived by the person as an adverse event.
Though core philosophy is shaped in early childhood, its repeated construction and reconstruction (*indoctrination* is the term used by Ellis (1994a)
becomes an integral part of the worldview. In his words (1994a),

> Once I had clearly begun to see that neurotic behavior is not merely
> externally conditioned or indoctrinated at an early age, but that it is also
> internally reindoctrinated or auto-suggested by people to themselves
> until it becomes an integral part of their presently held (and continually
> self-reiterated) philosophy of life, my work with my clients took on a
> radically new slant. (p. 30)

Clearly, a philosophical approach aimed at helping people change the
meaning they attribute to their past experiences replaced a psychodynamic
orientation where the therapist's aim is to help clients focus on their past.

How does emotional disturbance develop? It is likely to occur when individuals evaluate, based on core philosophy, their strong wishes to actualize themselves in a demanding and absolutist manner. There are three main categories: Demanding directed toward the self, toward others, and toward the world; demanding (absolutist musts, shoulds, and oughts) that takes the form of self-devaluation, devaluing others, and devaluing the world; and low frustration tolerance (LFT), and "awfulizing."

In the REBT model of therapy, Ellis (1994a) stressed the universality of the tendency to think "irrationally," the demand-based interpretation that self, others, and the world should be the way one wants them to be, and that human construction of demanding is carried out in an idiosyncratic manner.

Originally the model was called Rational Therapy to indicate the role of cognitions in understanding emotional disturbance, and to distinguish it from more traditional psychodynamic therapies that viewed emotional symptoms as the sole key to understanding disturbance. Philosophies, especially of the positive stream, were Ellis's inspiration in shaping his therapeutic model, one that throughout the years has undergone changes and revisions to its latest version, now referred to as Rational Emotive Behavior therapy (REBT). Interestingly, although the title did not always indicate the function of emotions, Ellis has strongly advocated the cyclical interaction between the Activating event (A), the Beliefs, and the Behavioral and Emotional Consequences (B-C).

The interaction between beliefs and emotions (and behaviors) has been referred to as the B-C connection in the ABC model. In the first version, the distinction between emotions related to "rational" and "irrational" beliefs was described in terms such as "appropriate" and "inappropriate" emotional consequences, later to become "healthy" and "unhealthy" ones. More recently, the different emotions are referred to as "functional" and "dysfunctional" emotional consequences, minimizing the judgmental element and emphasizing the subjective component of interpretation. In as much as the terms represent linguistic changes of the two types of emotional consequences, they indicate more importantly the covariance of interpretation to a given event rather than merely describing a symptomatic state of the individual. Stated differently, sadness and depression are both negative emotional consequences, each related to a particular interpretation which differs from what Ellis has called rational and irrational beliefs.

The REBT model postulates that emotional consequences (C) are not solely determined by the activating event (A) but largely by the beliefs (B) they have about the event (see figure 4.1).

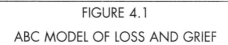

FIGURE 4.1

ABC MODEL OF LOSS AND GRIEF

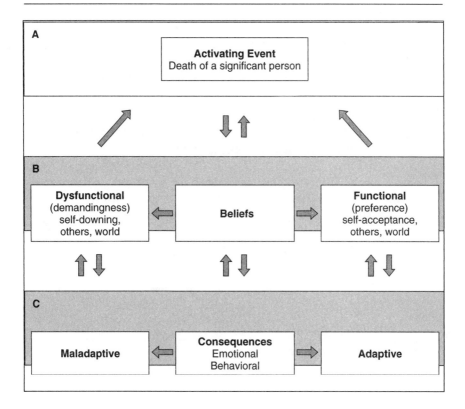

Loss (especially sudden and unexpected death) may be regarded as an adverse external event (A) that affects one's belief system (B), and consequently, one's emotions and behaviors (C). "People's cognitions, emotions, and behaviors are not pure but part of an organismic or holistic interaction" (Ellis, 1994b, p. 217). A cyclical interaction occurs among the event (A), the beliefs about the event (B), and the emotional and behavioral consequences (C) (Ellis, 1962; 1994a).

Absolutistic evaluations at B (irrational beliefs) are dysfunctional not in or by themselves but because they largely result in emotional upsetness at C (Consequence). "Awfulizing," low frustration tolerance, and self-condemnation are forms of irrational demandingness that are often followed at point C by emotional upsetness such as depression, anxiety, extreme shame, and guilt. The human tendency to irrational evaluation often reaches a peak following a death event, because of the thought held by bereaved individuals that the death should not have happened to them or that it is too painful for them to withstand (Ellis, 1976, 1994c).

If thinking, and in particular thinking about thinking, is a central component in emotional disturbance, then an important way to change these irrational beliefs is to use cognitive methods of which disputation has become associated with REBT.

REBT in Grief Therapy: The ABC of Constructing Rational and Irrational Meaning to the Loss

REBT in grief therapy integrates ideas about the human tendency to think irrationally when experiencing an adverse event, and a constructionist perspective that stresses a search for meaning that was shattered or threatened as a result of traumatic experiences.

A few elements underlie REBT in grief:

1. A loss through death is an irreversible adverse event which can be evaluated and interpreted in many different ways.
2. The distinctions between two types of thinking (rational and irrational) imply that the human tendency to irrationally evaluate the experiences can also be rationally interpreted. Evaluations and interpretations are a matter of choice.
3. The reciprocity between the event, the belief, and the emotion is related to the evaluations made about them.
4. REBT in grief distinguishes between adaptive emotional consequences (sadness, sorrow) and maladaptive ones (depression, anxiety).

Cognitive processes following a loss through death are central to REBT: how the event is processed will determine the emotional and behavioral consequences that in turn affect the cognitive process. In grief that follows a loss the emotional consequence will remain negative, but its quality (i.e., as a functional or dysfunctional emotional consequence), depends on whether the cognitions are adaptive (rational) or maladaptive (irrational). Rationality and irrationality do not equal positive versus negative thinking that are followed by positive or negative emotions. Rather, it is a substance that is comprised of each type of belief. Both rational and irrational beliefs are predictions and conclusions that persons draw about events in their lives which are generated from their schemas or core beliefs.

As an objective negative event, it is unavoidable that loss through death will involve negative evaluations and emotions. However, REBT distinguishes between negative evaluations that increase emotional distress and those that moderate it. The predisposition to think "irrationally" in an almost automatic manner tends to increase after experiencing an adverse event and is usually followed by extreme emotions such as avoidance ("I don't want to think that this happened to me") or intrusion ("I can't stop thinking why, why did it happen?"). The more traumatic the event, such as death from road accidents, wars, terror attacks, and natural disasters, the more likely is it that there will be a tendency to think in extreme patterns. Although temporarily less profound, "rational" thinking continues to be a source of a more realistic appraisal of the event and its consequences in one's lifetime. The tendency of individuals who experienced a traumatic event to compulsively repeat their memories and perceptions of the event is explained from a psychodynamic framework, as the ego's attempt to master the overwhelming effect of a traumatic experience in efforts to assimilate it through repeatedly reviewing the event (Horowitz, 1986). Both psychodynamic and cognitive frameworks identified a human tendency of extreme response to traumatic events, and each observed the pattern of reaction to the event and the process that follows, but each emphasized different components or mechanisms for its explanation.

The distinction between the occurrence of an adverse event and its evaluation has always been a major tenet in REBT. Ellis, in his early writings used the word *catastrophizing* to indicate the person's tendency to think irrationally and to exaggerate the evaluation of an event (any event perceived by the individual to be negative), and later changed it to *awfulizing* to signify that catastrophes, over which one has no control, do occur but their evaluation is a cognitive "choice." In other words, Ellis emphasized that it is the evaluation of an adverse event rather than the event itself that explains the individual's response. Moreover, evaluations are always subjective and idiosyncratic and take many forms. This in turn explains the variety of emotional, behavioral, and sensational consequences. The question then is what are considered the adaptive and maladaptive forms of grief?

Processing Adverse Events: "Rational" and "Irrational" Ways

How does REBT view adaptive and maladaptive grief? According to REBT, adaptive grief involves more flexible, realistic evaluations of the event, whereas maladaptive grief takes the form of distorted inflexible thinking, thereby increasing emotional distress. As mentioned earlier, REBT stresses the reciprocity between the belief system and emotional response. Hence, a dysfunctional emotional response is related to a dysfunctional evaluation that intensifies the distress, which then strengthens the cognitive processing, thus forming a continuous distress loop.

A major factor in emotional disturbance is linked to negative evaluations or dogmatic demandingness relating to oneself, others, and the world (Ellis, 1962, 1993). For example, bereaved persons with distorted thinking may interpret loss as an intended rejection ("How could he or she have done this to me?") (Beck, 1976) or as a confirmation for being worthless ("I am guilty and a worthless person for not saving his or her life") (Malkinson & Ellis, 2000).

Based on the main tenets of REBT, overreaction or a lack of reaction to the death of a loved one are not in themselves "right" or "wrong," neither preferred nor undesirable, but rather are related to a specific set of beliefs that result in either functional or dysfunctional (adaptive or maladaptive) emotional consequences. In the case of loss through death, negative emotional reactions (e.g., sorrow, sadness) are viewed as normal and adaptive "rational" cognitions.

Rational, functional beliefs (B) are realistic evaluations of adverse events (e.g., "Life has changed forever, it's sad and painful"; "The doctors did all they could do to save my child, I don't blame them"; "I know we did everything to keep him alive but that didn't help and he died"; "How sad and unfortunate that this happened to me"), and their related emotional consequences (C) are negative but not as upsetting: sorrow, sadness, regret, frustration, and concern (Ellis, 1994b, 1995).

The REBT approach to grief is that it is a normal and healthy reaction to a very stressful life event. As distinguished from depression, grief is a process of experiencing the pain of the loss and searching for a new meaning to life without the dead person, and it is also a process of restructuring one's irrational thinking to a more rational, realistic mode. Unlike depression, it is a process of searching for alternatives for a life without the loved one, who is the center of the pain and yearning. It is an oscillation between grieving the loss and having to make choices regarding the reality of the loss (Neimeyer, 1999, 2000; Stroebe & Schut, 1999).

Put differently, within the REBT conceptual framework, the grief process is a healthy form of thinking and emoting that helps the bereaved person organize his or her disrupted belief system into a form of adaptive acceptance. Thoughts about the death are not avoided, nor are they constantly remembered; rather, they are rearranged into a system that includes sadness and pain. Thus the bereaved person is enabled to adapt and live with the great loss. Grief that has a healing effect and that adapts to the sad reality, which no longer includes the deceased, involves pronounced negative emotions such as sadness, frustration, and pain. Yet it minimizes maladaptive, self-defeating feelings of depression, despair, horror, and self-deprecation.

Although the REBT model considers a more traumatic activating event or adversity (A) to render a greater effect on one's beliefs (B) and on one's emotional and behavioral consequences (C), it also considers the nature and closeness of the relationship to affect the bereaved's response. Parental loss of a child is particularly stressful when compared to other losses (Rubin & Malkinson, 2000), but it is not unlikely that an expected death of a close friend will be evaluated in a way that can evoke a strong reaction (Doka, 1989; Neimeyer & Jordan, 2002; Attig, 2004). The combination of the circumstances, the nature of closeness to the deceased, past experiences with losses, as well as other demographic variables, are likely to yield individualistic and idiosyncratic evaluations, and emotional responses will be in accordance. Different evaluations have the potential of increasing or moderating emotional responses. REBT postulates that when evaluations are exaggerated they are dysfunctional, because they increase the distress of an already stressful event over which the person has less control, as compared to the choice of its interpretation that can exerted. Thus, in this case, the Belief-Consequence connection will most probably result in overreliance on irrational beliefs that in turn will increase stress and reduce the individual's coping resources.

How does REBT view complicated grief? It is seen as an irrational evaluation, with distressing emotional consequences held by the bereaved over time; these evaluations are referred to as "irrational" maladaptive cognitions (e.g., "Life is not worth living without my loved one"; "I can't stand my life without my loved one"). From this perspective complicated grief is defined as prolonged and persistent over time with distorted, irrational beliefs as the dominant set of cognitions affecting the intensity of emotional consequences (Malkinson & Ellis, 2000).

In addition, while those individuals with functional beliefs are still traumatized and feel very badly about their loss, those with dysfunctional beliefs not only tend to feel continuously devastated, but also to create secondary symptoms about their primary bad feelings. As Moore (1991) pointed out, not only does irrational thinking tend to promote upset feelings, but one's traumatically upset feelings also tend to lead to irrational thinking: "Not only does cognition significantly influence emotion but emotion appears to significantly influence cognitions" (p. 10). Following a traumatic death event, people tend particularly to have both self-defeating (irrational) evaluations of the event, and self-defeating evaluations about their disturbed emotions (second-ary symptoms or disturbances). For example, a mother who lost her teenage son in a road accident (Adverse event) feels angry with her son (emotional Consequence); she is telling herself that he was careless and he should have taken a better care of himself (Belief). She then tells herself that she shouldn't think this way about her son and becomes angrier at herself for even consid-ering such a terrible thought. The mother's self-directed anger at her son is a secondary symptom or secondary disturbance anger about being angry (Walen, DiGiuseppe, & Dryden, 1992). In such cases, an irrational pattern of response is often more dominant than a rational one.

Bereaved individuals often respond extremely rigidly to the level of pain tolerance following an adverse event and develop a disturbance over a distur-bance. At times when the experience of grief is perceived by the bereaved to be too painful and unbearable ("Grieving is too painful") or when the reality of the loss is too difficult to comprehend ("I don't even want to think about him or her as dead"), avoidance of experience is an emotional consequence. In other words, having a secondary reaction over the primary one is a distur-bance over a disturbance (Walen et al., 1992).

"Reason" and Emotion in Grief

Grief therapy following a loss, unlike other forms of therapy, begins when a change in the person's life has occurred. Thus, the process of grief therapy is the result of a change rather than a process of change (DiClemente & Procheska, 1982). It begins with a problem or distress that the client wishes to solve or change. Grief therapy is then initiated because of a change.

By its very nature, the normal process of grief entails sadness, pain, yearn-ing, anger, guilt, shame, and envy, which are negative emotions, all or some of which can be experienced by the bereaved individual; the occurrence and intensity of these emotions is not only likely to vary from individual to indi-vidual, but will also vary during different phases of the individual process. As was suggested earlier, the persistence of intense negative emotions over time that increase emotional distress is considered maladaptive. Depending on the phase, the goal of therapy is either to normalize or moderate negative emo-tions in order to facilitate a more adaptive process. Characteristically in grief, the flooding effect of emotions tends to be associated first and foremost with the adverse event and less with the way it is being evaluated ("I am angry because he or she died"). The tendency is to undermine the role that cogni-tions play ("I tell myself that I shouldn't have agreed to him taking the car") in mediating between the event and the emotions one experiences. Underlining the centrality of cognitions is a significant source for helping the bereaved to regain an inner control where the external one existed at a minimal level if at all.

A closer look (Table 4.1) at different emotional consequences will reveal differences in cognitive evaluations between functional and dysfunctional emotional consequences such as sadness and depression, concern and anxiety (importantly, the meaning ascribed to the terms can vary from individual to individual signifying not only linguistic differences but also perceived and experienced life events).

If the evaluation of the event is critical to understanding the course the process takes, what is the B-C connection of the experience of loss? The cognitive pattern related to sadness through a negative evaluation of the event is a realistic and flexible one: "Life has changed forever," or "I will miss my loved one very much"; this is distinct from depression, which is also a negative evaluation but is typically stated in a more absolute, rigid self-focused and total manner: "Since she died my life is worthless, I therefore don't want to live any more, I feel worthless."

Inasmuch as sadness is seen as an obvious and natural response to loss, pain is also common and natural but often is avoided only for the bereaved person to realize its dominant part in healing. The inclination to avoid the pain is the evaluation of its associated suffering ("I can't bear the intensity of the pain"). Similar to sadness, pain is assigned different meanings by bereaved persons as they search for a meaning to life without the deceased. Unlike sadness, pain is thought to be a fear-provoking emotion that should be avoided. Not only is pain a normal reaction in grief, it is an inevitable part of its experience. The process of realizing that the presence of the loved one in everyday life is no

TABLE 4.1
Grief related evaluations and emotional consequences

Sadness: Life has changed forever.	**Depression**: My life is worthless.
Anger: He or she didn't think about the outcomes.	**Rage**: How could he have done it to me?
Pain: It's painful to think that I will never see her again.	**Anxiety**: It's too painful, I don't want to think about it, I can't stand the pain.
Concern: I couldn't help it, I will miss her greatly.	**Guilt**: It's my fault. I wish I were dead.

longer tangible, necessitates a shift toward a presence of memory and an inner representation, and is very painful. Many routine activities that involved the loved one are valid no longer. Detaching from what life has been with the deceased to life without him or her is a painful journey. It entails deconstructing a reality and reconstructing a memory. Minute decisions are taken almost everyday, especially during the acute phase. They involve "undoing" or "unweaving" the lost relationship to redoing and reweaving the fields of memory.

Pain can take many forms. Among bereaved individuals there are those who avoid the pain of the loss because it is too painful and is evaluated such that they will be unable to withstand what is considered unbearable ("I avoid going to places that he used to go to do shopping because its too painful"; "I took all the pictures away because seeing them is having to accept that he is dead, which I rationally know but the feeling is too painful and I can't stand it"). But pain can also be associated with a strong wish not to forget the deceased. Such is the case with bereaved individuals who want to or must maintain the pain as a way of remembering the deceased ("That's the only way to remember him or her"). In REBT terms it is the bereaved's evaluation of the pain and the reason for maintaining or avoiding it which is the focus of assessment to determine its functionality or dysfunctionality ("I must remember . . . and suffering the pain is the only way to do so" ; or "The pain is so overwhelming that the only way to survive it is by avoiding it").

Similar to sadness, pain as an integral part of the process of searching for a meaning to life without the deceased, can partly be avoided as an adaptive way (a functional avoidance), but when avoidance is absolute it can result in increased emotional distress. "It is painful to think that I will never see/hear/talk to my beloved," will result in experiencing a moderately, less intense pain, whereas, "I can't stand the pain, it shouldn't be so painful, and it's not fair that I have to suffer so much," or "I deserve the pain for not preventing the loss," are cognitions that are most likely to increase distress and need be avoided.

The same can be applied to anger, a normal and common feeling in grief but the distinction is made between functional and dysfunctional anger, each related to a certain set of cognitions. "When I think of the circumstances of the death of my beloved I get very angry at him or her for not being more careful" (rational thinking); or "How could he or she have done it to me, I will never forgive him or her" (irrational thinking). Guilt, shame, and hostility can be viewed in a similar manner, assessing the functionality or dysfunctionality of the emotional consequence to identify the set of cognitions, self-worth, or self-defeat, that maintains each one.

Without doubt, feelings are viewed as having a function in the process of reconstructing what was shattered and inasmuch as we know their intensity during the acute phase of grief, we also understand that the cognitive process of assembling the pieces and their assimilation will result in a reduced intensity of feeling.

From a cognitive perspective, teaching clients the B-C connection is also a way to help them regain control over an uncontrollable loss. Moreover, it is a painful journey of making choices in reconstructing an alternative worldview about one's life after experiencing a loss.

Constructing a Rational Meaning of the Loss

Ellis has been criticized for his "rationality" approach, which has been understood to exclude emotions from human experience (Ellis, 1994a, 1994b). In REBT terms beliefs are "rational" or "irrational" not in and of themselves, but are defined to be so because of the emotional consequences they elicit that can be either functional or dysfunctional. Stating it differently, emotional consequences (more or less distress) will indicate how rational or irrational beliefs are.

Another criticism raised by constructivist therapists is that REBT and other forms of CT assume that distorted thinking can be "restored" or "corrected" rather than, as they emphasize, created (Mahoney, 2004; Neimeyer, 2000). But a closer look reveals that cognitive therapies and REBT in particular hold that cognitions are constructed and affect emotions and behaviors; emotions and behaviors also affect cognitions by interaction. They are interrelated in that each affects the other in a circular way.

In Ellis's words (1994a):

> Unlike most other therapies, REBT clearly distinguishes between healthy negative feelings like keen sadness and grief when one suffers a great loss— and unhealthy negative feelings such as serious panic and depression when one suffers a similar loss. It therefore encourages strong negative feelings (C's) about unfortunate Activating Events (A's), but doesn't favor all negative emotions. It discourages unhealthy negative feelings by showing clients their functional and dysfunctional Beliefs (B's) about their unfortunate A's and by teaching them how to maximize the former and minimize the latter. (p. 309)

Moreover, people largely create their emotional distress by strongly adhering to an extreme and inflexible way of evaluating events in their lives, what Ellis has termed *irrational beliefs* (1994a). These constructions are partly learned and influenced by the cultural context in which the individual is set, and partly are innate biological tendencies which intensify under stressful circumstances. If man creates self-defeating constructions, he can change these constructions into less disturbing stress-producing ones. In this respect we can assume that evaluations are bidirectional and can be constructed in either a rational or an irrational manner.

Experiencing the loss of a loved one is a life event that triggers stress-related evaluations; certain types of evaluations, especially if they are rigid "musts," potentially increase distress, while other less rigid and more flexible evaluations may lead to a moderate level of distress. The flooding effect of emotions increases the feeling that one has no control; this in turn intensifies emotions and increases the sensation of loss of control. Helping individuals to regain an inner control involves "teaching" them the connection between evaluations and emotions and showing them the difference between "rational" and "irrational" beliefs and the related emotional consequences. As proposed by Ellis, the psychoeducational approach has become strongly associated with cognitive therapies, REBT included. Although criticized for its active, directive style, which minimizes the individual's "natural" desire to adopt an alternative self-model, the psychoeducational approach does not contradict the constructionist perspective, but rather complements it. Oftentimes, traumatic events are followed by a temporary sense of helplessness, weakening existing inner resources, which from a cognitive perspective can and need to be strengthened or even restored. Learning to construct an alternative evaluation is essential. For example, a woman who has lost her husband in a terror attack and is left with three children now believes she has the responsibilities of both mother and father, a thought which is probably at least partly true. However, she can be shown how to be less demanding of herself as a mother and as a person, and this will enable her thereby to moderate an already stressful situation. She describes how this feeling increases her stress when she cannot attend to her children's needs, which results in failing herself by not coping as she must. She further criticizes herself because she must respond in the way she did in the past when her husband was alive and could balance her demands.

Viewing individuals as story-tellers for whom loss severs their narrative, and grief as the process of its reconstruction, as posited by constructivists, integrates well with the REBT notion of individuals developing a philosophy about life whereby they evaluate events that are especially adverse in their lives. Cognitive grief therapy as presented in this book approaches intervention as a process of both reevaluating one's distress, increasing emotions, and changing related cognitions to "rational" ones, and reconstructing and renar-rating a life story that was disrupted as a result of loss.

The following is an illustration of integrating REBT that focuses on dys-functional cognitions (correction) and a constructivist's concept of meaning construction (creating). It is the case of a woman who had suffered the sud-den and unexpected loss of her husband some months earlier from a heart attack. The devastation of the loss was experienced on several levels, as the woman tried to make sense of life without her beloved husband. Although she was active functionally, made decisions, and considered her future with regard to work, she was sad, found herself crying frequently, talked about how much she missed her husband, and wondered how her life would be without him. She mentioned that she avoided doing certain activities, not because she didn't know that her husband was dead, but doing these things was too painful and was a reminder of the reality of his death. It was almost as if she needed to control her own stream of thoughts by determining what she could and wanted to think about. She seemed to know what thoughts elicited pain and tried to avoid them. Her way to regulate and control the level of pain that she feared she would be unable to withstand, was by avoiding it.

Two elements are salient in the client's account of her life following the loss: Disruption of her life story, and elements of distress-increasing evalua-tions of the reality that excluded her husband.

> I don't buy apples because my husband loved them. And if I buy them they will be kept in the bowl in the kitchen so I will see them all the time and it will be too painful. It will remind me that he is dead, something that is too painful. If I don't see the apples I can avoid thinking about it, avoid the pain and avoid the reality of the loss that I rationally know I am wrong about, but thinking about it is too painful. I am trying to "control" the pain by avoiding things like that.

During therapy the aim is to lessen, but not avoid, the experience of pain. Paradoxically, experiencing pain is the way to heal the fear of not being able to withstand it. Explaining how the loop of avoidance does not result in "no pain" but on the contrary might increase it, the client has information about her dysfunctional evaluation: "It will be too painful and I can't stand it, I am suffering enough" and change it into a more adaptive way of thinking. It is painful and perhaps I can try to buy apples and see how I feel." A few sessions later the client said laughingly: "I bought apples." She experimented with an alternative evaluation and behavior to realize that avoidance maintained rather than prevented the "awfulness" she was experiencing in continuing to search for meaning to life without her husband in a less disturbed way.

The therapist gives information about dysfunctional beliefs and encourages but does not force the client to experiment. This is especially important in cases of avoidance, which like many other distressful responses, tend to be habituated. The importance of a detailed cognitive assessment is stressed: What does the client do or not do since the loss, what is the intensity level (overdoing, moderate, or excessively doing it), and what are the emotional consequences of each?

Thus from the cognitive constructionist perspective it is the combination of both psychoeducational interventions such as information giving, with what is considered to be constructivist ones, that may yield effective outcomes in assisting the client to deal with the changed reality and to find a path to learning to live with adaptive pain.

Elements of correcting dysfunctional thinking with elements of searching and creating new meaning are apparent. Often the reason for maintaining a certain belief is related to yet another belief that "if this is so, then it must be right or true."

Like other CBT and CT models, REBT uses a variety of interventions—cognitive (disputation, thought restructuring, and reframing), emotional (guided imagery), and behavioral (practicing skills as homework assignments)—to improve the person's coping, reduce emotional disturbance, and increase self-control, especially when circumstances are uncontrollable. As a psychoeducational model it relies on the individual's active involvement both during and between sessions (homework assignments) in changing and adopting a more rational evaluation of the event, resulting in more functional emotional and behavioral consequences.

Conclusion

REBT as developed by Albert Ellis suggests that the origins of emotional disturbance are cognitive, emotive, and behavioral and that cognition is a mediator between an event and its emotional consequences. Dysfunctional emotions largely follow from irrational thinking (demandingness). A central tenet in REBT is that human beings are born with a biological predisposition to think irrationally. Some are born with a greater tendency to think irrationally and will therefore exhibit more distorted evaluations. The biological tendency to think irrationally coexists with the healthy human tendency to actualize oneself (Ellis & Bernard, 1985).The premise that emotional disturbance and behavioral symptomatology are maintained as a result of dysfunctional evaluations is central to REBT and cognitive therapy. It has been adapted to cognitive grief therapy, distinguishing between the adaptive and maladaptive course of grief. Its belief was that these can be modified through a variety of cognitive, emotional, and behavioral techniques both during the sessions and between the sessions in the form of homework assignments. These can be applied in cases of acute and prolonged grief following death, such as combining guided imagery, exposure techniques, thought stopping, cognitive restructuring, breathing exercises, and skill acquisition that are all aimed at assisting clients to adapt to the new reality without the deceased. Interventions include helping the bereaved to construct more adaptive evaluations and to reconstruct new meanings. This integrated approach emphasizes the idiosyncrasy of cognitive processes, while recognizing the universality of grief reaction following loss. From the REBT perspective, viewing cognitions as central to understanding emotional disturbance indicates the choice a person has in interpreting a "choiceless" event such as a loss event (Attig, 1996, 2000).

Thus in cognitive grief therapy, a distinction is made between "rational" adaptive thinking, which results in the emotional consequence of sadness, and "irrational" maladaptive thinking, which results in prolonged distress and at times depression. Grief therapy is a multifaceted process of assisting the bereaved to cope with the stress that follows the loss and to cognitively construct a more balanced or rational inner relationship with the deceased. A variety of cognitive (thought restructuring), cognitive emotional (imagery), and cognitive behavioral (learning new social skills) interventions are at the disposal of the therapist.

Part II

The Practice of Cognitive Grief Therapy

Chapter 5

Assessment and Interventions

"For me a meaningful accomplishment as a result of therapy is that I learned not to fear the pain of the loss and to live with the continuous yearning." –A woman widowed after the prolonged illness of her husband

As was noted, earlier empirical investigations revealed that not all interventions following loss are necessary or effective. Based on meta-analyses of evidence-based studies, the recommendations pertaining to the efficacy of grief therapy suggest that it is more effective in cases where the circumstances are traumatic, and when grief takes a complex form; also, the effectiveness of therapy increases when the bereaved self-refer themselves for help (Jordan & Neimeyer, 2003).

In general, the goal of grief therapy, regardless of its theoretical adherence, is to normalize, legitimize, and provide information to the client about grief, its processes, components, and possible outcomes, and to facilitate an adaptive (even though painful) process of grief in a life that has changed for ever.

Cognitive grief therapy is a short-term, phase-related mode of intervention. In most cases the focus is on the present and the establishment of a therapeutic alliance for a collaborative relationship between therapist and client, and a mutual understanding of the process of therapy and its expectations. In cognitive grief therapy, the therapeutic alliance is used to encourage clients to reevaluate and change their distorted thinking. Moreover, in addition to cultural sensitivity, cognitive therapy approaches the therapeutic alliance as a vehicle that needs to be tailored to each client's idiosyncratic needs. Whereas some clients will benefit from a more formal type of therapeutic relationship, others will be more comfortable with an informal one (Dryden, 1991). The establishing of an effective therapeutic alliance in working with the bereaved is particularly critical because clients are vulnerable and susceptible to the way the therapist responds to their distress. Also, the alliance is viewed as a dynamic process so that its reevaluation along the course of therapy is recommended. Similarly, in cognitive therapy the choice and application of intervention is in accordance with each client's idiosyncratic needs. Some clients benefit from a more cognitive type of intervention (an inner dialogue) whereas others do better with rational emotive imagery.

Triple Assessment

By employing a thorough assessment in the initial phase and throughout therapy, the therapist becomes more attentive to how the client responds to therapy and whether any accommodations need to be discussed for it to proceed in the desired direction. There are a number of methods that determine which interventions are best suited to assist the client in the process of adapting to the loss—the demographic one is most frequently applied. It includes a set of questions pertaining to the client's past and present experiences, especially those relevant to experiencing losses. For example, it is possible that clients may relate to a variety of experiences of losses, not necessarily death related, but the fact that those experiences are perceived as losses makes them relevant to the assessment. There are several ways to conduct an assessment; these include the use of standardized measures or self-monitoring, as well as projective methods. Of the three, two types of assessments will be elaborated for purposes of determining the level of adaptability to life following loss and subsequent grief: those based on The Two-Track Model of Bereavement (TTMoB) and on a cognitive assessment. Each one provides a specific view of bereavement, and when combined they offer a comprehensive perspective necessary for planning and applying cognitive grief therapy.

Assessment Based on TTMoB

Assessment based on TTMoB has already been outlined in chapter 1 while pointing to the importance of assessing the various components along each axis (the functional and the relationship to the deceased axes); the interaction between them; the presence or absence of specific components; the magnitude, intensity, frequency, and duration of responses for purposes of determining the course and choice of intervention; as well as dominance of either one in the way the story is told. The following are case illustrations which will be assessed based on TTMoB.

A 50-year-old man was referred to therapy following the death of his 21-year-old daughter who had committed suicide a few months earlier. He said: "She made more than one attempt to kill herself and each time we believed we had convinced her not to take her life away as we loved her so much. During the last few days of her life she had felt somewhat better and we were hopeful that a new beginning was awaiting all of us. That evening we went out to visit friends and left her by herself. When we returned home later that evening we could feel that something terribly wrong had happened, there was that quietness in the air. We found her hanged in her room. Although it was not unexpected we were shocked and devastated. Life became a nightmare, I can't stop thinking "why" she did it, and I am flooded with rage and guilt. I can't sleep at night, and when finally I do fall asleep the image of her keeps on returning and my efforts to calm myself are futile. I keep on thinking that I could have saved her if I had stayed at home, and I can't forgive myself for going out. She was just beginning to feel a little better about herself and her life, and although I know that she had a long way to go before I could say that she was feeling more secure and settled, I was hopeful that she was on the right track. I have given up my work as I have been too distressed to function and life has lost its meaning for me. I feel I am a failure for not preventing her death.

We can see here an example of a traumatic loss, which is also described as a violent death (Rynearson, 2001). Although not unexpected it was nevertheless shocking and devastating.

From the description by the bereaved father of his experience following the tragic death of his daughter, the dominance of the functioning aspect was apparent, although there was some evidence of interaction between the functional and the relational tracks as well. Components typical of the functioning track include restlessness and anxiety, depression and sleeping difficulties, combined with feelings of helplessness and extreme sadness to a point of disruption in functioning that led the father to give up his work. The intensity of preoccupation with the circumstances of the death of his daughter was indicative of features associated with acute stress disorder (ASD) which is a variation of PTSD, but as the name implies, refers to the acute phase (Foa & Rothbaum, 1997). The description of components of the relational aspects, though partial, were indicative of possible areas of conflict about the nature and quality of the relationship with the daughter as described by the father: they include the daughter's past attempts to take her life, alongside the hope that things would improve. These areas would have to be explored further as therapy proceeded and when the timing was assumed to be appropriate. The various components, their presence or absence, magnitude and intensity would be reassessed as therapy progressed. However, in accordance with the working method of the model, what determines the priority given to either track depends on the bereaved's narrative therefore in the specific case, functional and trauma elements in particular should receive priority in the initial phase of therapy.

In her book *The Blessing of a Broken Heart* Sherry Mandell (2003), the mother of Koby, told how he and his friend were stoned to death by Arab terrorists:

> "Mourning my son has similarities to labor. The contractions of pain rush through my body like a knot that is tied tighter and tighter so that I am unable to breath, dead along with my son. My womb becomes a grave. I feel the pain of him in my belly, a pressure bearing down in me. It will always be inside of me. And although I hope and pray that one day I will not be as great with pain as I am now, the pain will never leave me.
>
> Still, it feels like I am pregnant, pregnant with death, giving birth to a new self—a self that can navigate the depth of suffering, and yet go on with life. . . . I try to remember my son's face. It is difficult for me to picture him clearly in my mind, to retrieve his physical presence. I will no longer gaze at his beautiful face, admiring his almost-man's contours. . . . I took pleasure in his growth, admired his ever increasing height. . . ." (p. 13)

Track II focuses on the bereaved's experience with the deceased and looks for a clue to understand the construction of the inner relationship with him or her. Mandell's description is an example of the cognitive and emotional construction of the loss, describing the enormous pain by using the metaphor of labor and the womb as a grave. Though this description is not a part of therapeutic assessment it best captures the magnitude and continuity of the inner relationship with the deceased child.

Both TTMoB and cognitive assessment are seen as dynamic multidimensional processes that evolve during therapy and include a variety of domains. Applying TTMoB to determine the centrality of either track enables the therapist also to identify some cognitive and emotional elements. These too will need to be assessed.

Cognitive Assessment

Cognitive assessment, unlike more traditional forms that assess the individual's motives and drives (which are often unconscious), is concerned mainly with what the person thinks and the meaning he or she attributes to various life situations. Cognitive assessment is an attempt to evaluate how individuals process, organize, and construct their perceptions of events that occur in their lives. Information (schema) is organized by the individual based on past experience and its representations and is the person's worldview. Adverse events shake the person's worldview and the new information will be processed, partly assimilated, and partly accommodated, in the search for an alternative meaning that will be reconstructed throughout the process of adapting to life without the deceased. There are several ways of conducting a cognitive assessment, including structured questionnaires such as the Beck Depression Inventory (BDI) or structured interviews.

A combination of creative and corrective considerations will be applied for assessing and planning an intervention. Constructivist therapy emphasizes the creative rather than the corrective aspect of intervention. According to REBT, intervention in cases of complicated grief combines creative and corrective components. If we assume that individuals have an innate tendency to construct dysfunctional beliefs, it is necessary to help them identify this tendency, and show them how to modify these beliefs into more realistic ones so as not to increase their distress but rather moderate the pain, the outcome of which is a decreased emotional distress. In traumatic losses the worldview is often shattered and the tendency to think in an exaggerated manner prevails. Hence, identifying distorted cognitions and assessing the shattered elements of the narrative will enable the choice of an intervention to correct and reconstruct the story. Thus, the assessment of the bereaved's perception of the loss will include details about the adverse event, the individual's beliefs, emotions, and behaviors, the structure of the narrative, and the bereaved's use of idiosyncratic language (DiGiuseppe, 1991).

Assessing the ABC of the Story and Exploring the Belief–Consequence (B–C) Connection

In cognitive assessment, as in any other form of assessment, attentive listening to the telling of the story, the language used, and choice of words (a sigh, a pause or a moment of silence, facial or body nonverbal elements, emotional moments when tears appear or efforts are made to avoid tears), are of particular importance, as they are details through which related cognitions and emotions can be explored. Exploring through the use of questions may elicit the thoughts that are linked to the emotional or physical consequences of the B–C connection, such as: "I noticed you were very emotional just now, I wonder what went through your mind?" or "You kept silent after mentioning your son's name, what were you thinking about?"

To formulate a hypothesis regarding the client's thinking and its interaction with emotions and behaviors (Beck, 1976; DiGiuseppe, 1991; Kavanagh, 1990), the therapist should first seek to explore details concerning the activating event (A), the telling of the story. In cognitive therapy and REBT in particular, cognitive assessment is focused on establishing a hypothesis regarding the relationship between thoughts and emotions. According to Ellis (1994a), this does not require a lengthy and elaborate Activating event (the telling of the story); in the case of grief, however, an elaborate Activating event is not only necessary for understanding the meaning of the loss, but is also a way of venting thoughts and emotions that in many cases are told for the first time (Malkinson, 1993; Malkinson & Ellis, 2000).

The client's detailed perception of the death event should be elicited during the intake sessions and should be reassessed as therapy progresses, in conjunction with the collection of general demographic information and the person's underlying schema or assumptions about the self, others, and the world, so as to identify the individual's dysfunctional beliefs (Ellis & Bernard, 1985; DiGiuseppe, 1991; Dryden, 2002). A detailed assessment of the client's perceptions of the activating event (A) will assist the therapist in identifying the client's loss-related irrational beliefs (B) that underlie specific emotional consequences (C) (Malkinson, 1996), and will also enable the therapist to make a distinction between functional and dysfunctional responses (B, C) to the death. This distinction is especially pertinent to sudden, traumatic events, which are characteristically negative and overwhelming. As Ellis (1991, 1994b, 1994c) emphasized, dysfunctional thoughts about the adverse event ("How could she have done it to me? I will never forgive her for leaving me," "It shouldn't have happened to me," "This shouldn't have happened at all," "I should have prevented it") coexist with functional, healthy thoughts ("It's so painful but I did all I could to help her").

What and How to Assess?

In addition to assessing the cognitions and emotional consequences, exploring the death event in detail may have a cathartic effect, because telling the "story" includes one's interpretation of how one feels about it, while offering an opportunity for the client to express rational and irrational thoughts he or she may have about the event itself or thoughts about the self, others, or the circumstances surrounding the loss (Malkinson, 1996). It is essential to explore with the client the personal meaning of the loss event (e.g., "She was all my life, my life is worthless without her") and of the lost person (e.g., "He was the only one who cared for me") (Freeman & White, 1989). This includes how the loss is verbalized and what specific words do or do not mean to the client (e.g., "I am tired of life"). These will assist the therapist in proposing an alternative interpretation, paying special attention to the person's linguistic style. As was stated earlier, the purpose of the grief process is to make sense of the loss and construct a meaning to the death and to life without the loved one who died, and integrating this meaning in rebuilding one's beliefs, which had been shattered. It involves a painful search for what was lost and never to be regained, and what could be remembered in spite of the pain these memories elicit. In this sense the grief process is similar to weaving, where each thread is of importance.

Cognitive assessment includes the person's thoughts, feelings, and behaviors. Frequently we refer to the observed behavior (avoidance) as the focus of our intervention, but avoidance can be related to a variety of thoughts: "I avoid going to the grave because if I go it means that she is dead and I don't want to think of her as a dead person," or "Since he died I no longer bake his favorite cake because it is too painful to think that he will never be here to eat it," or "I left my husband's clothes the way he left them, it is a vivid reminder of him which I don't want to give up." These thoughts will be assessed as rational or irrational according to the emotional consequences they elicit and vice versa. What is the thought behind the behavioral or physical consequences that will determine the course of the intervention?

The risk of experiencing PTSD-like symptoms such as intrusion, avoidance, and hyperarousal following a violent and sudden death requires special attention during the assessment. Exploring cognitions related to these symptoms may reveal that they are loss related. In grief therapy, the meaning of these symptoms has an unique function, which varies from person to person, thus necessitating a careful assessment. Whereas for some bereaved avoidance may include details of the loss events, for others it can include reminders of the deceased. Some will avoid entering the deceased's room, or other reminders such as photos, certain food, music, or places that were of special interest to the deceased. For others any reminder of the circumstances of the loss is avoided because of the difficulty in confronting the finality of the loss; the belief that if one avoids certain reminders it is a way of not having to deal with the "knowing in the heart" that he or she is dead. This is common among the bereaved. Also, for a similar reason, visiting the grave is sometimes avoided. The same applies to intrusion; for some, intrusion is perceived as a way of remembering the deceased, while for others this very behavior is perceived as an exaggerated form that increases the pain of grief and is therefore avoided. Clearly, each response needs to be assessed as part of the narrative which has a past (" She was the closest to me"), a present ("I think of her all day and every day"), and a "lost future" ("If he lived he would have been a famous scientist"). Persistent avoidance or intrusion are observed responses (symptoms) maintained by distorted cognitions that often appear to be evaluations about evaluations (secondary symptoms). In the eyes of the bereaved, these are "right" evaluations (thinking about the deceased as if he or she was alive) but increase emotional distress and may hinder retelling the story in a less disturbed manner. Thus, assessing a secondary symptom and providing information about its potential increase of emotional distress is necessary if an adaptive grief process is to be facilitated. This is how a woman described the anxiety experienced when she suddenly saw a picture of her late husband: "In my head I know he is dead. I go to the cemetery every week and talk to him, but at home there are no pictures of him. I can't see a picture of him around or watch any video of him because they are reminders that he is not here and that he is not alive. It is my way of avoiding the terrible pain of the realization of his absence."

A Case Illustration to Determine the Dominant Cognitive Elements

The following is an illustration of how death as an activating event is perceived and recounted by a bereaved father during the first intake session. Typically, it involves questions about the circumstances of the loss as well as additional demographic details, but most importantly, it is the father's interpretation of the event:

Therapist: Tell me, what brought you here?

C: It is hard for me to tell you. My only son was killed in a road accident. He was the youngest of three. He was a very sensitive child and difficult to discipline but lovable. He didn't like school and had few friends. Only recently, upon entering the regional high school where he stayed during the week, did he outgrow many of his insecurities. He had matured, and we became closer, enjoying each other as real friends. It was only recently that I began to enjoy him, his personality, and his company. He used to come home for the weekend, and we spent quite a lot of time together, which was a new experience for me. It's very painful and sad. Since his death a few months ago, I cry a lot and can't bring myself to stop as I should be able to. What worries me most is when bereaved parents warn me that it's going to get worse. This thought frightens me more than anything else. For me, who's always been strong and rational, such a response means that I am getting weaker and weaker. I tell myself that I must be rational. Tears and crying have no rational explanation, and that's why I'm terrified.

This bereaved father's account of his loss demonstrates how a detailed account of A does not necessarily have to focus on the event itself (i.e., the traffic accident), but may instead be comprised of personal factors exacerbating the client's loss, such as the sudden and painful loss of the newfound father–son relationship and the son's personality. In presenting what had happened, the father vacillated from past to present on the one hand and experienced both rational and irrational thinking on the other. Vacillation from past to present, from preoccupation about the deceased to attending to life tasks is part of the process of comprehending the loss and reinterpreting it (Rubin, 1999; Stroebe & Schut 1999). This excerpt also reveals diagnostic information concerning the client's belief system (B) and its emotional and behavioral consequences (C).

From this assessment the therapist can hypothesize that the bereaved father holds maladaptive (irrational) beliefs about himself and his grief: "If I cry, that means I'm a weak person, and I must be strong," and "I should be able to stop crying because I'm a rational person." In this case, using as an example the father's crying (C), a normal, healthy response to a sudden loss, is interpreted by the father as weakness, and the father is angry with himself for not being able to control his emotions. The father has a secondary disturbance of anger over his crying and being weak.

The information provided can be mapped and summarized in ABC form to assist in formulating a hypothesis regarding the client's thinking and its interaction with emotions, behaviors, and physical reactions. It can also be used to teach the client about the ABC model and is given in a self-help form to be used as a between sessions assignment. The father's ABC summary is presented in Table 5.1.

In view of this father's assessment, a treatment plan was developed to include explanations about the adaptive, healthy aspects of sadness, normalization of feelings of pain and grief, and pointing out the inappropriateness and needless disturbance of the client's self-condemnation over his crying. A distinction between adaptive feelings of grief and maladaptive feelings of depression was made and discussed throughout therapy, and the father was helped to accept his grief and pain as a part of a normal process of coming to terms with his son's loss, rather than viewing himself as a failure for not being able to stop crying.

TABLE 5.1
Assessing and Mapping Death Related ABC

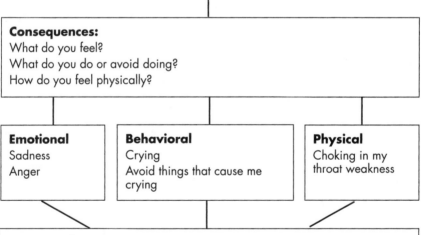

Activating Event:
My only son was killed in a road accident few months ago. The youngest of three, a very sensitive but loveable child and only recently we became closer. Thinking about his death makes me cry. Crying is a weakness. I know myself, I am a rational person and I should be able to stop crying.

Beliefs: assess both functional (rational) and dysfunctional (irrational) ones:
I never cry. If I cry it means that I am a weak person. It's very painful and sad. What worries me is when bereaved parents warn me that it gets worse. I loved my son and this thought frightens me more than anything else. For me, who's always been strong and rational, such a response means that I am getting weaker and weaker. I tell myself that I must be rational. Tears and crying have no rational explanation, and that's why I'm terrified.

Consequences:
What do you feel?
What do you do or avoid doing?
How do you feel physically?

Emotional	**Behavioral**	**Physical**
Sadness	Crying	Choking in my
Anger	Avoid things that cause me crying	throat weakness

An Example
I tried to look at my son's picture album. The moment I take the album out I begun crying and I was furious with myself for not being able to control my crying. I was so devastated that in the end I gave the idea up. I felt so weak.

Interventions

Acute-Phase Intervention through REBT:
From Experiencing Anxiety to Experiencing Pain

The acute phase will include a demographic assessment (including previous losses and how they were perceived and grieved) a TTMoB-based assessment (with questions pertaining to functioning as well as questions about the deceased—Track II) and a cognitive assessment based on telling of the story, how the relationship is described, and any thoughts and feelings about the circumstances of the death. Essential in any intervention—but specifically so during the acute phase as a preventive measure that sets the course of grief— are the following: normalizing, legitimizing, and giving information about the grief process; cognitive, emotional-behavioral, and physical responses; evaluating the existence of a support system as a reminder that to the bereaved that he or she is not alone. Very often, though not always, a short and focused intervention is sufficient to reduce the emotional distress related to the painful thoughts of going crazy due to the emotional flooding during the grieving process.

An important element in grief therapy is dealing with the pain of coming to terms with loss (Malkinson, 1996; Malkinson & Ellis, 2000; Sanders, 1993). This element of pain is similar to the catastrophic misinterpretation observed in panic disorders and PTSD (Clark, 1986; Moore, 1991; Warren & Zgourides, 1991). The REBT approach legitimizes pain and sadness as functional, healthy, negative emotions that are a normal part of coming to terms with traumatic and tragic loss. Pain is the emotional expression of the understanding and recognition of the fact of death. Moreover, the process of giving up old beliefs regarding the dead person and adopting new ones based on the new reality cannot be experienced without pain and sadness.

In dysfunctional, acute, and prolonged grief, a secondary symptom (e.g., stress, anxiety) regarding pain may stem from irrational beliefs (demand-ingness), such as, "This death is so sad in itself that it shouldn't also be painful," or "I must be able to control the pain or else I will go crazy." In some cases, people even demand from themselves that they must have great pain, especially when they blame themselves for possibly forgetting the deceased. In all, the human quest to avoid pain and increase pleasure is seriously disturbed when experiencing a traumatic event such as death (Ellis,

1962, 1986; Epstein, 1993). Dysfunctional pain can originate from thinking that "I mustn't suffer pain" to expressing a wish to suffer as a way to remember the beloved one.

REBT-based interventions for the acute phase have six aims to facilitate an adaptive process, in addition to its normalizing and legitimizing functions:

1. Identifying dysfunctional irrational beliefs (demandingness directed at the self, others and the world) and their emotional (e.g., anxiety), behavioral (e.g., avoidance), and physiological (e.g., breathing difficulties, heart palpitations) consequences.

2. Explaining and teaching the connections between beliefs (B) and consequences (C) and correcting thinking errors by providing corrective information (Foa & Rothbaum, 1998).

3. Identifying and assessing individual specific consequences (i.e., specific language to describe emotions, behaviors, and specific physiological reactions).

4. Teaching and practicing adaptive (rational) cognitive, emotional, behavioral, and physiological grief responses (Ellis, 1994; Ellis & Dryden, 1997; Malkinson, 1996).

5. Assisting in beginning a search for ways of retelling one's shattered story.

6. Searching for ways to continue bonds with the deceased (memories, memorabilia, commemoration etc.).

The following clinical illustration of acute grief demonstrates how clients' beliefs and consequences in terms of the ABC model can be identified. A women requested therapy a few months after the sudden, traumatic death of her 18-year-old son in a road accident during his military service.

An assessment based on TTMoB revealed dominance of Track I components, namely anxiety and difficulties in functioning at work, sleeping difficulties, and avoidance of reminders of the deceased son. Talking about the son was too painful in the initial phase of therapy because it was associated with the lost future of a talented musician and sensitive young man. According to her, the decision to come to therapy occurred when she realized that her initial decision to be strong and carry on with life "as if nothing happened" turned out to be too difficult, painful, and, in fact, impossible.

Client: I don't understand what is happening with me. I have difficulties in concentrating at work, at home. And I force myself to function, only to realize that it doesn't work.

Therapist: What do you tell yourself about not being able to concentrate?

Client: I tell myself that I must concentrate because I promised myself that life must go on as if nothing happened.

Therapist: And when this doesn't work, what do you tell yourself?

Client: I don't even want to think about it because it's awful! I hate myself for not being able to control myself. I can't stop crying, and I tell myself that I must stop crying, and if I don't, I am a weak person.

Therapist: Are you experiencing any other reactions which you dislike about yourself?

Client: Yes, I don't want other people to pity me, so I didn't tell my colleagues about the loss. Not telling them makes me feel very tense because I am afraid they will ask me questions that will be too painful for me to hear. I've lost my appetite and I can't sleep well.

This bereaved mother was experiencing dysfunctional acute grief and needed intervention to help her grieve in an adaptive, healthier way beginning with identifying her irrational thoughts (Aim 1, e.g., "I must not cry because, if I do, I am a weak person", "I must be strong and in control") and to explain to her the connection between each of these thoughts and their different consequences (Aim 2), whether emotional (e.g., feeling anxious when crying), behavioral (e.g., avoiding situations that might elicit crying), or physiological (e.g. choking, panic attacks, and sleep disturbances). Irrational beliefs and consequences expressed in her idiosyncratic way were explored (Aim 3) during the intake sessions and revealed the mother's other distorted interpretations referring to self (e.g., "I must not give up, strong is my motto") and the unrealistic expectation that life could proceed unchanged despite the loss. Additional idiosyncratic avoidance behaviors were also identified, involving reminders of the dead son: refraining from mentioning the son's name, moving his photographs, or not driving near the cemetery where he was buried. The irrational belief underlying this avoidance was discerned as: "This way, I don't have to confront the overly painful reality of my son's death. Also, it's my way of keeping my son alive. I don't want to think of him as dead."

Avoidance of talking about the deceased or refraining from certain behaviors several months after a sudden and traumatic death, as in the above illustration, is common among grieving persons and is an example of irrational thinking according to the REBT model on the primary level. It is a way of cognitive construction to deal with a reality that is "too painful." The mother also created a secondary symptom (a disturbance about the disturbance) by putting herself down for not preventing herself from overreacting to the pain, for being a weak person rather than the strong one she must be. Her demands (B) might have stemmed from the family's decision to continue with life "as if nothing has happened." Avoidance (C), as interpreted by the bereaved mother, became "functional" in escaping from experiencing the unbearable pain, and when her efforts "to be strong as she must be" failed, she was critical and self-damning and became anxious. The cycle of events includes the woman's demands that she must not experience the pain, but based on her accumulated experience she anticipates her failure in avoiding the pain, which in turn increases her fear of loss of control, and the consequence is anxiety.

The fourth aim of intervention was to teach the mother the difference between her irrational demands ("I must not cry") and her feelings of anxiety if she cried, as compared to more rational thoughts such as "I wish I wouldn't cry," which would lead only to feeling frustrated if she did cry. Training and practicing rational thinking (e.g., "I cry because I am sad, not because I am weak") were initiated to help the mother acquire healthier grief responses.

The fifth aim of intervention was to help the mother to search for ways to retell the shattered story following the death of her son, which was loss of the future and the death of a promising musical career: "I think the most painful thought to come to terms with is the thought that he will never actualize his musical talent, which he was so much looking forward to doing."

The sixth aim was to search for ways to continue bonds with the deceased child, which evolved as the mother overcame her avoidance by baking the son's favorite cakes, discussing with family members his love for music, and publishing his letters in booklet form.

In general, REBT therapy for this bereaved mother comprised three major processes. The first process was to help the client change her self-condemning thoughts to ones of self-acceptance (from self-demands that she must be able to control her pain, to a less critical view of her efforts to cope with the pain). She learned to differentiate between functional and dysfunctional beliefs and their related consequences. She realized that her "functional" avoidant behavior not only did not prevent her suffering but actually added to her pain whenever she encountered an unfortunate external event, a stimulus over which she had little control.

Second, the focus was on guiding the client in helping herself experience unavoidable, bearable pain and in overcoming her anxiety attacks; this took the form of an intervention focused on teaching her to increase her sense of control, both cognitively and physically, over her pain. Third, search for alternative ways to weave the loss and the pain it elicits into a sufferable meaning. Fourth, help the client find ways to continue bonds with her dead son, in a balanced way.

In the first and second processes, a variety of cognitive and behavioral strategies were employed to increase the client's sense of control over her pain, as well as the use and rehearsal of rational-emotive imagery (REI) (Ellis, 1993; Maultsby, 1971; Maltsby & Ellis (1974)). Rational emotive imagery will be described in detail.

Rational Emotive Imagery and In Vivo Exposure

Rational emotive imagery (REI) (also referred to as imagined exposure) and in vivo exposure are forceful cognitive and emotive strategies (Ellis, 1993). Both REI and in vivo exposure interventions are widely used with clients suffering from PTSD and anxiety (Foa & Rothbaum, 1998) as ways to relive the trauma, and through repeated exposures decrease the intensity of the emotions, to a point where avoidance of the feared trigger or feared loss of control is reduced or at times even abolished. Imagined or in vivo exposure combines cognitive and emotive elements and enables the client to repeat and relive the event and the related emotions as they change and "measure" the change in intensity at his or her own pace. People who experience a trauma are aware of the intensity of the pain that follows and often assume that avoidance will help them forget both the horrendous event and its emotional consequences, and thus ease the pain. Mistakenly, they believe that avoidance will help them regain control over the event. In most cases, regaining control over the event is impossible: "If I avoid thinking, feeling, or doing anything related to the event I will feel better." Furthermore, the fear of encountering any reminders of the event (or of the deceased person) is likely to result in a secondary symptom, namely, avoidance of what is perceived as unbearable pain. The efforts of avoidance are ineffective and a distorted cognitive loop with dysfunctional emotional consequences is formed. Using REI to moderate emotional intensity increases the inner control.

In REBT, rational emotive imagery and in vivo exposure are interventions that enable the client to experience cognitively, emotionally, and physically the centrality of his or her thoughts and also explain the connection between cognition and consequences (B–C connection). Applying REI focuses on changing a dysfunctional emotional response into a more functional one as the bereaved imagines the traumatic loss. With the therapist's assistance, the bereaved learns to replace a self-sabotage response through changing the related belief. Using REI enables the therapist to lead the bereaved into understanding and experiencing that emotional responses can be modified, an understanding that in itself increases the sense of control one has over one's thinking, emotional expression, and physical sense. Additionally, REI is an experience in which the bereaved can vividly "see" as he or she relives the experience as it takes place, as well as "see" the event the way she or he would like it to be through "imagery experiments" of various alternatives. In both, the client is asked to relive an experience (either an avoided one or one that floods), and pay attention to the thoughts and associated emotions (or emotions and the accompanying thoughts B–C connection). REI and in vivo exposure after a careful cognitive assessment can be applied in a variety of ways to different events that increase emotional distress as reported by the bereaved. In both imagined and in vivo exposure, the client is instructed to assess the emotional intensity on an imagined scale, and reassess it again after reliving the event, changing the thoughts or emotions to emphasize the choice one has over thoughts and feelings (inner control) in contrast to the adverse event in which one has no choice.

Imagery or in vivo exposure interventions are aimed at helping the client regain an inner control by learning new ways of experiencing the avoided event. At times there is a fear of loss of control over physical responses (pain in the chest, hyperventilation etc.), which can be identified and modified with the employment of REI.

REI involves three stages: preparation, application and follow-up. In the preparation stage, information is provided about the procedure in general, the link between cognitions and emotions, and the use of the subjective units of distress (SUDS) as a measure of emotional distress, where 1 represents a low level of distress and 10 a high one. Additionally, the client is taught the difference between regaining control over her or his *responses*, which is an attainable goal, in contrast to the unrealistic goal of regaining control in "a safe place" over the *event*. In REI or in vivo exposure, the client is actively involved in the process and is being led very carefully by the therapist who encourages and supports the client as she or he progresses in the session and between sessions.

The preparation phase includes the following:

1. Information about REI and its purpose as well as information about the subjective units of distress (SUDS), an imagined scale to measure emotional consequences as REI progresses.
2. Assesing the client's level of preparedness for reliving the adverse event is important. Make the client aware that there is also a possibility of an unsuccessful effort to recount the event. Normalizing such an outcome is recommended.
3. Prior to applying REI, assessing possible obstacles the client foresees.

Application of REI involves guiding the client through the event:

1. Recollect the event and the emotional response you experienced as close as possible to the one you had when it happened. You can choose to do this with your eyes closed or open. Signal with your head or finger when you are through.

2. On the imagined scale, measure the intensity of the emotion you experience as you rethink the event, 1 being low intensity and 10 a high one.

3. Concentrate on the measured intensity and moderate or decrease the intensity. Take as much time you need to do this. Signal me when you are through.

4. Measure the intensity on the imagined scale once more. Tell me where you are on the scale. (At this point the therapist needs to be aware that one of three outcomes is possible: no change, a slight change, or a marked change. In case of no change, it is important to assess what cognitively prevented change [what went on in the client's head?]. There may be different thoughts to explain it, but it is most important to legitimize the difficulties and suggest further trial.)

5. Reporting a slight change is often an indication either of the client's evaluation of the belief that he or she can change the nature of emotions, or disappointment over the degree of change. After assessing the client's thoughts it is important to reaffirm the direction of the change rather than its size.

6. A change in the intensity is carefully examined as to what was done or said that enabled the change: "What did you do or say to yourself that changed the intensity? What was the self-talk? Now as you say that to yourself what do you feel? Can you measure it by SUDS?"

   By asking the client to repeat it once more, the therapist identifies the effective strategy, which will be further employed by the client, and emphasizes the B-C connection by comparing the belief that increases intensity and one that decreases it.

7. Ask the client to "go back" to the previously experienced high intensity emotion, while exploring its related cognition and applying the new cognition with its reduced intensity emotion. This is another way to guide the client toward a sense of increased control and introduce the element of practicing. During the imagery the therapist observes nonverbal cues as well as changes in breathing.

Follow-Up and Between Sessions Assignments

The therapist reviews with the client the overall REI experience and specifically probes cognitions, emotions, and physical reactions before, during, and after employment of the imagery. The therapist encourages the client and reinforces accommodation of the change, assigning between session practice. The client sets aside time for practicing the REI to be discussed in the following session.

In the acute phase, REI is focused on assisting the bereaved in experiencing grief in a more balanced way as a result of the change that life has taken, as well as to accommodate to these changes. In complicated grief REI can be applied by focusing on the past relationship with the deceased as well as developing a future focus.

Rational emotive imagery strategy was applied with the bereaved mother. The REI and in vivo exposure included the following:

1. A cognitive assessment of the client's avoidance of driving past the cemetery: What does she tell herself? How does she feel?
2. Information about REI, B-C connection, and SUDS (imagined scale to measure the intensity of the response). Exploring with the client her various emotions, explaining the differences between adaptive healthy emotions (sadness, concern) and maladaptive unhealthy emotions (depression, anxiety), identifying the cognitions that go with each, and practicing the changes many times.
3. Explaining to her the healing effect of the "painful treatment" and the long term benefit of the experience.
4. Encouraging the client to think about the avoided behaviors and ask about her preference regarding keeping her eyes open or closed (she chose to keep her eyes closed), and to let herself experience the dysfunctional feeling associated with her avoidance. The therapist pays attention to the client's pace through her nonverbal cues, encourages her, and checks whether she encounters any difficulties.
5. The client is asked to focus on the emotional consequence and measure it on the imagined scale from 1 to 10 (with 1 being low intensity and 10 most intense feeling).
6. The therapist explores the client's imagery processing: "What are you feeling right now?"
7. The client is asked to change the emotion to a less intense (more functional) one and measure it by SUDS.
8. The therapist evaluates the process with the client.

9. The therapist explores with the client what she did or told herself in order to change the intensity of the emotion. What was the most difficult part for the client, when did she feel less tense? Whatever the client did or thought becomes a key statement and a resource for rehearsal and practice in the following weeks to maintain the change: "I told myself to calm down."

10. Follow-up: Cognitively, the mother was guided to identify and rehearse (in the session and between sessions) the distinction between unbearable (anxiety) and bearable pain, a distinction which helped her determine her own level of pain tolerance and have much more control over her feelings.

In subsequent sessions the client reported the outcome of her practice: "I tell myself that though I would have preferred not to have the pain, I understand that pain is part of the loss, and having said that it becomes much more bearable with less anxiety."

Additional behavioral strategies were prescribed between sessions as assignments, and were used throughout the therapy. Each time she felt like crying, she was instructed to detect her thoughts and write them down and identify those that increased her distress and those that moderated it.

REI of overcoming her avoidance of driving past the cemetery preceded the client's in vivo exposure. Once the client estimated that she could bear the pain, she asked her husband to join her in driving the "avoided" route, past the cemetery. When the mother reported her experience she said that it was particularly significant for her to overcome her avoidance of driving past the cemetery, the mere thought of which caused panic attacks with pronounced physiological responses, including choking sensations, numbness, and irregular breathing. Using REI imagery and rehearsing the details of the route, the worst thoughts about what she feared, and the most intense feelings of pain she imagined she would experience (the B-C connection), the client rehearsed and learned to use coping statements to stop "awfulizing" and to continue her driving. "Thought stopping" was also applied as a way of preventing herself from panicking: "Telling myself that I can't stop thinking about my failure to prevent pain, increases my anxiety, so I am going to tell myself to stop thinking this thought each time it goes through my mind." Breathing exercises were added to help her overcome her choking sensations.

When the client felt confident that she was able to control her thoughts and emotions, she agreed to drive by herself on the road by the cemetery. She reported crying and being very sad while driving her car. She said she forcefully used the coping statements and breathing exercises, and she did not choke that time. When telling her experience in the session, she described a feeling of being at peace with herself. She added that she wished she would never have had to drive past the cemetery but felt a lot less tense because she had done so. As can be seen, the mother's irrational expectations and beliefs about driving past the cemetery were modified to rational, adaptive, and healthier grieving responses.

Similar procedures were adopted to overcome the mother's avoidance of thoughts about carrying out or actual avoidance of certain behaviors that in her mind were associated with memories of her son or the pain involved in thinking of him as dead. These involved a careful monitoring of her activities, cooking her son's favorite food, looking at his photographs, talking about him with other family members, entering his room, and so on.

Circular Questions, Socratic Questions, and Meaning Construction

As can be seen, the first two processes focused mostly on correcting distorted thinking, whereas the third process dealt with the mother's efforts to reassemble a life that was shattered by the sudden death of the son, a life that no longer contained hope for the future. The third process was carried out through the use of circular questions as developed by Palazzoli, Boscolo, Chechin, and Prata (1980) as a way to elicit information through the exploration of cognitions, emotions, and behaviors about relationships among family members. In working with bereaved individuals and families, the therapist assumes that the death of a family member impacts the relationship among living members, as well as each member's inner relationship with the deceased. Circular questions can provide an opportunity to explore the complexity and richness of relationships, especially when families encounter difficulties in openly discussing them. These circular questions were developed further by Peggy Penn (1985) to also include future circular questions as well. Circular questions tackle relational issues that can then be explored cognitively, emotionally, or behaviorally.

For example, in a family session the therapist asked the brother of the deceased son "When your mother says that the dream she had about your brother becoming a musician will never happen and she hopes maybe you will carry the dream, what did you think? Or what did you feel?" or, "If your brother could comment, what would he have said?". The assumption behind circular questions is that family members are preoccupied not only with thoughts and emotions concerning the deceased, but also thoughts concerning how the deceased affects relationships among living family members, an issue that is either neglected or difficult to raise, resulting in avoidance. In other words, formulating circular questions can be relationship-focused, time-oriented (past, present future), and can be explored cognitively, emotionally, and behaviorally.

In cognitive therapy Socratic questions are applied as a way to guide the client to explore thinking alternatives (Wallen, Diguiseppe, & Wessller, 1980). These are hypothetical questions, which are not intended as a search for the "right" answer, but rather to generate an additional perspective on an existing situation. Socratic questions introduce yet another way of thinking about the reality without judging the bereaved's thinking as wrong. For example, the therapist might ask, "How does thinking about the fact that the dream of your son becoming a musician will never come true change your life? Has it lost its meaning or changed it?" Circular and Socratic questions enable the therapist to explore and elicit thoughts and feelings that family members have about present and imagined future relationships, including imagined relationships with deceased family members, both for assessment and intervention: "If Bob were alive what do you think he would have said about mom and dad feeling so devastated?" The mother was asked what she would say if she could have said something to her dead son. After a few moments of silence the mother said she would have told him how sad she feels when she thinks that his dream of becoming a musician will never be actualized but remains an unfulfilled dream. However, she hopes that his brother, who is also involved in music, will continue along the same path. Asking circular questions enables the therapist to conduct the session less judgmentally and in a more exploratory manner. Questions can be time-related and focus on relationships at different times (past, present and future), different circumstances (if the loss hadn't occurred how would your family look these days?), different roles (how has the loss affected relationships between you and your parents?), or closeness and distancing (are you less, the same or more close to each other since your brother died?).

In the case of the bereaved mother, therapy lasted six months with one-hour sessions, and as it progressed she became less anxious and less depressed but was sad, grieving, and significantly less avoidant of her pain, which was associated with the realization of the loss, and painful realizations about the future that would never happen.

In summary, the range of strategies employed with this client in the acute phase of grief included cognitive ones related to the ABC of the REBT model with special attention to the following: Identifying and learning to differentiate between rational and irrational beliefs; focusing on the emotional consequences; seeing the connections between thoughts and emotions; and using REI to rehearse modifying a dysfunctional emotion into a functional one, as well as changing an irrational belief into a more rational one. Other CT strategies were employed aimed at increasing the sense of control over pain, learning and rehearsing the cognitive distinction between unbearable and bearable pain, use and rehearsal of rational emotive imagery, thought stopping, and breathing and relaxation exercises. Also, using circular and Socratic questions was aimed at assisting the client in the process of meaning reconstruction for life following the loss as well as expressing the pain of the "lost dream".

As can be seen, cognitive strategies are central to the intervention because they help the bereaved person regain a sense of control over a shattered reality; it is assumed in the REBT model that behavioral changes will follow cognitive ones. Practicing between sessions in the form of homework assignments is an essential strategy in the REBT model in order to increase the effect of the cognitive, emotional, and behavioral changes (Ellis & Dryden, 1997). During acute grief it is of special importance to assess the client's physical reactions and address them in the course of therapy because loss through death involves physiological reactions as part of grief (Sanders, 1989). Learning appropriate breathing and relaxation can be most beneficial in facilitating a healthier course of grief, especially in the case of panic-stricken individuals. Teaching progressive relaxation (Jacobson, 1938) is often of special importance because it has the potential for improving the bereaved's functions and sleep.

As the term implies, *acute grief* refers to the initial reactions to the loss event, which at times include intense emotional reactions combined with a sense of flooding. Therefore, interventions during this phase are aimed at facilitating an adaptive, healthier course of grief and helping the bereaved individual gain a greater sense of control over his or her life. Suitable strategies for this phase also include cognitive rehearsal and reframing (Ellis & Dryden, 1997; Meichenbaum, 1986), without actually challenging the irrationality of the individual's beliefs. Interventions in prolonged grief, (see chapter 6) apply more forceful types of Socratic questioning to introduce the idea that irrational beliefs maintain the distress rather than relieve it, and so prevent an adaptable grief process.

This case illustration of cognitive grief therapy focused on the distinction between adaptive process of grief involving functional negative emotions, and a disturbed unhealthy process which is maintained by adopting distorted interpretations resulting in dysfunctional emotions. Normalizing and legitimizing pain as a normal part of coming to terms with traumatic and tragic loss is a central part of the intervention. The therapy was a process of regaining partial control, and of reestablishing an acceptable equilibrium between mind, feeling, and behavior as well as learning to live with the pain of the loss and all that was lost with it (Malkinson, 2000).

Conclusion

As a short-term phase related intervention, the ABC model of REBT is a form of cognitive therapy, which aims at facilitating an adaptive though painful process of grief, and focuses on the distinction between functional and dysfunctional thinking.

In addition to the therapeutic alliance, three general components were identified as essential interventions regardless of the grief phase: (1) normalizing; (2) legitimizing the process; and (3) providing information about its components and outcome.

There was a general demographic assessment and two additional types relevant for planning an intervention were elaborated: a TTMoB-based assessment to determine the dominancy of either track (functional or relationship with the deceased), and a cognitive one to assess and formulate a hypothesis regarding the client's thinking. Similar to the dynamic character of the grief process, both TTMoB and cognitive assessment are dynamic, and as therapy progresses, reassessment may result in modifying the initial assessment.

The aims of interventions included identifying distorted beliefs, explaining the reason for their being distorted via the B–C connection, correcting them, and practicing alternative thinking, as well as interventions aimed at helping the client create a meaning to her life, as well as ascribing meaning to the loss event. There is no "right" or "wrong" or a preference of one over the other, but rather the decision as to the choice of "correction" or "creation" orientation is client-dependent: What does the client connect with at a specific phase of therapy that could either be changed or supplemented as therapy progresses? Aims were verified and modified in accordance with the phase.

Interventions were focused on the acute phase of grief and described as a combination of correction of distorted thinking and creation (construction) of an alternative narrative to fill the void created by the loss. Interventions of the application of the ABC model were illustrated with case examples of the acute phase of grief. In the acute grief stage, avoiding the pain, which is common among the bereaved, was an obstacle to an adaptive grief process, and necessitated an intervention that helped the client to overcome it. Rational emotive imagery, in vivo exposure, and the use of circular and Socratic questioning were demonstrated and explained. From a cognitive perspective, the assumption underlying persistent avoidance (secondary symptom) is the client's developing a thinking error over a feared pain (primary symptom). All interventions were combined cognitive-emotional ones that were used as tools to identify distorted thinking and modify it into a more realistic evaluation of the event, enabling a more functional emotional processing. The use of a variety of cognitive (thought stopping, thought restructuring), behavioral (driving past the cemetery), and physiological techniques (breathing and relaxation) were also applied. The use of between-session assignments was demonstrated as an effective element to enhance therapeutic aims and gains. A basic tenet that underlies all interventions is that the client is an active collaborator in the process of change, and has the choice and ability to change distorted thinking as a way to create order in a world that has been shattered.

Chapter 6

Constructing a New Meaning to Life: A Case Study

"You know that you have reached a balance between the pain of the loss and continuing with life when you have made room in your heart for your loved one and he or she is there without having to take them in and out all the time." –Joe, a widower

In this chapter, a case study will be presented to illustrate the application of cognitive grief therapy with a woman who requested professional help following the loss of her male partner. The application of the course of therapy from the moment of referral to its completion will be described. Some interventions mentioned in the previous chapter will be expanded, giving the reader the opportunity to follow the process of intervention more fully.

As was mentioned previously, therapy is found to be more effective in one or more of three conditions: Traumatic loss, complicated grief, and in cases of self-referral (Neimeyer & Hogan, 2001).

The following is a case description of therapy following self-referral within the first few months of grief that was based on an assessment considered as suitable for intervention to facilitate an adaptive process.

The Referral

Sheila, a woman in her late 50s, requested therapy following the loss of her male partner, who was 20 years older then her and had suffered from chronic heart disease. He was 75 when he died and had been ill and under her care.

Months prior to his death he was hospitalized a number of times and said that he would rather be dead than suffer so much, fearing that his health would deteriorate to a point of incapacitation and total dependency on others.

Sheila had been married once before and divorced her husband after meeting the love of her life, a father of two children who had also divorced his wife. She had two grown, married children from the previous marriage. Her story revealed a loving relationship, which turned into one focused on caring when he took ill. She was so absorbed in caring for him that she ignored signs of deterioration in his health. In her story she talks about feeling angry toward him and feeling guilty for ignoring the signs of his deteriorating condition. She referred herself to therapy when she realized that her depression was persisting. Over the phone she said that the death of Rocky (her partner) had been so devastating that she felt she could not live without him. She was depressed and felt that she was going crazy by refusing to think that her beloved partner had died.

Sheila's therapy is an example of cognitive grief therapy adapted to her pace.

The Telling of the Story

This is what Sheila told in the first session. Her story was related in a soft voice as she cried quietly:

> I come from a family of four children, my father left my mother with four children and she raised us alone. I have two brothers and a sister. I am the oldest. It was my mother who arranged my marriage. When mother thought it was time for me to get married she arranged with her cousin who had a son that we would marry. I was young, nearly 20 and hated the situation, but felt helpless and couldn't go against my mother. I was all alone with nobody to turn to because my siblings, as I understand it today, could not support me and go against Mom's decision. The man I married was a good person; the only thing was that I didn't love him. Two children were born from that marriage. When I met Rocky a few years later I knew I had to leave my husband and go after my heart. I asked my husband for a divorce which he unwillingly accepted and left with my two children who were 5 and 2 years old, and moved to live with my beloved man against my mother's wish. She refused to talk to me after that. My siblings did not support me either, and for years I would visit my family without the man I loved so much. Our life was not easy, Rocky himself had to fight for a divorce from his wife who refused. His children (a son and a daughter) did not speak to him because they felt he had deserted them. Although it was

not easy, we had each other and our love only grew stronger. I have no words to describe the love we had for each other. He loved my children as though they were his own and they returned their love as to a father. During the last year we moved to a more comfortable apartment with the thought that it would be easier for Rocky to manage as his heart was giving him a lot of trouble. He loved the new place and we felt that we were given an opportunity to enjoy the coming years together in a comfortable place (in contrast to the small apartment that we had lived in before). He had a pacemaker and suffered from breathing difficulties—I think that was because he smoked a lot. He was hospitalized a number of times and I didn't miss an opportunity to consult with the best cardiologist available, for Rocky's love for me was limitless and so was my love for him. He loved life but mentioned every now and again that if his condition deteriorated his wish was to die rather than live incapacitated. In retrospect I think that during the last hospitalization he felt tired and knew that his condition was worsening. He took an overdose of pills, and the nurse found him. He was reluctant to discuss it with me but hinted in other ways that he would rather die. I refused to listen to those words, and in retrospect I feel bad for ignoring his attempts to talk to me about it. During the last day of his life I stayed with him, shaved and washed him, and gave him a big hug of love. The look in his eyes was one of great love. I left him to go home for the night. He died that night. When they called me from the hospital I didn't suspect anything but thought they wanted to tell me about an additional treatment that they considered giving him. When I arrived at the hospital I knew something wrong had happened and refused to believe that my Rocky was dead. I was in a shock. How could he have done it to me?

During the months that followed Sheila described how life became unbearable for her; she lost her appetite, cried a lot, and lost interest in life. She went to work only because she had to and felt she became a burden on her children, who expected her to overcome her sadness and comfort herself with her grandchildren, whom she loved. But even the grandchildren could not comfort her. She couldn't stop going over and over the last moments she spent with Rocky and blamed herself for not paying attention to what he wanted to say to her. For her, accepting the fact of Rocky's death was not an option. His death was the death of a significant part of her self.

The Initial Phase of Therapy

The initial phase of therapy was focused on establishing a therapeutic alliance with Sheila, conducting assessment, teaching her the ABC model of

REBT, and applying techniques aimed at increasing self-control. This lasted for about 10 weekly sessions. Sheila's telling of the story was an additional element in establishing rapport between her and the therapist. Letting Sheila tell the story uninterrupted while listening attentively and nonjudgmentally was not only an important source for therapeutic bonding, it also provided information relevant for assessment and for developing hypotheses; it enabled the therapist to capture the narrative in its fullness, both verbally and nonverbally. Catharsis was an additional outcome. Demographic, TTMoB, and cognitive assessments were made.

A demographic assessment included details about her family of origin, relationship between sibling and parents (her father understood her more than her mother), education, work status, and social life.

A TTMoB-based assessment of Sheila revealed a dominance of the relationship to the deceased (track II); the description of the circumstances of the loss and the deceased had elements of shock and disbelief. Sheila was immersed in the representation of the deceased, since she had left the apartment where they lived and had gone to stay with her daughter ("It's too painful to be there"). She avoided listening to music that reminded her of Rocky, and refused to think that she would ever be able to enjoy life, go on vacation, or have fun ("these were Rocky's favorites").

Also, some depressive responses were apparent with thoughts and feelings of extreme sadness and hopelessness, but without disruption of her ability to function at work (Track I). Did Sheila's thinking about the deceased result in her negative self-view ("I feel guilty whenever I think that he wanted to tell me something and I avoided it")? How much of her condemning herself for this explains her feelings of hopelessness? A psychiatric consultation for medication prescription was considered and discussed as a possibility to help her; it was decided that this option would be reconsidered as therapy progressed, if necessary.

A cognitive assessment for formulating a hypothesis included assessing (1) Sheila's "story"; (2) the functionality of the cognitions that included details about the activating event; and (3) Sheila's beliefs, emotions, and behaviors. Although the circumstances of Rocky's death were not considered to be traumatic, Sheila's reaction of shock and disbelief had elements of trauma—a subjective experience without an external trigger as suggested by Rubin et al., (2003), as if something in her life was shattered. Her cognitive construction of "Why did he do it to me?" increased her anger toward Rocky, creating a cognitive-emotional loop where the question of "why" is not only left unanswered but increased her anger.

The initial hypothesis was that Sheila's life story had been shattered and her reaction to the loss was avoidance: she expressed her refusal to accept it. Acceptance as far as she perceived it meant facing her guilt for not listening attentively to Rocky's efforts to talk to her during the last days of his life, and admitting her anger at him for "doing it to me." The loss was enduring and painful, and this was her way "to freeze" reality and repetitively ask "why" as a way to relieve the unbearable pain. She wrongly believed that by doing so she could change the reality of the loss or partly correct it ("If only I had joined him on his daily walks whenever he asked me to"; "If only I could I ask him why, why did he leave me").

As therapy progressed, Sheila unfolded her story and it became clear that Rocky's death was the death of a loved one and the death of a relationship that was a source of self-efficacy. It was Rocky whom she loved so much and for whom she left her husband, with two small children, against the will of her family of origin, whom she also loved. She made a choice between remaining "faithful" to her mother and family, who expected her to stay married to a person she didn't love, and being "faithful" to her love by deciding to leave and join Rocky. Between the two loves, the one for Rocky was her choice. His death was a double one as she experienced it : the death of her loved partner and the "death" of a chapter in her life which symbolized her choice and reflected her strength to follow her heart even at the price of breaking off her relationship with members of her family. Could life without her beloved partner have any meaning?

Interventions

Acute grief is often characterized by intense emotional reactions combined with a sense of flooding. Therefore, interventions during this phase are aimed at facilitating a more adaptive, healthier course of grief, and helping the bereaved gain a greater sense of control over his or her life, which is often necessary, as the immediate family often believes that they should encourage the bereaved to return to a pre-loss routine as soon as possible.

The five aims of REBT-based interventions for the acute phase and complicated grief toward facilitating an adaptive process were applied during the course of therapy:

1. *Identifying irrational beliefs:* "How could he have done this to me?" "I should have listened to what he tried to tell me," and their emotional (anger and guilt), behavioral (e.g., avoidance of any memories of

Rocky), and physiological (e.g., breathing difficulties, loss of appetite) consequences.

2. *Explaining and teaching* Sheila the connections between her beliefs that "He shouldn't have done it to her," and that she "Should have listened to him" (B), and emotional and behavioral consequences (C) of anger and guilt feelings and avoidance of situations that might elicit pain,loss of appetite, and breathing difficulties.

3. *Identifying and assessing individual specific consequences* that could become a source of strength. Sheila said: "My life is worthless, if it weren't for my children and grandchildren I would rather die." Although on the face of it this was a negative statement, it was evaluated as a potentially resourceful cognition.

4. *Teaching Sheila adaptive* (rational) cognitive, emotional, behavioral, and physiological grief responses, and practicing as a homework assignment.

5. *Assisting Sheila in searching for a way to retell and reconstruct her story* where the deceased is included ("This part of my life seems like a new chapter in my life story which excludes my beloved partner; and I realize that all my life I was a compliant person, but since his death I have rebelled against the world's injustice!").

Also applied is (1) *information* about grief, its components and process, its intensity and frequency of thoughts and emotions; and (2) *normalizing* its emotional and behavioral consequences and their pace. The overwhelming effect of the event created an additional stressor: "Something must be wrong with me if I can't stop crying." A possible response that focuses on normalizing this experience is, "It's human and normal to feel like that when one has experienced such a loss," or "How can one not cry or feel 'crazy' when one's world has shattered." This also included (3) *legitimizing* the *temporality* of feelings of helplessness and loss of confidence that one gets with the pain and sadness. When Sheila said: "I don't believe I will ever get over it, the loss of Rocky has ended my life and I see no point in carrying on," the therapist's reply was: "You have a full right *as of now* to think and feel that way."

In the initial phase of therapy, the focus (in addition to teaching the ABC model) was to increase Sheila's sense of control over her flooded thoughts and emotions, a common response in the initial phase of grief. The overwhelming feeling of loss of control over one's life following a death event is common among the bereaved. The centrality of cognitions as applied in cognitive therapies is pertinent in assisting the bereaved to increase the sense of control over their thoughts and emotions. There are several useful strategies available for that purpose: Distraction and thought stopping, cognitive rehearsal, reframing (Ellis & Dryden, 1997; Meichenbaum, 1986) without actually challenging or attempting to change the irrationality of the individual's beliefs (Malkinson, 1996). Teaching deep breathing: difficulties in breathing are frequently reported by bereaved individuals. Awareness of one's breathing can be exercised at any moment of experiencing stress or flooding and increases the client's sense of control and reduces the stress (Foa & Rothbaum, 1998; Meichenbaum, 1986). Breathing, in contrast to relaxation, is not perceived by the bereaved as inappropriate ("How can I be relaxed when it is so painful?"), and when applied and practiced helps the bereaved to identify moments of stress and attend to them. Breathing is also a physical way to thought stopping. Sheila practiced deep breathing and applied it at times of distress and "heavy chest."

Distraction and thought stopping are especially effective as "a first aid kit" to teach the bereaved how to regain an inner control over an external, uncontrolled one. Sheila rehearsed both distraction ("I tell myself to do something else") and thought stopping ("Thinking about it over and over again makes you exhausted. Take a pause").

What characterizes these interventions is that they are focused on the "here and now" and help the bereaved regain a sense of control over a devastating event. It helps the bereaved in making an initial distinction between not having control over the external event and not losing the inner one.

The flooding effect that is frequent during the acute phase following the loss event is expressed as repetitive questions, such as "Why?" or "How could it happen to me?". In addition to distraction and thought stopping aimed at teaching Sheila, especially when she felt so flooded, to distance herself even momentarily from thinking about Rocky's death and her life without him, a dialogue with repetitive thoughts was applied. Creating a dialogue with a "why" question is another way of increasing cognitive control over an inner sense of not having one. If distraction and thought stopping aim at distancing oneself from the disturbing cognition, a dialogue with repetitive "irrational" thoughts involves attending to and confronting the thought and searching for a more "rational" reply.

A Dialogue with the Repetitive Thought

Following normalizing the sense of flooding of the question "why," the therapist distinguishes between the loss as an external uncontrollable event and its cognitive processing as a way to increase the feeling of control. This is followed by an introduction of the dialogue idea, wherein answering the "why" question minimizes its flooding effect and increases a sense of control. In

Sheila's case it was a way of introducing an alternative way of thinking about her anger at Rocky for leaving, and her feelings of guilt for not cooperating with his efforts to talk to her on his last day.

Here is an excerpt of this intervention with Sheila.

Sheila: I can't stop thinking why, why did he die? How could he have left me? I know that his condition deteriorated and he always said his greatest fear would be to sit in a wheelchair and be incapacitated, but why, why did he die?

Therapist: This is a justified question and how could you possibly answer it?

Sheila: That's the problem, the question keeps popping over and over again.

Therapist: Let's think of an answer because without an answer the question as you described it will keep popping up.

Sheila: I have no answer to that question.

Therapist: In a way this is an answer, can you tell yourself when the question "why" pops again, "I have no answer to that question"?

Sheila (*says loudly*): "Why, why?" And she answers: "I have no answer to that question." (*She adds*): "Rationally, I know that it is irrational. I realize that I need not insist on finding an answer."

Therapist: You are right in realizing that as of now there is no point in insisting (I must have an answer) on finding an answer. How do you feel now with the answer of, "I don't have an answer and I need not insist on finding one?" Do you feel more, less, or the same level of flooding?

Sheila: Less.

Therapist: Good, that helps you take better care of yourself in moments of great pain and sadness. Paradoxically, not answering the question increases your sense of helplessness. So, I suggest you practice and apply it when you feel distressed, as well as in between these feelings so you master its use.

In the next session Sheila told the following :

I cried and couldn't stop thinking that he left me never to return. My life is worthless and I couldn't stop thinking, "Why?" And then I remembered what you told me, and said to myself that I don't have to insist on finding an answer. It helped because then I could think that actually he didn't want to see himself deteriorating and being dependent. He loved life and dreaded the thought of being incapacitated. I also told myself that I wouldn't want to see him in such a terrible state of not functioning. It helped me to feel less overwhelmed. In a sort of a way it eased the pain, which was mixed with yearning for Rocky. The yearning was most intense and at times unbearable.

Therapist: So you felt more in control over your questions but experienced intense yearning for Rocky. What did you tell yourself over feeling the yearning? If you could choose between the two (yearning mixed with pain or feeling flooded over "why" questions), what would your choice be?

Sheila: I was asking myself the same question. I don't know whether I am strong enough to withstand the pain of yearning.

Therapist: Would you like to explore it?

Reflections

1. Yearning for Rocky causes pain which Sheila believes she cannot tolerate.
2. Sheila's way to "overcome" the unbearable pain is to avoid thinking about Rocky or any memory of him.
3. The emotional consequence is a loop of avoidance which does not bring relief to the pain, but on the contrary retains it.

Gaining control over the "why" question was made possible by giving up the insistence on finding an answer. However, at this point in therapy it was perceived by Sheila as partial and specific, and not yet generalized. Therapy will proceed by further exploring the meaning of inner control and the issue of the choice one has over feelings of pain (a secondary symptom) that comes with the yearning and searching for ways to deal with the pain involved in thinking about Rocky.

Intermediate Phase: Facilitating an Adaptive Grief Process — Balancing Negative Emotional Responses

Following the establishing of therapeutic collaboration, conducting an assessment, and formulating an initial hypothesis, the focus of intervention during that phase was to help Sheila regain a sense of control over her shattered life. Therapy in the intermediate phase (until the first anniversary of Rocky's death) was aimed at further facilitating an adaptive process so that Sheila's life without Rocky continued as she searched for its meaning. From a cognitive-emotional perspective, avoiding the pain that came with yearning for Rocky actually increased the pain, which resulted in further avoidance. A dysfunctional loop of thoughts and emotions blocked a more adaptive process. Interventions thus were aimed at helping Sheila realize that a choice of alternative thoughts is possible, and probably would elicit moderately negative emotions. The therapist's belief in the appropriateness of negative moderate responses, as distinct from inappropriate ones, was essential for helping Sheila adopt alternative cognitions. The therapist was aware of the fact, which is often found among bereaved persons, that Sheila was thinking in an "all or none" manner: "It is not possible to stop the pain after experiencing such a loss." Explaining the difference between intense (overresponse), and a moderate (controlled) pain, was followed by practicing it using the subjective units of distress (SUDS) as an imagined scale to measure the level of intensity of the pain, thus legitimizing pain but controlling its intensity. This is a potential pitfall for therapists who want to help a client rid herself of pain as a source of suffering rather than viewing pain as a part of grief and a part of learning to absorb the loss into one's life. Empathizing with the client's pain as part of grief leads the therapist to cognitively explore with the client ways of moderating it. Legitimizing pain, learning the difference between adaptive and maladaptive pain, and exploring ways to moderate it, was applied in Sheila's case with the use of a number of interventions of which REI and continual letter writing will be elaborated further.

Rational Emotive Imagery (REI)

Rational emotive imagery was used as a way to help Sheila experience negative dysfunctional and functional emotions, and notice the difference between the two and their related cognitions. Sheila avoided positive thoughts or memories of Rocky because she feared experiencing the pain that it aroused. Pain was a primary emotion and the fear of pain was a secondary symptom.

Sheila: I can't think of Rocky. I am afraid it will be too painful.
Therapist: How intense is your fear?
Sheila: Very intense. It feels heavy in the chest.

(The therapist explained the idea of controlling (reducing and increasing) the intensity of emotions and suggested using an imagined scale of SUDS to measure it, and explained the procedure).

The therapist *then explained the steps of the imagery:* imagining the fear in its max-imum intensity, measuring it on an imagined scale, and reducing it by doing something imaginative as well. Note that the fear of pain is normalized but its intensity is the focus of the REI. Thus a distinction between an adaptive and maladaptive reaction was made. Stressing the reduction of the intensity while normalizing the fear of pain was the way to help Sheila learn and explore in her own way the difference in experiencing adaptive and mal-adaptive reactions.

Therapist: Can you measure the intensity?

Sheila: Yes, nine.

Therapist: Take your time and try to reduce the intensity. You can close your eyes. As you try, think of something that will help you reduce the intensity. Take your time as you try. Just give it a try and see where it takes you.

(Sheila closed her eyes and concentrated for a long moment. When she opened her eyes there was a look of disappointment).

Therapist: Can you share with me what you experienced? Did you manage to reduce the intensity? You seem to be disappointed.

Sheila: Yes, I did reduce it to eight. I was hoping to reduce it even further.

Therapist: Can you tell me the difference between nine and eight?

Sheila: Nine is heavier in the chest. Eight is a little less heavy.

Therapist: That's important. What did you do?

Sheila: I said to myself Rocky was the great love of my life.

Therapist: That is very significant and when you said that to yourself what happened to the pain?

Sheila: It was less then I feared.

The therapist discussed the disappointment Sheila expressed in that she only managed to reduce her pain from nine to eight on the imagined scale. This feeling is a common response among the bereaved, who want to elimi-nate pain altogether. In applying REI the client rehearses the different levels of intensity of pain, and by changing irrational cognitions to rational, func-tional ones, he or she learns to accept pain as part of his or her life without their loved one, and also to gain control over it.

Sheila cried and talked about all those things that she could have done with Rocky and those that she would never be able to do. In subsequent sessions Sheila could distinguish between her avoidance of memories as an inefficient way to prevent pain and her concern for feeling the pain which was part of remembering her great love.

In one of the following sessions Sheila shared her fears of going for the first time on holiday without Rocky. "How can I go without him? It will be awful!" Sheila was weighing up the short- and long-term outcomes of joining her children and grandchildren versus staying alone at home. Sheila could see the sadness and pain involved in going on holiday without Rocky, but at the same time she realized how important this was for her children. She chose to join her family knowing that sadness would be experienced, sadness that was part of missing her loved one.

Between session assignments included practicing a thought dialogue, exercising deep breathing, and REI. Writing was suggested to Sheila as a way of keeping therapy's continuity when the therapist was away for a number of weeks. Sheila agreed to write once a week for half an hour at the time of the session "as if" she was talking to the therapist. Writing included keeping a diary and writing to Rocky at times when she thought about him. Sheila continued her writing throughout therapy. Writing is an intervention that can be applied in a number of ways and will be elaborated on in detail in the next chapter. Some excerpts from Sheila's continual writing follows:

The first writing is addressed to the therapist:

> It is difficult for me to start writing and that's why I postponed it until Saturday, and I am trying to imagine that you, Ruth, are sitting in front of me. The week that passed since leaving the last therapy session was not easy for me. I started the week feeling great distress and crying that never ended. My yearning was so intense with thoughts and memories from the past, what we did together and what I missed. On Sunday I felt devastated and cried endlessly all day. In the evening I contacted Rocky's family and the only thing I wanted was that they would talk about him. I took some pills to relieve the pain (Kalmanervin, a homeopathic pill).
>
> Ruth, since you are not here at the moment there is no one to answer and direct me to continue the talk. I am trying to imagine what you would have said in moments like these, anyhow I will try. You probably would have asked what I did when I reached this situation. What did I answer to myself?
>
> Well, Ruth, I didn't answer. I simply tried to push things aside and think and ask myself if I really wanted to see Rocky reaching difficult situations like incapacitation and using diapers. I managed to get over it for two days and then invited Rocky's niece and talked about the good days we had with him. This refilled me with pleasant memories that were forgotten because of my present situation.

Ruth, I miss him terribly and would like to go out with him to hug him and tell him all the things I missed telling.

I dreamed about Rocky and that I am with my children and grandchildren in the room, and I called him at home at about 9:50 in the morning, even though I knew he woke up at 10:00 and was surprised to hear him happy, relaxed, and alert. We talked for a while and then my daughter-in-law took the telephone and talked with him. Then I took it back, walked upstairs to the room, and continued to talk to Rocky who asked about my daughter-in-law's birthday, which had happened three days earlier. "Yes," I replied "It was her birthday." Rocky said: "Then get her a present on my behalf." I answered that it took place three days ago and we already bought her a present so it is not necessary to buy another one. "No," replied Rocky, "it doesn't matter, buy her something special from me." I woke up feeing wonderful. Is it natural Ruth, that I regret all those things that I missed with Rocky, the most wonderful time in my life that passed so fast?

Ruth, it is so difficult to continue without him. Even though I carry on with life and try to overcome the loss, it is hard without him. Something shook me up one day this week. On one of those days I was crying a lot and talked with my daughter, asking her what will happen, to which she replied: "Mother you don't notice but I don't have my mother, Rocky died and took with him my mother and it's hard." I was shocked for a moment and even asked myself what do they want from me at the moment I am with my grief. After having a second thought I found that my daughter is right, and I have to do something about it, and give them a little of the mother they had; it's hard Ruth. Is it too early or am I a lost case? If Rocky was here next to me I would be full of happiness, and then together with him I would be the same mother I used to be, full of the joy of life and ready to help and enjoy day-to-day experiences.

One thing Ruth, as you suggested that I stop to ask myself the question, "Why." When it pops through my head I answer to myself: Sheila, don't ask "why" because there is no answer.

Ruth, I still miss your response. I hope that until you return Rocky from up above will help me to get over the pain and fill me with new energy as he did all his life. It is so sad that such a beautiful life ended in the middle and for everything is still too early (that is how I feel).

Meanwhile my daughter is of some help.

We will continue our "talk" next week.

On resuming sessions we discussed Sheila's writings, and some elements reflecting Sheila's grief process can be identified there:

1. Life without Rocky is worthless and yearning for him is painful.
2. Talking about Rocky brings a momentary comfort.

3. Dreaming about Rocky was followed by a mixture of joy and sadness, drawing the line between the painful reality without him and the dream world where he was very much alive and involved in their life only for it to fade away.

4. An increasing inner control over the emotional flooding affects of thoughts about "why" and "what if" questions.

5. Giving more room to the thought about Rocky's wish not to be dependent as his health was deteriorating, in contrast to the thought that she would rather have him stay alive regardless of his condition. This would become an important issue as therapy progressed, with Sheila examining her anger toward Rocky who was "inconsiderate" for not wanting to continue to live as a chronic patient, realizing that his death saved him from feeling degraded.

The following is a letter to Rocky:

Today is Saturday; I woke up feeling very bad and flooded with memories and yearning for you my dear Rocky. Over and over again I keep asking myself how to continue without you, my sweetheart. You filled my life with your love and gave me so much attention, and all of the sudden it all disappeared, and I am trying to get hold of something that will help me keep my head above water. It is so hard my love (no one could ever understand what a special person you were). It was so short. Rocky, you taught me that life is strong and one has to continue. I suppose I was a lousy student because today when I have to apply it I realize that I learned nothing from your school of life. You covered me with so many layers of love and now that you are gone the cover was torn off and I feel vulnerable. You knew and sensed how difficult it was going to be for me and tried to hold onto life until the last moment of your life, and I still refused to accept it. Life without you is not the same. Kissing and hugging the grandchildren feels like something is missing. My wonderful children take care of me and are sad when they see me in such pain. For them and for your memory I will make an effort to continue. I remember that this was your wish that I would take care of myself. You also asked my daughter to look after me, which she does but she can't understand the pain that I experience whenever I think that my life with you has ended. I love you and you will always be mine.

Reflections

1. At this stage of therapy the hole left by Rocky's death is so big and painful, and efforts in searching for ways to fill it seem fruitless.

2. Rocky's wish that Sheila would take care of herself is remembered, but its fulfillment seems beyond her.
3. Sheila is immersed in her grief.

A letter from Sheila to her children:

My dear children, I would like to share with you a little bit of what I am experiencing these days. It is like an emotional storm, like waves in the sea; like stormy waves crashing the pier, my emotions are crashed facing the new reality. I want to tell each one of you how ashamed I feel at letting you down for not being the strong mother that always cared for you and inspired you to be what you are. All this has changed with the death of Rocky. Rocky was the one whom you loved and trusted.

My dear children I try to lift my head above water and carry on with life as you expect me to do. The thoughts of being alone don't leave me and pull me back down. I know how much you try and care but I see your dismay. This is where I am at the moment, still grieving the loss of my beloved Rocky. While you think that continuing life is going back to the same routine I had before, I still feel the urgent need to talk about Rocky, even though you think it prevents me from functioning. You are wrong my dear children. Your avoidance of the subject of Rocky pushes me into a corner from which I cannot move. On the outside I am trying to show you that I am making progress and am functioning, but inwardly I am in pain, which sometimes results in my thinking why do I continue? Where will I get without Rocky whose love was the source of my life? The kind of help you are offering is important but I am not yet ready for it. I feel ashamed that what I taught you, to be strong and look forward, I myself have failed in doing so. It feels like you lost both Rocky and me. The unknown future frightens me and I still need to work it out for myself. I can hear you saying to me: "You are not making an effort to continue, you need to carry on; take some of the legacy Rocky left and apply it to your own life." I try, sometimes it works and sometimes not. When I reach a moment that it doesn't work it is fearful and sad. I need time, and for that you need to be patient with me. I promise to talk to you after the first anniversary. I hope not to disappoint you. Please understand and forgive me, your mother who loves you endlessly.

Reflecting on Sheila's letter to her children a number of issues are identified:

1. Sharing with her children the shattering of her life following Rocky's death.
2. Sheila's close relationship with her children and her feelings of betrayal for not being available to them as in the past.

3. The warm relationship between Rocky and Sheila's children.
4. The children's expectation from Sheila "to be strong."
5. Sheila's explanation of what kind of help she needs at present.

Final Phase: Learning to Live with the Pain of Yearning

The first anniversary was a difficult event for Sheila, but nevertheless a turning point. Sheila wrote a letter to Rocky in which she expressed the difficulties in resuming life, missing his love for her, and yet her commitment to the family in spite of the sadness. As therapy progressed, Sheila became less anxious and less depressed, but was sad, grieving, and significantly less avoidant of her pain. She resumed previously avoided activities, such as returning to a holiday resort they had visited when Rocky was still alive. Most importantly, she no longer condemned herself for yearning for him and feeling sadness whenever she thought of how her life had changed. The therapy focused on helping Sheila search for ways to construct the new chapter in her life, one that physically excluded Rocky but not the memories of his love for her. Can being a mother and grandmother become a source of meaning? Sheila noted that she had changed from being a dependent woman to being a more independent and assertive one, and she wasn't certain whether she liked her "new self." Her new self meant that she could at times say "no" to people around her because it was less crucial to please everybody. She decided on early retirement and devoted more time to her grandchildren. Life was never the same, but a blend of moments of contentment, yearning for Rocky, sadness, and pain.

The intervention in Sheila's case focused on the distinction between grief as a painful process involving functional negative emotions, as opposed to a disturbed painful process which is maintained by adopting distorted interpretations that result in dysfunctional emotions. An important element in the adaptive process experienced by Sheila was coming to terms both with the loss and the pain that it elicited; and with it came the understanding that although her life had changed for ever she could still find meaning in it as a mother and a grandmother. In a follow-up a year later, Sheila talked about her life and her thoughts about Rocky. In her own words she described the process of balancing continuing bonds with the deceased.

Yearning and Pain

These are Sheila's words that explain the change in her life describing her acceptance of pain as a part of life:

> Life is like a pack of cards that was scattered and was picked up in a different order; learning to live with the pain is the ability to distance myself from it. On one hand I accept the fact of Rocky's death: Now I know that I wouldn't have wanted to see him suffering and I know that this was how he wanted things to happen. I know that I did everything possible, the maximum. I regret that during the last few weeks of Rocky's life I didn't understand that it was the end. My children did, my daughter said after the electric shock, "This is the beginning of the end." The physician said to me: "I will do whatever I can," but there was very little that could have been done. My family convinced me that if I were to accept it I wouldn't have done all I did for him. On the other hand, I am very lonely. I even told my son, sarcastically: "You know there is something good in Rocky's death—I can go to bed early!"
>
> My sister and brother-in-law forced me to join them on an outing. There were sad moments. All of a sudden I saw that I am strong. There was a moment where I couldn't hear the music of the dances and I said to myself: "Rocky is with me—not physically but within me." I talked to myself whenever memories came and said: "I don't know the way my life is shaping and I need to be positive." I felt pain remembering how much Rocky lived in those places. Rocky was with me every single moment of that outing, but not physically. For example, when we stopped at one of the places we used to visit together, I felt as if Rocky was with me and heard him telling me: "Learn to enjoy life, you need to relax," and so I did. I feel that being with Rocky today is from a "clean" place.
>
> Rocky is in my heart I am not so angry at him. I realize now that it is OK to be sad and to yearn for Rocky. I feel I am ready to immerse myself more in life and give more of myself. There are still things that I find difficult to do, reading books is one of them but I also know that I have the choice to do it when I feel like it. I don't criticize myself for not doing it. Perhaps the major change is that I am aware that this is my life and I have the strength to choose and decide how I want to live my life. I was lost and felt betrayed. I was afraid from the change. Now I feel more confident in myself.

Reflections

Sheila's anger towards Rocky has subsided considerably. Adopting a rational attitude enables her to explore alternative meanings to her life that has changed so much.

During the last session Sheila mentioned that the anger she felt towards her mother, who forced her to marry a man she didn't love, has lessened dramatically and she has forgiven her mother. Sheila said she came to realize that her mother's act many years ago, although against Sheila's will, was intended to ensure her daughter's financial security.

Sheila's therapy was a process of regaining inner control over the pain associated with yearning. In reestablishing an acceptable equilibrium between mind, feeling, and behavior she adopted a more rational attitude. From the perspective of the TTMoB, Sheila developed a more balanced inner relationship with the deceased (Track II).

Chapter 7

Complications in the Normal Course of Bereavement

"And Reuben returned unto the pit; and, behold, Joseph was not in the pit; and he rent his clothes. And he returned unto his brethren, and he said: 'The child is not; and as for me, whither shall I go?' And they took Joseph's coat and killed a he-goat, and dipped the coat in the blood; and they sent the coat of many colors, and they brought it to their father; and said: 'This have we found. Know now whether it is thy son's coat or not.' And he knew it and said: 'It is my son's coat; an evil beast has devoured him; Joseph is without doubt torn in pieces.' And Jacob rent his garments, and put sackcloth upon his loins, and mourned for his son many days. And all his sons and all his daughters rose up to comfort him; but he refused to be comforted; and he said: 'Nay, but I will go down to the grave to my son mourning.' And his father wept for him." –Genesis, 37: 29–35

Traumatic Loss and Complicated Grief

The majority of bereaved individuals find ways to continue life without the deceased, but for some, bereavement increases the risk of developing complications (Henesley, 2006; Prigerson, 2004). What then characterizes an adaptive adjustment? There are a number of factors that are recognized as affecting bereavement process and its outcomes: demographics, personality, circumstance and the socio-religious-cultural context within which bereavement is experienced (Raphael & Martinek, 1997; Shuchter & Zisook, 1993). From a relational perspective, the level of adaptation to a loss is related to the bereaved's attachment patterns, his or her ability to make sense of the loss and to life without the deceased (Neimeyer, 2006), and his or her ability to weave the loss with the pain it entails into everyday life. In the words of Strocbe & Schut (2001) ". . . oscillation between positive and negative (re)appraisal in rebalancing not only the loss—but also restoration orientation" (p. 396). With the passage of time the process becomes less intense but never really ends; (see the three phases of grief proposed by Malkinson & Bar-Tur, 2004–2005). Although this is true for most bereaved individuals who experience longing for the deceased accompanying with sadness and pain, for others the loss might result in an enduring experience of anger, guilt, shame, depression, and anxiety that do not subside over time, thereby indicating difficulties in adjusting to life without the deceased.

Compared with bereaved individuals who incorporate the loss, yearning, and pain into their lives, those with complicated grief are immersed in their grief, unable to adapt to life without the deceased and take part in interpersonal relationships or any other activities that for them represent continuing with life. Their continuing relationship with the deceased tends to preoccupy them, and they are immersed in thoughts about the loss, the deceased, and the circumstances of the loss. They have difficulty finding meaning to life without the deceased. The level of distress they experience does not dissipate over time. In Bowlby's terms, efforts are being made to activate the attachment figure in search of physical proximity, and to realize that separation is irreversible. In adaptive grief the fruitless efforts to physically rejoin the deceased die away gradually, and are accompanied by reorganization of the internal representation of the deceased. In contrast, disbelief that the person is dead (Field, Gao, & Paderna, 2005; Pivar & Field, 2004; Prigesron, 2004) or a prolonged difficulty in accepting reality without the deceased's "real" and physical presence, and a failure with the passage of time to reorganize the schema of attachment, are indicative of complications. Both the relationship with the deceased and the enormity of the event are central issues in understanding adaptation to loss, and have been identified as potential risk factors (Stroebe, Van Son, Stroebe et al., 2000; Stroebe & Schut, 2006). Moreover, it is not the mere existence of a relationship, but the manner of its expression (flooded, avoided or balanced), and the intensity of preoccupation (over or under) with the inner representation or the attachment quality that affects adjustment to loss (Mikulincer & Shaver, in press). In other words, the interaction between the loss and the bereaved's perception of who was lost, and the attachment system that is being activated, will affect the course and outcome of grief. Also, the traumatic circumstances of the loss affect grief. The term "traumatic grief" was coined to indicate that interpersonal loss and life injury co-occur (as a result of direct or indirect exposure). The occurrence of loss and a life-threatening experience increases the distress (such as in the terrorist attack on the World Trade Center), and affect the process of reworking an inner relationship with the dead person (Green, Grace, et al., 1990; Pynoos, Nader, Fredrick, Ganda & Stuber, 1987; Lehaman, Wortman & Williams, 1987; Pivar & Field, 2004; Rubin et al., 2003). The sense of loss of a secure, comforting, and love-providing attachment figure, especially under traumatic circumstances, has brought to light the need to reconsider what were two previous separate fields: namely, trauma and loss.

The question is, when should grief and trauma be viewed as separate entities, and when as linked? What are the implications for assessment and intervention?

Mr. Moses recalled the loss of his daughter Lora, who had been killed one night when driving home six years earlier. In a soft voice he retold in detail how for several years he had taken her to school on his way to work, and a very special relationship was formed; on the last evening he saw her, he had asked her not to drive home when the party ended. Lora promised not to drive and made arrangements to stay with a friend, but for some unknown reason she had decided to drive home, and was killed. For six years the vision of her promising not to drive had not left him: "Why?" he asked, despite knowing that the answer would never be found. The memory of Lora's face and voice remained as vivid as they had been six years earlier. While Mr. Moses wished to retain these memories as a way of remembering his beloved daughter, signs of reaction to the traumatic event were also identifiable.

We can see that both loss and trauma are experienced as stressful and painful events that disrupt life patterns and functioning, requiring a process of adjustment to the changes that they cause. Although most people experiencing loss or trauma find a pathway to work through the event, this is not true for everyone. In viewing these two classes of events, we can see how each produces multiple responses which account for individual differences; also, numerous events can result in seemingly similar response patterns that were often overlooked when focusing on the shared elements of life crises and shared symptomatologies (Malkinson, Rubin, & Witztum, 2005; Rubin, Malkinson & Witztum, 2003).

There are multiple ways in which trauma and bereavement interface, and at times it is difficult to distinguish between them, although both are experienced. Thus, conceptualizing traumatic bereavement as a combination of external life stress and relationship to the deceased enables both elements to be addressed as possible risk factors, without focusing on one and neglecting the other.

There is increasing interest among researchers and clinicians from both fields in studying similarities, distinctions, and overlapping between bereavement and trauma, (referring to it as traumatic bereavement) as a way to understand better the nature of the relationship between the two (Green, Krupnick, Stocktom, Corcoran, & Petty., 2001; Raphael & Martinek, 1997; Rubin, Malkinson & Witztum, 2003; Stroebe et al., 2001; Stroebe & Schut, 2006). There are those who emphasize the similarities between the two processes (Brom & Kleber, 2000; Harvey, 2002; Stroebe, Schut & Finkenauer, 2001), while others emphasize that "the phenomena of trauma and loss differ in important ways" (Raphael & Martinek, 1997). There are yet others who see loss as part of the trauma (Kaltman & Bonnano, 2003). It is too early to reach definitive conclusions, but there can be little doubt that cross-fertilization between these evolving areas can be mutually beneficial. Such a trend will reflect our professional sensitivity to the interplay of traumatic conditions and processes of bereavement in both research and clinical work. From a clinical point of view, the bereaved, who experienced a traumatic loss and seek therapy, are preoccupied with both the circumstances of the loss and the relationship with the deceased in their search for a meaning to what they refer to as a meaningless loss while the dominance of one over the other, as told by the bereaved who comes to therapy, will determine the initial intervention. Thus, adopting a multidimensional view that considers the circumstances of the event, the subjective internal experience that includes both functioning and its derivatives, and attending to the nature of emotional, cognitive and psychological relationships with the newly deceased is essential (Rubin, et al., 2003, p. 680) (see also Malkinson, Rubin, & Witztum, 2005, 2006).

Such an integrated view of loss and trauma provides additional connotations that affect the way we assess complications in the process and outcomes, and our approach to therapeutic interventions. In traumatic bereavement, as a result of direct or indirect exposure, the bereaved's experience includes both the event and images of the deceased and causes a disruption of the worldview of self, others and the world. The emotional consequences include fear, anxiety, and discomfort, which are typically trauma-related, as well as sadness, yearning, and a sense of rejection, which are loss-related. Impairment in functioning in social and other domains is likely to occur. The complication of traumatic loss is termed complicated grief (CG) which is a threat if co-occurring with PTSD (life threat) symptoms. Other possible outcomes of combined loss and trauma that are likely to be evaluated as traumatic loss can include occasions of very extreme (objective, traumatic) events that are subjectively experienced as very intense, or an extreme objective event can be experienced subjectively as less traumatic at the moment of its occurrence, but develops later into an intense experience; or a less extreme objective event might be experienced subjectively as very traumatic. These differences are crucial for evaluating whether an outcome is adaptive or maladaptive, and in determining the need for further evaluation, treatment course, and its timing.

Complicated Grief: The Work of Holly Prigerson and Colleagues, and Horowitz and Colleagues

Among the researchers studying grief and its forms and outcome, the work of Prigerson and associates, and Horowitz and associates is the most prominent (Prigerson, 2004; Prigerson, Frank et al.,1995; Prigerson, Shear et al.,1999; Horowitz, Siegel et al., 1993). Their contributions in the following areas are of special significance:

   a. Delineating a cluster of grief specific symptoms characteristic of complicated grief reported to be distinct from any other generalized distress (Major Depression Disorder, PTSD, Generalized Anxiety Disorder) (Prigerson, et al.,1995; Pivar & Prigerson, 2005). Symptoms such as yearning, disbelief, and preoccupation with the deceased are grief-specific indicators, whereas depressed mood and low self-esteem are depressive symptoms and symptoms of hypervigilance; preoccupation with the fear-evoking traumatic event are indicators of PTSD (Prigerson, et al.,1995, Prigerson, et al., 1997; Boelen, Van den Bout, Keijser, 2003).
   b. Distinguishing uncomplicated from complicated grief reactions were all symptoms that are attachment related, and evolve around the relationship with the deceased: yearning, pining, and disbelief that the person is really dead. Such delineation emphasizes that continuing bonds with the deceased can become complicated if not balanced by continuing with life (Prigerson, 2004; Horowitz, Siegel, Holen et al., 1997).
   c. Based on studies resulting in a novel proposal for a diagnostic DSM criteria, its aim was to specify both psychological and behavioral dysfunctions that impede the bereaved's life following the loss, and also to examine similarities and differences between depression, anxiety, and posttraumatic stress disorder as ways of providing an accurate assessment of the individual's adaptation to the loss.

Complicated Grief: Proposed Diagnostic Criteria

Once a distinction between aspects devoted to the deceased (CG), the self (depression), or the traumatic event (PTSD) was established, the path was set for a consideration of a proposal of diagnostic criteria for inclusion in the *DSM-V* (to be published in 2010). Though some concerns arise about medication and stigmatization of grief as a result of the introduction of a diagnostic criterion, with estimated prevalence of complicated grief at 10 to 20% of the bereaved population, it is believed that the introduction of a specific diagnostic criterion for grief can potentially result in more focused and effective interventions for the at-risk bereaved (Jacobs, 1999; Malkinson, Rubin, & Witztum, 2005; Prigerson et al., 1995; Rubin, Malkinson, & Witztum, 2003). An additional element for supporting a specific diagnostic criterion is related to the fact that bereaved individuals who encounter difficulties as a result of the loss are less likely to ask for help because of their grief, but they may seek help at times for health problems. A diagnostic criterion can alert both family members and family physicians to encourage the bereaved to seek help for grief-specific issues.

Prigerson and Colleagues' Proposed Diagnostic Criteria for Complicated Grief

In their studies Prigerson, Field et al., (1995), Prigerson, Burhals et al., (1997), and Prigerson (2004) and Jacobs (1999) delineated two central features that were included in their proposed diagnostic criteria for complicated grief. They are *separation distress* and *traumatic distress*, with the former representing aspects of the relationship to the deceased, while the latter is concerned with aspects of changes in a worldview following loss. Both are specifically related to the death of a loved one. This means that these proposed criteria combine attachment concepts and stress theories. From the attachment perspective they emphasize a human need to attach that remains throughout their lives (Bowlby 1960, 1980). A threat or separation from an attachment figure that remains unavailable results in anxiety, grief, and mourning. Thus, separation anxiety is a normal human response to a threat of loss or separation, but can also become a risk factor for complicated grief.

From this standpoint, emotional numbing, yearning, searching for the deceased, and disbelief are normal responses of separation anxiety which are very intense during the acute phase, and subside over time, lasting one year or more depending on the circumstances of the loss. On the other hand, excessive separation anxiety or its absence provides indications of a maladaptive form of grief, justifying diagnostic criteria (Prigerson, Shear et al., 1999; Prigerson & Maciejeawaski,2006). Based on the two clusters of separation distress and traumatic distress, four criteria are proposed:

Criterion A: yearning, pining, longing for the deceased. Yearning must be experienced at least daily over the past month to a distressing or disruptive degree.

Criterion B: specifies eight symptoms, of which four have to be experienced at overwhelming or extreme levels: 1. trouble accepting the death; 2. inability to trust others since the death; 3. excessive bitterness or anger about the death; 4. feeling uneasy about moving on with one's life (e.g. difficulty in forming new relationships); 5. feeling emotionally numb or detached from others since the loss; 6. feeling life is empty or meaningless without the deceased; 7. feeling the future holds no meaning or prospects for fulfillment without the deceased; 8. feeling agitated, jumpy, or on edge since the death.

Criterion C: refers to the level of disturbance in dysfunction in social, occupational or other important domains caused by the specified symptoms.

Criterion D: specifies the length of time (six months) that the disturbance must last.

As can be seen, the most pronounced features of the criteria are attachment-based symptoms associated with difficulties in relationship with the deceased, manifested in separation anxiety and distress caused by the death event. Duration and severity of symptoms are two indicators for determining adaptability to the loss.

Horowitz and Colleagues' Proposed Criteria for Complicated Grief

Yet another conceptualization of deviation from the normal course of grief is proposed by Horowitz, Siegel, et al., (1997) who observed that in some cases grief does not take a normal course, and the occurrence of complicated grief is evident.

Similar to Prigerson and colleagues' observation, they also found that symptoms typical of complicated grief differ from those seen in major depressive disorders, and proposed criteria for complicated grief disorder. The criteria include, "the experience (more than a year after the loss) of intense intrusive thoughts, pangs of severe emotions, distressing yearning, feeling excessively alone and empty, excessively avoiding tasks reminiscent of the deceased, unusual sleep disturbances, and levels of loss of interest in personal activities" (p. 904).

The approach formulated by Horowitz, Siegel and their associates (1997) uses the extremes of a continuum to define complicated grief. At one end is intrusion, and at the other, avoidance, with failure to adapt to the specific loss event (1997, p. 905). Difficulties in the relationship to the deceased and the dysfunction that may follow loss are stressed as indicative of difficulties in the grief process, produced without resorting to the trauma dimension.

In a model formulated by Horowitz (1976), he described the response to extreme life events experienced by the individual, which he termed *stress response syndrome*. The major features of his model to explain how the individual copes with stressful life events includes two categories that alternate or may occur simultaneously: *intrusion* and *avoidance*. In the normal course of coping with the stressful event there is an oscillation between the tendency to avoid memories, and repeatedly returning to them, or intrusion. Gradually the event becomes processed and integrated into an existing belief system. A maladaptive outcome based on this conceptualization is when avoidance and intrusion are prolonged in the form of too much or too little of each. As can be seen, the proposed diagnostic criteria of complicated grief are based on the stress response syndrome model of coping with trauma and loss.

The proposed criteria include two clusters of grief-specific symptoms, the first of which describes the event and proposed timing for applying the diagnostic criteria:

1. Event criterion/prolonged response criterion: Bereavement (loss of a spouse, other relative, or intimate partner) at least 14 months ago (12 months is avoided because of possible intense turbulence from an anniversary reaction). The second one describes symptoms of intrusion and avoidance divided into seven categories according to their duration.

2. Signs and symptoms criteria: In the last month any three of the following symptoms have occurred with a severity that interferes with daily functioning. The list of symptoms includes: (a) unbidden memories or intrusive fantasies related to the lost relationship; (b) strong spells of pangs or severe emotions related to the lost relationship; (c) distressing strong yearning or wishes that the deceased were there.

The list of signs of avoidance or failure to adapt includes: (d) feelings of being far too much alone or personally empty; (e) excessively staying away from people, places, or activities that remind the subject of the deceased; (f) unusual level of sleep interference; (g) loss of interest in work, social caretaking, or recreational activities to a maladaptive degree.

There are three sets of symptoms: intrusion, avoidance, and failure to adapt to the specific loss event. Five of the categories of intrusion and avoidance symptoms center on the deceased either by way of being excessively preoccupied or avoiding people, places, and reminders of the lost person. Categories f and g are descriptive of functioning difficulties.

A closer examination of the two proposed diagnostic criteria reveal that both establish a specific concept as distinct from uncomplicated grief; both stress the uniqueness of the cluster of grief-related symptoms that differ from those of depression. However, each highlights a specific aspect of bereavement, along with some similarities.

Horowitz, Siegel, et al. (1997) applied intrusion or avoidance symptoms to assess complicated outcomes of grief while Prigerson, Shear, et al. (1999) and Jacobs (1999) have proposed criteria to measure complicated grief that are based on the concepts of separation anxiety and distress anxiety. Both regard those symptoms that reflect the inner involvement of the bereaved person with the deceased as central.

Clearly, we can see in both cases the integration of various theoretical resources into a cohesive framework applicable in a complicated one (Neimeyer, Prigerson & Davis, 2002). It is only natural that approaching and conceptualizing maladaptive forms of reaction to bereavement have emerged in parallel to changes regarding adaptive and normal responses to bereavement.

The proposed criteria for complicated grief signify the recognition that grief may at times go awry and justify specific diagnostic criteria for those bereaved who are at risk. In its adaptive course, grief following loss through death is a process with a sequential order and is socially recognized and legitimized. However, when there is a prolonged distress and impairment assessment of complications, and grief-specific interventions are needed, the proposed diagnostic criteria are an important contribution to serve this purpose.

Perhaps a combination of the two might yield well-integrated diagnostic criteria. Undoubtedly, an overlap between adjustment disorders of depression, PTSD, and anxiety disorder exists, but studies repeatedly indicate that grief specific symptoms are distinct, and more importantly cannot be explained by depressive symptoms.

Conclusion

In defining the outcome of bereavement as adaptive or maladaptive it is important to note that: (1) grief is seen as a normative personal and social experience which takes place within a specific cultural context; the experience involves a painful process of adaptation to changes in life (psychological, social, financial etc.) as a result of the loss; (2) complicated grief is observed among individuals who experience, in addition to the difficulties in accommodating to changes in their lives following the loss, a life which cannot be amended. Additionally, in determining adaptive and maladaptive bereavement outcomes, the enormity of the event and factors such as the sociocultural context, family relationships, gender, and age need to be considered. The range of possible outcomes includes adjustment to life without the deceased, resilience, and complicated grief.

Another important development concerns the study of the relationship between loss and trauma, leading to the establishment of the concept of traumatic grief, and maladaptive forms such as complicated grief, as distinct from PTSD.

Although trauma and loss studies developed separately, there is a growing interest today among researchers and clinicians in their interface and the various combinations in the form of traumatic loss and traumatic outcome. An event such as the terrorist attack on September 11, 2001 introduced a new perspective from which to view and study traumatic life events that are both attacks on the individual and are shared by the local community and the rest of the world.

As a result of the accumulated empirical evidence, there is a better understanding of the existence of multiple variations of traumatic events and the multiple ways of experiencing them. The many possible variations of outcome as a result of objective traumatic circumstances of the event and perceived subjective experience of the relationship give further support to the notion that both need to be assessed based on objective criteria as well as on the individual's interpretation. Proposed diagnostic criterian seem to be warranted.

While posttraumatic stress disorder (PTSD) has attained the status of diagnostic criteria of complications resulting from trauma in the *Diagnostic and Statistic Manual of Mental Disorders* (APA,1994/2000), complicated bereavement has not yet gained a specific diagnostic criterion, although there seems to be increasing support among researchers and clinicians for such a criterion.

Thus, proposing diagnostic criteria is noteworthy because it recognizes the existence of a group at risk among mourners, whose size can vary from 10 to 20% of the cohort. Clinically, early detection of individuals at risk can be followed by effective intervention. Researchers and clinicians in the field are therefore attempting to characterize complicated grief as a diagnostic criterion to be included in the updated edition of the *DSM*. These suggestions parallel the overall approach to grief and to inter modular integration, of which the prime examples are stress and attachment.

Furthermore, integration of concepts derived from attachment and stress theories, and loss and trauma, have encouraged the viewing of grief following the death of a significant person and its many forms of adaptive and mal-adaptive outcome as a multifaceted process with a much wider perspective.

Studies by Prigerson, Frank, et al. (1995), Prigerson, Shear, et al., (1999), and Horowitz, Bonanno, & Holen (1993), have led them to consider that maladaptive forms of bereavement deserve diagnostic criteria. Identifying grief specific symptoms, as distinct from those of depression and PTSD, and the proposed diagnostic criterion in the *DSM-V* for complicated grief, are therefore landmarks in the field of bereavement which should assist therapists in attending to their clients' specific grief-related complications.

Chapter 8

Cognitive Intervention with Complicated Grief: "As if" Strategy and Letter Writing

Coauthored with Eliezer Witztum, M.D.

"After I finished writing to him I felt a relief and the following night I dreamed about him for the first time since he died." –A woman widowed for two years

In this chapter we describe a combined REBT and strategic cognitive-constructivist integrative therapeutic model which uses "as if" strategy and continuous letter writing as a leave-taking ritual to help clients who suffer from complicated grief.

The Question of Intervention in Complicated Grief

As noted earlier, those experiencing a sudden and traumatic loss are at high risk. These risks, mentioned in connection with parental loss, include the development of a depressed state, a rise in the suicide rate, higher smoking rates and drug and alcohol consumption, an increase in morbidity (including outbreaks of existing illnesses and the onset of new illnesses), and an increase in the number of nonpsychiatric hospitalizations (Clayton, 1975;

Clayton, Halikas, & Maurice, 1972; Witztum, Malkinson & Rubin; 2005; Zisook & Shuchter, 2001).

In light of these results, questions crop up, such as, is there a reason to treat grief? If intervention is to take place, at what point should one undertake it? Should one treat all the complications or only some of them; all bereaved persons or only those at high risk? If one does treat, what is the optimal therapy? Is therapy effective at all?

We have mentioned in chapter 7 that complicated grief is one of the conditions for which grief intervention was found to be efficacious (traumatic violent death and soliciting help were the other two) (Jordan & Neimeyer, 2003; Stroebe, Schut, & Van der Bout, 2000). It seems that a combination of such conditions may yield a variety of therapeutic methods that can ease much suffering, facilitate an adaptive process especially for those suffering from complicated grief and interconnected depressive syndromes (Witztum & Roman, 2000). Follow-up and continued preventative treatment for high risk groups is vital.

The therapeutic implications of these reconsiderations presented cognitive and cognitive-constructivist therapies as efficient modes for grief intervention, viewing cognitions as significant in understanding human disturbances (Beck, Wright, Newman, & Liese, 1993; Ellis, 1993) and the need to reconstruct a shattered story (Fleming & Robinson, 2001; Neimeyer, 1996, 2000) when a loss through death occurs.

REBT therapists view complicated grief as a form of dysfunctional grief and defined as a persistence over time with no diminishing effect of dominant irrational (distorted) beliefs regarding the loss event, the deceased, and the self (Malkinson, 1996, 2001; Malkinson & Ellis, 2000) indicative of some sort of "stuckness" in the search for the meaning of the death and life following death. The client's difficulty, failure, or disbelief in his or her ability to reconstruct an alternative "assumptive world" (Parkes, 1993) or belief system are manifested as crying, anger, and protest. Similar to other therapeutic models, from an REBT perspective prolonged dysfunctional grief is related to such factors as the circumstances of the loss event, past experiences with loss and availability of support. However, REBT stresses the centrality of the cognitions as mediating between the loss event and the emotional consequence. Response to the loss event is mediated by the individual's cognitive tendencies that lead to distorted constructions. "This loss never should have happened to me and I will never get over it"; "Life is not worth living "; "I would rather die than go through this terrible pain," are typical cognitions (Ellis & Dryden 1997; Malkinson, 1996, 2001; Malkinson & Ellis, 2000).

According to REBT, during the acute phase of grief, the bereaved require help in accepting their grief and pain through general cognitive-behavioral strategies (e.g., using coping statements, thought stopping, cognitive rehearsal, REI, and cognitive reframing), combined with provision of information. In contrast, in cases of complicated grief, challenging irrational beliefs is more appropriate, and the employment of rigorous "disputation" interventions, combined with behavioral strategies (Ellis, 1994b) and diverse cognitive-behavioral methods (Ellis, 1994b; Kubany & Manke, 1995), may be more effective. Changing irrational beliefs is known in REBT as disputation (D), which refers to challenging the client's dysfunctional belief system using cognitive, emotive, and behavioral strategies (Walen, DiGiuseppe, & Dryden, 1992). In general REBT such strategies challenge and at times include arguing with the client's rigid beliefs, so that he or she can internalize a more rational, desirable set of beliefs (Ellis, 1994b; Malkinson, 1996). When complicated grief has taken a prolonged form and is dysfunctional, REBT interventions will most likely include rigorous use of Socratic questions, and logical empirical, pragmatic disputation combined with employment of other forms of empirical disputation (i.e., REI, thought stopping, reframing, practicing rational statements, and alternative behaviors). The wide range of strategies in cognitive therapy has been described at length by Beck (1976), Ellis and Dryden (1997), and Freeman and White (1989).

REBT-based complicated grief interventions have four aims to facilitate an adaptive process:

1. Identify irrational beliefs (demandingness directed to self, others, and the world) and their emotional (e.g., anxiety), behavioral (e.g., avoidance), and physiological (e.g., breathing difficulties, heart palpitations) consequences.

2. Explain and teach the connections between beliefs (B) and consequences (C).

3. Identify secondary symptoms and assess individual idiosyncratic consequences; that is, a specific language to describe emotions, behaviors, and specific physiological reactions and change distorted thinking constructions into "rational" adaptive ones through the practice of cognitive emotional, behavioral, and physiological strategies.

4. Assist the client in a search for alternative ways of retelling his or her shattered story.

5. Explore ways to continue bonds with the deceased (e.g., ways of remembering, keeping memorabilia, commemoration).

From Complicated to Uncomplicated Grief:
Applying an As If Strategy

G. Kelly (1955/1991) introduced the "as if" option. He asserted that there are infinite ways to construe the world and people need to apply alternative constructions. With his "as if" position Kelly sought to encourage people to apply different constructions to events and then test these new possibilities and experiment with them. Death of a loved one is such an event. Fleming and Robinson (2001) discussed the cognitive functioning of counterfactual thinking among bereaved people. Counterfactual thinking is "the generation of imagined alternatives to actual events" (p. 657) in the form of an "If only— then" statement which is an inaccurate evaluation of the traumatic event but "offers the potential benefits of providing relief from suffering, preparation for the future, and enhancing the illusion of control" (p. 664). Applying the "as if" option in grief therapy can help the bereaved person experiment with alternative constructions as he or she searches for the meaning of death, and life without the deceased. Also, as Dryden suggested, "as if" can be used as a technique to dispute irrational belief. In grief therapy as if allows the bereaved to "talk," write, think, and do things as if the deceased were present, and express those thoughts and feelings which may block a more adaptive course of grief (Neimeyer, 1998). "As if" technique can be formulated as cognitive focused, behavioral, or emotive, emphasizing each component in accordance with the bereaved's specific needs (Fleming & Robinson, 2001).

Application of the "as if" cognitive strategy was found to be effective when working with the bereaved, especially in cases of prolonged grief (Ellis & Dryden, 1997; Malkinson, 1996; Van der Hart, 1987). In line with the REBT tenet of normalizing grief responses, the application of this strategy provides a means to legitimately allow the bereaved to express otherwise unexpressed "crazy" thoughts or secrets that he or she may hold or experience.

A phenomenon that has been described to occur among the bereaved is that of inner talking to the deceased person, at times of either stress or yearning (Raphael, 1983). The inner dialogue can take the form of questions and answers or of sharing good or bad news, indicating a continuing relationship with the deceased. In applying the "as if" strategy, it is necessary to keep a structured framework so that client's thoughts directed at the deceased are externalized and verbalized. Through an "as if" dialogue, irrational beliefs about the self ("It's my fault, I am guilty"), the deceased ("She shouldn't have left me"), or the world ("It shouldn't have happened") can be explored, with challenges being made as if the deceased is responding. In prolonged and complicated grief, an "as if" strategy can be applied to provide the bereaved with the tools to experiment with a number of alternatives of meaning construction or interpretations of the loss.

The following case illustrates the use of this strategy combined with others to help the client experience pain and yearning as part of an adaptive grief process instead of guilt and depression.

> Linda, in her late 20s, requested therapy because, she said, she felt depressed, cried a lot, had given up her work, and had lost interest in life. A detailed assessment was conducted on the circumstances that had led to her feelings of depression and her related cognitions. The client revealed that, one year prior to her requesting therapy, her brother, who had been suffering from severe mental problems, and was under treatment, had committed suicide upon his discharge from the hospital. According to the client, she and her brother were very close. Bursting into tears, she said she felt guilty because she didn't prevent her brother from jumping to his death ("It's my fault"); also anger was expressed at her brother for killing himself the way he did ("How could he have done it to me?"); and she feared she would never be able to forgive him. But even more painful were her guilt feelings for not saving her brother, and the awful feeling of having to live with the thought that he would never forgive her. Linda also revealed that she was condemning herself for her inability to overcome her intrusive thoughts (secondary symptom), convincing herself of how bad a person she was for neglecting her brother's call for help. Complicated prolonged grief was assessed as related to the cyclical interaction between irrational beliefs (demandingness) and disturbed emotions (depression), apparently preventing a healthier course of grief. Self-blame ("I should have noticed his distress, since I didn't, I'm a terrible person") and anger toward the deceased brother ("He shouldn't have committed suicide"; "How could he have done this to me?") were the emotional consequences of the distorted interpretation. It seemed from the client's disclosures that the brother was "present" within her, and the way she was thinking about and remembering him could explain some of the irrational beliefs she was holding onto.

According to TTMoB-based assessment there is no clear-cut dominance of either track; on the contrary, an oscillation between the two tracks is apparent. Linda disclosed a disruption in her ability to function, she had given up her work, and felt depressed, and had lost interest in life. Yet, she also felt that her beloved brother was inside her, and when she described their close relationship the memories of him were blended with guilt feelings for failing to save him and anger toward him for taking his life away. The forthcoming first anniversary was a determining factor in choosing to focus on the relationship with the deceased (Track II) components.

Linda's distorted thinking was identified (aim 1: "I should have saved my brother and if I didn't I am a terrible person"; "He shouldn't have done it"). The connection between her self-condemnation and her depression was explained to her (aim 2). Linda cried a lot and moved from talking about herself as a terrible person to feeling guilty for being angry with her brother. She also developed a secondary symptom (aim 3: "I shouldn't think these thoughts and if I do I am a bad person").

In the intervention with this client (aim 3), alongside logical disputation (mostly circular and Socratic questions to empirically evaluate the event and how sad it was, logically arguing with the client's distorted thinking, and challenging it), the as if technique was the main strategy employed (Ellis & Dryden, 1997).

The as if technique (aim 4) was used with this client to explore her cognitions related to past circumstances, to focus on the here and now, and as an appraisal of the future. The technique also enabled a distinction to be made between facts ("My brother died") and her if only thoughts or interpretations about these facts ("If only I had stayed with him as I should have"; "If only I knew what he had in mind"; or "If only he had asked me"). Talking to him in an as if manner, as if he were here, telling him all the thoughts that she wished she could have said, was a way of assisting her in verbalizing those "terrible and wicked" thoughts that were running through her mind. The imagined dialogue was rehearsed and practiced with a focus on functional emotions (sadness, pain, and frustration). As she practiced the difference between functional (rational) and dysfunctional (irrational) thoughts, she was able to emotionally experience sadness as distinct from depression. As sad as the death event was and obviously had remained, it was the client's evaluation of it that had to be changed into a more adaptive and healthier one.

In accordance with REBT routine (Dryden, 2002), between-sessions assignments were given to Linda with the aim of preparing her cognitively, emotionally, and behaviorally for the forthcoming anniversary, as well as to enhance therapeutic gains and create continuity between sessions.

Toward the end of the third session, a between-session assignment was given to write an as if letter to her brother. It was suggested that, as the anniversary of his death was approaching, she would go to the cemetery with someone of her choice and read the letter aloud as if to her brother. The assignment was prescribed as a way of practicing rational (functional) thinking and also as a leave-taking ritual (Van der Hart, 1987; Witztum & Roman, 1993). Preparation for her visit to the cemetery included going through the details she feared would be too painful and thus she might have avoided. Pain was to be part of the experience. In order to overcome a secondary symptom (pain is the primary reaction and her irrational thought that "It must not be painful" led to a secondary symptom of avoidance of the pain: "It shouldn't be too painful") it was crucial to attend to the client's pain tolerance and show her that, though painful, she could stand the anticipated pain of the letter-reading visit.

In the following session, the client described the visit with her sister to the cemetery. She related how, in spite of being tense, she had told her brother all the thoughts and feelings she had experienced following his death, her concern and love for him, and her regret that she was not sensitive enough to see the pain he went through. She cried in the session as she was telling it and felt very sad, though less angry toward him and less condemning of herself for not preventing his death. She said she felt relieved and was emotionally overwhelmed to find that, for the first time since his death, she could visualize her brother the way she remembered him prior to his death as a healthy young man. As is often the case, the cyclical nature of irrational thoughts formed a closed cognitive system, where one erroneous thought was followed by another, reaching a point where it was terrible to think such thoughts let alone verbalize them ("I can't stop those thoughts"). Verbalizing those "evil" thoughts (disowning them) brought relief. Also, verbalizing was a way of overcoming the fear of what people might say upon hearing these thoughts ("If they only knew what I was thinking, what they would think of me"). In Linda's case the aim of the as if strategy was threefold: to help her verbalize her if only "wicked" thoughts, to rehearse the distinction between functional and dysfunctional thoughts, and create an alternative narrative through as if talking to her brother.

Therapy was terminated after two more sessions. At this point, it was apparent that the client had adapted and internalized a more rational way of experiencing her brother's death, and was able to retell the story of his death in a way that was less stressful.

Three months later, in a follow-up session, Linda reported being less depressed, saying that though she felt the pain of her brother's death and yearned for him, she was feeling significantly less guilty. She said that most importantly she realized that it was his choice and that she probably could not have prevented it. Linda said that for the first time her dream about her brother was a pleasant one and his face looked calm and smiling the way she wanted to remember him in her heart (aim 5). She said: "I know my brother loved me and was very concerned over my depression. I think he forgives me."

Grief Therapy through Leave-Taking Rituals

The idea of using rituals and symbols as a way of reordering what was shattered stems from Jewish tradition, which emphasizes the importance of ritual as a cognitive emotional and behavioral experience at different points in the life cycle, and especially in matters relating to death.

In line with the idea of a ritual as a way of reordering a life that was shattered, a therapeutic approach was developed in the 1980s that emphasizes the symbolic ritual components of the treatment of grief, highlighting the therapeutic affect of leave-taking rituals (Van der Hart, 1983, 1986; Witztum & Roman, 2000; Witztum, 2005). In the original formulation of this ritual-based approach, the bereaved individuals, aided by the therapist, perform a series of symbolic acts in which they separate (break the bonds) emotionally from people or situations in their past. By distancing themselves from the people or objects, a resumption of functioning and rebuilding relationships with other people or objects was expected (Van der Hart, 1983, 1987). Van der Hart pointed out that the common denominator of the various forms of this therapy is that they return to the two periods of traditional mourning ceremonies, described by Janet in the early 20th century (for a detailed description, see Van der Hart, 1987). At first, the clients are encouraged to speak about or to the deceased and to act as though she or he is still alive; next they are helped to change their position, vis-à-vis the deceased, free themselves, and take their leave (Van der Hart, 1983). First, there is a separation from or a change of old behavioral habits connected to the deceased; afterwards there is a separation from the deceased. The differences between the various therapeutic approaches are expressed in the different formulations of stages, in the coping with grief, and in the types of help offered to develop new behavioral patterns.

Originally the model constructed a structured framework for the mourning process using a variety of cognitive and behavioral strategies, including continued letter writing to the deceased, accepting a linking object from the client, and planning a leave taking ritual, in which the client was expected to bury or separate from their precious linking object (for example by giving the object to the therapist for ritual storage, which in Hebrew is termed a *Geniza*). This was a completion phase of breaking the bonds with the deceased. In its initial formulation, one of its main purposes was to help mourners express their feelings, resolve the inhibiting emotional block, and facilitate alternative ways of expressing the whole range of feelings so that the process of separation from the deceased could be completed.

With the growing empirical support for a continuing relationship with the deceased, this therapeutic approach has modified how it defines complicated grief and how it conceptualizes the aim of the employment of these strategies.

The main purpose of utilizing a leave taking through the use of letter writing is to facilitate an adaptive process of meaning making (Neimeyer, 2000a, 2002, 2005). One of the main purposes of this approach, as applied within the continuing bonds framework, is to help the bereaved express thoughts and feelings through writing as a way of searching and constructing alternative cognitive and emotional processes in creating a new meaning, so that life after the loss may take its adaptable course. Moreover grief therapy, and especially cognitive and constructivist approaches, view interventions as a means to reconstruct the disruptive life narrative and facilitate an adaptive process within which a meaning construction to life without the deceased is seen as a central theme in a continuous life narrative. Leave-taking rituals and continuous letter writing are applied within this framework.

Letter writing can be applied in cases of complicated grief in any phase; during the mourning process that may last a number of years and in the postmourning period in cases without a clearly defined time demarcation (Rubin, 1985). Horowitz's (1990) schematic description of the grieving process consists of seven specific phases: primary denial and avoidance of the loss; distress responses which occur as a result of the loss, restlessness and physiological complaints and an attempt to search for the dead loved one; the appearance of anger and guilt feelings; feelings of inner loss; adopting the customs and manners of the deceased; and acceptance and making peace with the deceased's death, which includes the appropriate changes in the mourner's identity. These phases can serve as an assessment framework within which the bereaved can be guided in letter writing. Phases which include the appearance of creativity in the grieving process and the phenomenon of arousing or reviving grief at significant dates (the "anniversary reaction") were added by Pollock (1989). The described therapy uses traditional frameworks of letter writing as leave-taking rituals to facilitate an adaptive mourning process. Thus the bereaved persons can organize and reorganize their emotional connections with the deceased, so that emotions can be invested in additional relationships (Malkinson, 1985).

Letter Writing in Grief Therapy

The healing potential of writing is well established (O'Connor, Nikoletti, Kristjanson, Faaaia, Melger & Demaso, 1988; & Willcock, 2003; Pennebaker & Beall, 1986; Pennebaker, 1993, 1997, 2000; Pennebaker & Beall, 1986 Smyth, Stone, Hurweitz, & Kael,1999). The act of writing puts into words thoughts and feelings about the writer's past, present, and future life. Dreams, hopes, traumas, and losses can be expressed through writing, which involves cognitions and emotions, and has psychological as well as physical health benefits (Smyth et al., 1999). The incorporation of writing in therapy in general (which is also referred to as expressive writing), and in grief therapy in particular has become widespread, and is applied in a number of ways. In some cases writing is done over a limited number of consecutive days, while others have prescribed that this technique be carried out daily for a period of time (Pennebaker & Beall,1986; O'Connor et al., 2003) or that a daily diary or journal be kept (Miller, 2002). Whatever the chosen structure or setting, writing is believed to help the individual express the pain in a "private" way with the writer choosing the words, the pace and emotions, and a reconstruction of the narrative in a more organized way.

A combination of "as if" strategy with one-time letter writing was described earlier in the chapter. Letter writing daily over a limited period was applied with Fiona (Mrs. Pain, whose telling of the story of the circumstances of her husband's death was described in chapter 1, and was assessed as dominantly Track I in TTMoB). In its initial phase, therapy focused on Track I components and what was assessed as avoidance of the relationship axis at that phase became the foci track of therapy as the first anniversary of her husband's death was approaching. As Fiona unfolded her story it became clear that her avoidance of talking about her husband was related to their complicated relationship. The traumatic circumstances of the loss of her husband, combined with a complicated marital relationship prior to his death, explained her difficulties in discussing the subject. Letter writing daily over a limited time was the intervention chosen to help Fiona find a sense of connection to her late husband, despite her ambivalent relationship with him. It was assumed that through writing to her deceased husband Fiona would be able to restore a sense of control over her double-layered difficulties—those pertaining to the traumatic circumstances of the loss, and those relating to the conflictual marital relationship (see Malkinson, Rubin, & Witztum, 2006).

The first letter opened with an explanation for writing the letter to her late husband, saying that she was asked by her therapist "to write to you and tell you what has happened to me after you died." The letter was mostly an informative one, a sort of touching base about life without him. Subsequently, letter writing was about their relationship and her ambivalent feelings of guilt about not stopping him from going that night to his friends and guilt over her feeling of relief from a conflictual relationship blended with yearning for him. She wrote about dreams she had about him, which conveyed her ambivalence and her love for him. She dreamed that he was looking for her and when he found her he looked at her and smiled. She explained that being able to talk and discuss her marital relationship had freed some fears she was carrying inside her and she is more confident in herself. Paradoxically, the more confident she felt the more her yearning for her husband increased. Letter writing continued until after the first anniversary when she wrote about the theme of forgiveness, which had been raised in one of the sessions in terms of whom she should forgive. Should she forgive her husband for the period in their life where he treated her badly or perhaps he should forgive her for thinking many times negatively about him? This is what she wrote in her concluding words: "I forgive you my dear for the way you treated me, for the suffering I experienced during so many years, and I cherish the last months of your life when our relationship had improved." Letter writing assisted Fiona in adopting a more balanced view of her past and her present life following the violent traumatic loss of her husband.

Applying Continuous Letter Writing

Structured treatment in continuous letter writing as a leave-taking ritual in grief therapy greatly resembles traditional mourning rituals. Van der Hart (1983, 1987) has outlined four steps of the leave-taking ritual: preparation, reorganization, finalization, and follow-up.

Preparation

This first step is sometimes called the cognitive building phase. In it the client is not yet ready to talk about the deceased. The therapist explains the different options for therapy and what will be asked of the client. The therapist also points out that therapy can be difficult, painful, and very emotional.

In this approach, a family evaluation is also recommended and, if necessary, the family can be included in therapy.

Reorganization

Most of the working through of grief is done in this phase. The mourner usually acts as though the deceased is still alive.

Continual letter writing at this point is one of the most important techniques that can be used (Van der Hart, 1983, 1986). The bereaved writes to the deceased every day, about feelings or anything else he or she wants to share. The letter is an important tool for expressing unresolved ambivalence vis-à-vis the deceased. The writing has its own dynamics, and some clients may also choose to write to additional people from their past.

The client brings the letter and sometimes reads it in therapy. At other times the client enlists the therapist's aid in dealing with traumatic or difficult experiences. Through the letter-writing process, the awareness of the death of the loved person changes and the cognitive and emotional way of relating to the deceased is less intense and more balanced. The intensive letter writing tapers off, as do the heightened emotions, and the client begins to reorganize both an inner relationship with the deceased as well as a functioning relationship with others.

In its original version the model included an additional important part connected to "linking objects"—mementoes and symbolic objects which were precious to the client and which the therapist requested during therapy. Handing over a symbolic object gives the client the feeling that he or she can cope and separate and that there were other ways to separate from the deceased (Van der Hart, 1983, 1987).

At the end of this phase, the client is expected to be able to truly separate from the deceased with the help of the leave-taking ritual. The cognitive approach emphasizes the continuing bonds perspective, the meaning attached to them, and the possibility of reevaluating and exploring how they can be integrated in a more balanced way.

Finalization

In the initial model, the important component was the leave-taking ritual. Its purpose paralleled the traditional ritual of a second burial or gravestone setting one year after the death. The purpose of the ritual was to validate the change that had occurred in the relationship to the deceased. Although the deceased was to be remembered and respected, there was also the expectation from the bereaved that he or she would resume life. In the leave-taking ritual, the symbolic objects, which might have been the notebooks or letters, were released. They were buried, burned, or thrown into a body of water.

The idea underlying the intervention was that through this ritual, the client acknowledged that life with the deceased belonged to the past. Other forms of the finalization phase contained a leave-taking ritual, a purifying ritual, and a unification ritual. Van der Hart describes a ritual that includes a ceremonial meal after the leave-taking ritual.

In continual letter writing, as it is now applied, the client is not asked to discard or bury the letters; it is assumed that the completion of writing represents a coming to terms with the idea that the deceased is part of the bereaved's inner world and that memories and commemorations are an integral part of life.

Follow-Up

After the completion of the letter-writing phase, staying in touch is important. During follow-up talks, a ceremony or a memorial can be discussed, as well as how the client could cope with future negative feelings like pain and sadness.

Applying Letter Writing in the Process of Grief

The phases of continuous letter writing therapy correspond in many ways to the process of grief. In the first phases of assessment and preparing the client, and in the initiation of the writing, the client is still unable to speak about the deceased. Intervention is within the denial framework that corresponds to Horowitz's phase of primary denial and avoidance of the loss. The writer writes to the deceased and talks to him or her as though he or she is still alive. Most of the working through of grief is done during this phase. In cases of avoidance of reminders of the deceased or conversely "clinging" to such reminders, the use of a linking object where the client is asked to choose an object and bring it to the session can help, as this symbolic object gives the client the choice of rearranging and rewriting the way the deceased is represented. Only then are the thoughts and feelings that follow experienced in a more adaptive way to life without the deceased. In the finalization phase, the mourner reorders not only the inner memories of the deceased but also the transformed identity.

The therapeutic process and the application of continuous letter writing as a leave-taking ritual in a search for meaning will be illustrated with two cases of loss: a woman who had lost her husband 10 years prior to seeking therapy, and a man who had lost his wife 10 months before coming to therapy. Both reported a variety of syndromes.

A Case of Complications in Recent Grief

Assessment

David was retired, 73 years old, had been widowed some 10 months previously, and was the father of three children. David came to treatment because he was suffering from serious distress, lack of appetite, disturbed sleep, and great sadness, which all began suddenly after his wife passed away.

DEMOGRAPHIC AND TTMoB-BASED ASSESSMENT

David had been married for 50 years, and had enjoyed a very good marriage. His wife had a non-life-threatening heart condition. While traveling in one of the Balkan countries, his wife complained in the early morning hours that she was short of breath and was feeling weak. She fainted, he called the doctors, but by the time they arrived, she had died. This sudden death while on vacation away from home was a very traumatic experience. He stayed behind to take care of the arrangements, and ran into many enduring bureaucratic difficulties when he wanted to transport the body home by air, but made efforts to overcome them because he was getting ready to return back home with his wife's body. He was barely able to surmount these difficulties for he was hit hard and was left completely exhausted. David was born in Jerusalem, and grew up in a very poor family, one of many children. He had spent his working life with one employer.

Despite the fact that his wife had passed away nearly a year earlier, the situation was one of complicated grief. Utilizing Rubin's TTMoB, in Track I, one could observe withdrawal, reduced functioning, and severe anxieties. He had stopped driving, he became clinically depressed, and he suffered from sleep disturbance and a loss of appetite. David described yearning and preoccupation with memories of his wife, and thinking about how much he missed her, and the difficulties he experienced in remaining alone at night. Since the death of his wife, David had been unable to sleep alone in his home. He remained secluded at home and had developed a dysphonic and anxiety syndrome. Track I components were prevalent.

Cognitive Assessment

Assessment of distorted thinking that increases emotional distress revealed that David saw no purpose in continuing to live without his beloved wife. The yearning he felt had became unbearable and painful (a secondary symptom).

Not only was life without his wife painful, David was also continuously reexperiencing the circumstances of the sudden loss of his wife while on holiday, and failed to avoid remembering the dreadful arrangements he had to make to fly back home with the body.

It was assumed that a combined intervention of correction of distorted thinking and creating a "sensible" narrative through continual letter writing would be effective in David's case.

The Intervention

In the process of assessment it became clear that cognitive restructuring of distorted thinking, that increases emotional distress but guides it into a more functional way of interpretation, would be a preferred mode of intervention. It would serve to explain and clarify to David what he was experiencing following the loss of his beloved wife, and also to facilitate a more adaptive bereavement process. David's problem consisted of at least two components representing the two tracks. The first was his depression, which was at the level of clinical depression and could have been treated effectively with appropriate antidepressant medication, and the second was related to his relationship to his deceased wife that also necessitated active participation. Asked by the therapist (Eliezer Witztum) about the possibility of taking medication, David replied that he would like to consider the suggestion of medication as a way to treat his depression, but concerning the second suggestion that he write letters to his deceased wife, he wanted to know exactly what the purpose of this intervention was. Providing information about letter writing was crucial. After explaining the assignment and its goals, we discussed it and agreed that its purpose was to assist him to experience a more adaptive grief process that would help him improve his functioning and he would be able to continue to maintain his independence and social contacts. The idea of continual letter writing was introduced and explained to him and he was requested to try as if he were writing to his wife. He agreed, but he was afraid that he would be instructed to sever his emotional connections from his wife.

The second session took place a week later. During the session, he said that he wrote his initial letter to his wife, in which he expressed his yearning to her, how difficult it was for him without her, and how much he missed her. He reported that it had been very difficult for him to write the initial letter, but upon completion of the task he felt relieved. He decided that he would use antidepressant medication and treatment was initiated.

David expressed the feeling that he needed time between sessions and asked that the interval be two weeks. His request was accepted by his therapist but he received an additional task, which was to resume driving as home-work. He promised to continue writing, he agreed to the additional task of homework, and agreed to come to the next session in his own car.

During the third session, the client reported that he had successfully resumed driving and had driven in his own car to the session. He continued to write to his wife, and during the session he read the letter, which described his symptoms and how difficult this period was for him, especially his yearn-ing and loneliness.

During the fourth session, two weeks later (by then he had already taken the prescribed dose of medication for four weeks), he reported that the drug was working and he felt better.

After assessing the improvement of David's function (the first track) the therapist decided to refer to the traumatic element and to touch upon the cir-cumstances of that "horrible night." While the therapist and David were dis-cussing the events of the death on that "horrible night," David suddenly remembered a forgotten memory from his childhood. At the age of 8 he went to visit his elderly grandfather, who was lying in bed. His grandfather fell out of bed, and when David tried to get him back into bed he saw that he wasn't breathing. He tried to shake him but his grandfather wasn't responding. He understood that something terrible had happened to his grandfather, who was motionless, and it turned out that he was dead. David was shocked and became very frightened and sad. While recalling the story David remarked in amazement that he had forgotten the story all these years and recalled it only now. To the therapist's question as to whether he understood the connection between the two episodes, David replied that he did indeed.

He came in his car to the fifth session two weeks later, in a better mood, able to be alone, even for a short period at night, with a significant improve-ment in functioning around the house.

During the sixth session, David mentioned that he felt better, capable of staying alone during the day. David reported that lately, without any obvious reason, he had stopped writing to his wife. He promised to resume writing and said he would try to write to her about the difficulties he was having after her death. At his request, the sessions resumed once a month.

At the seventh session, David reported that he felt better, his anxiety had completely disappeared, and he was more independent during the day. He wrote a letter to his wife about the difficulties. He brought the letter to the session and read it aloud.

David reported at the eighth session that he continued to feel better; his anxiety and depressive fears had almost completely disappeared. The only remaining sign was his inability to sleep alone at night, and he asked his son to come to stay with him overnight. The company of his son enabled him to go to sleep. He had brought the letter, and at my request read it out loud. He wrote to his wife that he was suffering and still could not sleep alone. He thought that he would shortly be all right, but he missed her and spoke about her with the children. He felt sad with a need to cry. He was unable to be separated from his son, who had to sleep over.

By the ninth session, the situation was improving; the son was late on two occasions and David didn't wait but went to bed alone. He hoped that he was on the way to being independent. This was the only vestige of his problems that remained. He would return two months later.

David reported at the tenth session that he continued to be fine, and although the son still slept over, he no longer depended on him to do so. David said that he was done with letter writing.

The eleventh session found David looking better and he said he felt well, he was indifferent to whether or not the son slept over; the son often did not come home. In the meantime, David had met a woman who was about 60 years old and a relationship was forming. He had not forgotten the deceased wife but wanted to alleviate his loneliness. He would come for a follow-up in two months time.

The twelfth session was a follow-up, and he said he felt better and had resumed singing in the choir. During therapy, the first anniversary of the death had taken place. David told the therapist that the memorial ceremony had gone smoothly and that nothing unusual had happened.

At the second follow-up, David looked and felt better. He reported that he was sleeping by himself, his son had gotten married, and David felt more energetic.

This is a representative example of an aged widower who lost his wife under traumatic circumstances and developed complicated grief. In terms of the TTMoB, Track I is dominant, with symptoms of clinical depression, reduced functioning, and inability to stay alone at home at night with Track II (relationship to the deceased) components. David described yearning and preoccupation with memories of his wife. Intervention strategically addressed both tracks: The first with medication and cognitive behavior intervention (correction of distorted thinking) and the second with continual letter writing, which allowed him to express his feelings (creation). David responded positively to the interventions, he recovered from his depression, regained functioning, and in a relatively short time was able to stay alone at night and released his son from the duty to stay with him.

A Case of Prolonged Grief

Assessment

Laura, a 60-year-old widow and mother of three, did not work as a result of an accident at home when she fell off a chair and broke her hand.

Laura's main complaint was anxiety with a decreased appetite, and problems sleeping. Her mood was normal, but because of her broken hand she had difficulties functioning.

Demographic Assessment

Laura was born in Israel, the youngest of eight children. Her parents immigrated to Israel from Turkey. She was a good student who completed elementary school but did not go to high school. She did not serve in the army (which is obligatory in Israel) for religious reasons. She felt she had missed opportunities in life and felt bitterness and anger toward her parents, whom she felt held her back. Laura married at 18 to get away from home, and in her words, picked a "good" husband, a successful man, who was a building contractor. Later in life she studied at the Open University. Then, 10 years ago, her husband became ill with cancer and passed away. Over time, there were additional losses: a brother who died one year after her husband, and a sister to whom she had been much attached, who passed away four years ago.

TTMoB-Based Assessment

Laura's grief can be described as complicated. Utilizing Rubin's TTMoB, Laura's breaking her hand resulted in her stopping work and made her feel fragile and helpless and reminded her how she felt when her husband died (Track I); this leads us to Track II. We can see that in Laura's case her life completely collapsed, in familial (she was ignored by the extended family), financial (they were almost bankrupt), and psychological ways (she felt depressed and emotionally broken).

A Cognitive Assessment

An analysis of the information revealed that grief and difficulties in adapting to the multiple losses was a central issue. Of particular importance were the familial and economic complications that occurred after the death of her beloved husband. He was a wealthy person, and following his death, her economic situation worsened noticeably. Also, her husband, as the first born son, was the authority figure in the extended family, and his death created a vacuum and confusion within the family where his brothers were competing for leadership.

Laura's reaction was one of devastation. She told herself that she should have acted differently in handling financial matters and that she should have listened to the advice given by her children. The losses of her beloved husband, her sister, and brother were painful and too much for her.

In the initial phase of therapy, a cognitive restructuring was initiated. Her distorted cognitions as affecting her emotional distress were explained by exploring alternative interpretations. The therapist (Eliezer Witztum) expressed empathy and explained how he understood the situation while emphasizing the difficulties she had experienced following the loss. Then the therapist suggested that she write "as if" to her husband in order to continue her dialogue with him and make him aware of her struggles and her feelings. Laura agreed.

By the first session, Laura had begun writing; her letters interwove the family narratives. Another complication evolved in that she chose to write about what took place after her husband's death. As mentioned earlier, there were severe difficulties in the family, as the two brothers-in-law had passed away. It also turned out that much of her husband's business had been based on oral agreements and that many business associates who owed him money denied their debts. Many of them even claimed that he had owed them money. As she explained in her letter to her husband, her wish to honor and maintain his reputation made her reluctant to declare bankruptcy.

By the second session, Laura was continuing to write and in her writing she dwelt on the issue of the blackmail by former partners and employees who claimed that her husband owed them money and continued to demand money, threatening and intimidating her. She felt guilty because she had refused to declare bankruptcy. Much of the pressure fell on the eldest son, who had worked in the company, and tried to help her deal with the financial expenses after his father's death.

Laura spoke more about her anxiety and her dependence upon her husband during the third session. Together, we concluded that part of her recovery was also an "occupational rehabilitation." The therapist reminded her how important it was that she get out of the house and involve herself in other activities. She told the therapist about her excellent reputation for childcare. For many years she was very successful at working in a nursery school. In the course of events the director had changed, and there was tension and competition between her and the new director, and after she broke her hand she decided to resign (Track I).

The fourth session found Laura continuing to write, and after being encouraged to do so by the therapist, she also wrote for the first time about the anger she felt toward her husband because of the way he worked, not leaving records in an organized manner. Her children argued bitterly regarding whether or not to pay the father's debts, some of which were false claims (the beginning of elaborating the relationship with the deceased, Track II).

The fifth session suggested, via the letters Laura wrote and then read aloud at each session, that there was a problem of boundaries with her children and the difficulties she faced in expressing herself. She wrote the following: "I feel guilty, particularly regarding my relations with my sons, where I gave in, even when I knew I was right." We analyzed that aspect in terms of thought process errors and searched for alternative ways of thinking.

The sixth session was dedicated to the difficult relations that had developed with her husband's family after his death, as a result of the financial problems. The result was sad estrangement from this side of the family and her feelings of being rejected. She thought that the family was ungrateful to her husband and was angry with them.

During the seventh session, Laura recounted a dream she had about her deceased husband of which she could not remember details, only the feelings. Then, suddenly she recalled a dream in which two of her cousins had visited; she was probably substituting her late husband, which actually points to her feelings of yearning and her wish that he himself would visit her in her dream.

The session was emotionally intense and toward the end of the session Laura asked that sessions be reduced to once every two weeks.

At the eighth session, Laura said she felt fine. She found she had very little to write about, apparently she was "wrung out". She could not decide what direction to take with regard to work, and thought about moving with her son who had been offered a job abroad. She asked to change the frequency of the therapy sessions.

Three weeks later, at the ninth session, Laura reported that she had decided to try to be a cosmetician. She had decided to stay in Israel. Her son would travel abroad alone for work. She shared with the therapist the emotional upheaval she experienced as the tenth anniversary approached. She hinted to the therapist that she would like to cope with the upcoming event by herself. The next session took place a month later.

Laura told the therapist at the tenth session that she had been at the memorial service for her husband. Afterwards, she said that she would like to share a special dream with the therapist. She dreamed that she was walking in her garden which was full of flowers, and she added: "Daffodils are my favorite flowers." The dream was so vivid that she ran to the garden to check if the daffodils had indeed blossomed. Together with the therapist Laura concluded that blossoming of the daffodils represented a return to life. She said that for the first time after a long period she felt more optimistic. And then she added that she had started to fix up a room (in her house) and had begun working as a cosmetician.

Follow-Up

One year after therapy was completed Laura was invited for a follow-up session. She looked and said she felt better. She reported that she tidied up the room in her house so it would serve as an office and she reported working successfully at home. While she still had to cope with many problems with her late husband's family and with her sons, she felt she had the strength to do so.

This is an example of a middle-aged widow whose husband's death occurred following multiple recent losses. The circumstances of her husband's death and her total dependence on him left her very anxious, with ambivalence and strong negative feelings like anger, guilt, remorse, and disappointment. According to the Functional Track of the TTMoB her symptoms were those of anxiety. As for the relationship with the deceased track she was very ambivalent, with negative feelings toward her husband, who had left her in such dire straits, but she also felt strong yearning and longing for him. The symptoms of each track were handled strategically, the first with cognitive restructuring and the second with continual letter writing and use of metaphors to express her feelings. The client responded well to the interventions and overcame her anxieties and feelings of dependency. She regained her functioning and in a relatively short time succeeded in becoming more assertive and was able to create a space for herself as well as resume work.

Conclusion

Interventions for complicated grief can take place during the process of grief or at any other time that the bereaved experiences distress related to the loss event. Therefore, interventions are aimed at identifying cognitive sources of distress and their distressed emotional consequences. Through the employment of a variety of interventions sources of distress are changed to negative though less stressful ones in order to facilitate an adaptive healthier course of grief. The application of "as if" and letter writing were demonstrated as suitable strategies to reconstruct a more coherent narrative wherein the inner dialogue with the deceased person (Track II in the TTMoB) is encouraged. All interventions involved a thorough assessment, preparation, implementation, and a follow-up.

These phases seem to be parallel to the process of grief, which is dynamic and ongoing. These parallels were clearly demonstrated in the application of the phases of continual letter writing that resembled those of the mourning process. In the phases of preparation and reorganization, the client is not ready yet to talk about or relate to the deceased; the writing is mainly at the level of denial. The client writes to the deceased and talks to him or her as though he or she is still alive. This phase is very intense for the client, as it is a way of working through thoughts and feelings about the deceased and about him- or herself. During the finalization phase, the client begins to be able to reorganize thoughts and feelings concerning the reality of life without the deceased on both axes: that of relationship with the deceased and that of functioning in life without the deceased, which involve changes in one's identity.

Chapter 9

Cognitive Grief Therapy with Couples: Parental Grief over the Loss of a Child

So far we have discussed grief and bereavement as experienced by the individual. Although loss through death involves a loss of a relationship, and grief occurs on both interpersonal and interpersonal levels, the vast literature is on individual processes probably because bereavement is viewed first and foremost as an intrapersonal experience, with its various forms of outcomes (desirable or nondesirable) and their various dimensions.

While in individual grief therapy the relationship with the deceased (Track I of the TTMoB) is the focus of therapy, and relationships with other living family members is treated indirectly as one of the components of reorganizing one's life (Track I), in couple grief therapy both types of relationship co-occur and need to be assessed and addressed. Moreover, couple grief therapy is initiated as a result of the shattered relationship with both the dead and the living. Therapy is aimed at strengthening attachments with the deceased as well as between the spouses. While attachment with the deceased is being cognitively and emotionally relocated inward, those with a living spouse need to be reorganized interpersonally. Also, the loss of a child destroys, often temporarily, the ability of each partner to provide support for each other. Each parent mourns the loss and searches for a meaning to life without the child, and "the loss of the future" (Malkinson & Bar-Tur, 2004; Rubin,1999).

Such was the case with Mr. and Mrs. Jonas, who came for therapy eight months after the death of their son Jo from cancer. Jo was the youngest of three and was 9 years old when he died.

Mrs. Jonas repeated what she had said over the phone as the reason for their asking for professional help. Jo's death was expected; the doctors informed them of his critical condition, they were prepared in a way, and yet when he died they were shocked and could not believe it. Since he died there had been a sense that everything was falling apart, it was so painful. Mrs. Jonas said: "I think we need to do something, but my husband doesn't believe that anything can be done." Mr. Jonas said he didn't want to come and added that he was only willing to come this one time.

To the question of how he saw life after Jo's death, he replied: "I keep telling my wife that life must go on and nothing can help us. Talking about it will never bring Jo back. I am here because my wife was insisting that I come, so here I am. I know that it is a waste of time."

We can see the differences between the husband and the wife in dealing with the loss. Whereas Mrs. Jonas wants to "continue a relationship" with Jo and talk about and with him as a way of sharing her pain, Mr. Jonas refrains from it and thinks that by doing as she wishes, their "task of continuing with life" cannot be carried on.

The therapist suggested that perhaps they would like to discuss these differences with the therapist's help. It seemed that both cared about their relationship as each was describing a similar wish of caring for the other and for their relationship following the death of the beloved Jo, but were doing so in different ways. Would they like to explore these issues?

Brief information was provided with regard to differences between men and women in expressing emotions. Also, Stroebe and Schut's dual process model of coping with bereavement and Rubin's TTMoB concepts (described in the introduction and chapter 1) were used to normalize the oscillation between "continuing with life" and "continuing the relationship with the deceased."

The couple was asked to each think about exploring these differences in therapy and, then discuss it between them. After reaching a mutual decision they were to let the therapist know what decision was taken.

The intervention was underlined by emphasizing their care for each other, acknowledging the pain of the loss, legitimizing the differences in how each experienced the loss, and allowing both to discuss whether therapy could be a source of help to them to increase their ability to be "a secure base" (Johnson, 2002) for each other. Each one of them was experiencing the loss and both were searching for ways to deal with the "silent continuing presence" of their dead child.

Therapy with couples who have experienced a loss brings to the forefront the issue of relationships. We have seen that the relationship with the deceased is the heart of the grief process. Having to reorganize the relation-ship with the person who died and who is no longer physically present requires a cognitive, emotional, and behavioral shift, one that may continue throughout life. We have discussed at length the process of moving from one type of relationship with the deceased to an inner one, and variables that affect that change. In couple and family therapy we are dealing with relation-ships and their multidimensional aspect. On one level, the bereaved are searching for a way to reconstruct an inner relationship with the deceased, and on another level it is the relationships with living family members that are affected, at times shattered, and need to be reorganized. In couple ther-apy following the loss of a child, this is of particular significance because the relationship with the dead child preoccupies each parent, while at the same time they have to attend to the ongoing spousal and other family relation-ships. Sometimes couple therapy focuses on strengthening relationships, other times the relationship between the couple has been conflictual prior to the loss and therapy then becomes an opportunity to repair intimacy. At other times therapy leads to a decision to formally end a relationship that reached a dead end years earlier.

Among the many types of losses, that of a child in particular has the potential to impose stress on the marital relationship and oftentimes is a cause for marital therapy. One of the identified risk factors is associated with the untimely event that occurs against the natural order of the family life cycle: "How could this happen to us that we bury our beloved child instead of bringing him or her up to adulthood," expresses the feelings of pain that accompany the untimely burying of a child (Christ, Bonnano, Malkinson & Rubin, 2003; Kissane & Bloch, 1994). Additional stress may come from gen-der differences, individual differences (grief-specific and depression-specific), past experiences with losses, and cultural differences that may exist between the couple. (Wijngaards, Stroebe, Schut, Stroebe, et al., 2005). All of these factors need to be considered and assessed in treating couples who experi-enced a child loss.

The statement "My wife wants to talk about the death of our son and I can't stand it as she goes over and over it," reflects differences in intensity and length of grief reactions between men and women. Whereas women tend to express their emotions more openly and intensely, it is assumed that male response is not as deep as that of the female. This assumption results in the mistaken conclusion that men (fathers) are generally less affected by the loss of a child compared to women (mothers). The differences stem from the way emotions are being expressed and not in the way they are being experienced. Women and men express their grief responses in different ways (Florian,

Kasher, & Malkinson, 2000). These differences have led to the myth that the loss of a child has increased the rate of divorce, but this has gained no empirical support—the rates of divorce among bereaved couples are no higher than those found in the general population (Rosenblatt, 2005; Wijngaards, Stroebe, Schut, Stroebe, et al., 2005). A survey carried out for the Compassionate Friend, in 1999 confirmed these findings. (NFO Research, 1999, p. 11).

Although the empirical assumption is supported, a child's loss is undoubtedly an event that produces difficulties and increases stress as a result of the traumatic change experienced by the parent-spouse. The individual stress and that imposed on the relationship are interconnected and are reciprocal—they are both affected and being affected by one another. The individual preoccupation with the loss is blended with the other's preoccupation, and the pain experienced is more intense as there is a sense of "an accumulated" pain which is greater than the sum of its parts. The level of closeness, past experiences of each individual, and the spousal system will affect the outcome of the process both on the individual and the spousal levels. Because individuals are saturated in their own grief, their sensitivity to each other is at least temporarily also fragile. In attachment theory this is what is referred to as the ability to provide a secure base for the other or the ability "to contain" the other's pain (Cudmore & Judd, 2001).

Compared to other losses, the death of a child represents a unique and irreparable loss. For parents, the loss of a child injures their role as parents. Thus the image of the deceased child is tied up in the historical self of the parent. It is not surprising that the literature describes the effect of the loss of a child as pervasive, with possible risks for chronic grief. In some ways, a parent continues to be a parent forever, and when asked if she or he has any children, will almost always include the name of the deceased child(ren). Parents carry the memory of their dead child and worry that their own death is a second death of their child (Malkinson & Bar Tur, 2005). In the words of Raphael: "Parenthood as a psychobiologic process ends only with the death of the parent" (1983, p. 185). According to Edelstein (1984), loss of a child entails some unique qualities: the loss of part of the parent, the loss of a link to the future, and the loss of illusions regarding life, death, and existential issues. Rando (1984) also discussed "survival guilt" and the "out of turnness" often experienced by bereaved parents. Both Edelstein and Rando suggest that the death of a child may be the most difficult death to resolve, and the intensity of the grief reaction may be of longer duration than other types of bereavement. The parents' pain and suffering of loss take on a central significance in their lives. How parents accommodate to the continuing relationship with the deceased child in the inner and outer worlds is of concern: "The greater the comfort and fluidity with which one can relate to the representations of the deceased, the more one can refer to resolution of the loss" (Rubin, 1985, p. 232).

Undoubtedly, differences in grief patterns among parents who search for a alternative meaning to the loss, and differences between male and female manifestations, intensity, and pace of individual bereavement, and spousal coping, all need to be considered in initiating therapy.

An examination of general couple therapy reveals that the aim of intervention is to strengthen marital relations, increase intimacy, enhance communication and problem-solving marital skills, and where there is "a parental child" or triangulation (Aponte & Van Deusen, 1981; Minuchin, 1974) to help the couple "free" the child from the parental alliance. Triangulation refers to a situation where one parent allies with the child against the other parent (a coalition). In other words in couple therapy the therapist assesses the level of the living child's involvement in the marital-parental conflict, and targets the intervention toward increasing intimacy between the parents independent of the child's involvement. In contrast, in grief couple therapy, intimacy between the couple, communication, and problem-solving skills center on the dead child. Is the memory and preoccupation with the dead child "owned" by one of the parents and forms "an inner coalition"? Could the memory of the dead child be shared by both parents and become a source of intimacy, rather than one of distancing and isolation? In other words, the aim of therapy will be to search for ways to keep the spirit of dead child as part of the parents' mutual life so that he or she becomes the child of both parents who continually search for ways to continue an inner relationship with their child.

Returning to Mr. and Mrs. Jonas: after discussing the therapist's suggestion to explore the meaning of their differences in light of their concern for each other following the death of Jo, they decided to continue therapy. In one of the first sessions Mr. Jonas sadly remarked that Jo will always remain his mother's boy, a statement that reflected his feelings of loneliness and caused further distancing from his wife, who felt lonely because she was not understood by her husband.

Intervention from an REBT constructivist perspective would address the effects of the loss of the child on the individual and the family as a system, with particular focus on the marital relationship.

REBT-based cognitive couple grief therapy interventions have six aims to facilitate an adaptive process:

1. Identifying each spouse's irrational beliefs (demandingness directed to self, others, and the world) and their emotional (e.g., anxiety), behavioral

(e.g., avoidance), and physiological (e.g., breathing difficulties, heart palpitations) consequences, and their effects on the individual and the marital relationship.

2. Explaining and teaching the connections between each one's beliefs (B) and consequences (C), while assessing individual idiosyncratic consequences and their effect on the marital relationship, as well as identifying secondary symptoms.

3. Identifying and assessing the spousal system's beliefs, myths, and consequences (i.e., are loss and death to be discussed or avoided?). How is grief experienced and expressed? Are there specific languages or gestures to describe emotions, behaviors, and specific physiological reactions, and can distorted thinking constructions be changed into "rational" functional ones through practicing of cognitive, emotional, behavioral, and physiological strategies and sharing of thoughts and emotions?

4. Assisting the couple in their search for alternative ways of retelling each one's shattered story as well constructing a shared one.

5. Exploring with the couple for ways (individual and spousal) to continue bonds with the dead child (ways of remembering, keeping memorabilia, commemoration).

6. Assigning between sessions homework to increase sharing of thoughts and emotions in a more adaptive way.

Two case illustrations will be presented. The first is couple therapy following a traumatic loss of a 22-year-old son. The couple asked to be helped to be able to continue with life for their daughter's sake. The other is a description of therapy following an anticipated death from cancer, the death of Jo, whose father reluctantly agreed to come to therapy.

Life Has Lost Its Meaning, How Can We Continue?

Mrs. L. requested therapy following the death under traumatic circumstances a few months earlier, of their son Ido who was 22 years of age when he died. It happened in an underwater diving accident that later appeared to be the result of damaged equipment. She expressed her worries over her husband's reaction to the loss. According to her, he had been very depressed and lost interest in life. She was very concerned about the way he was experiencing his grief and thought that professional help was needed.

During the first session the couple described the circumstances of the loss as the medical team described it to them, how they were notified, the funeral, and most of all their feeling that life had become empty and meaningless following the loss of their beloved son. Each talked about their son, his childhood, his friends, his talents, and his plans for the future, describing a young, energetic, and lovable person, and how hard it was to grasp the idea that he was dead and would not pursue his plans to become a musician. The mother was more verbally expressive of her emotions than the father, who was withdrawn and expressed his emotions nonverbally. In their early 50s, the couple were both professionals and worked full time. They had a daughter in her late 20s who was a student, and it was only for her sake that they continued functioning, but life had lost its meaning and purpose.

In line with TTMoB, we can clearly see that both tracks are identified in the parents' narrative, while Track II (relationship with the deceased) is the dominant one and will direct the therapist in planning the intervention.

Both wife and husband described a happy, loving, well-functioning, and harmonious family and a close marital relationship, which were destroyed when the news about the son's tragic death was broken to them. As they described the tragedy they shared, each expressed the pain and yearning for their son in a unique way. They seemed to be aware of each other's pain as well as the different way each experienced grief and tried to avoid what each believed would be imposing pain on the other, thereby increasing their own pain. Hence they had avoided discussing anything that reminded them of their son.

From their way of telling the story, the therapist hypothesized that the couple's efforts to support each other ("I must protect him from further pain" as the wife was thinking, or, "Her heart is broken, I mustn't discuss with her anything that will increase her suffering," which is what the husband was thinking), consequently resulted in avoidance of talking about the painful subject of their loss and sharing their thoughts and emotions of pain, and the dysfunctional loop continued. Each was preoccupied with thoughts about the dead child but was hesitant to impose the pain experienced on the other. Distancing was assumed to guard against the unbearable pain each experienced.

After identifying their thinking errors, the B-C connection was explained to the couple, along with the difference between functional and dysfunctional pain that would follow, and normalizing sorrow and pain as part of the grief process.

The following is an excerpt from the first session:

Therapist: You have each talked about the pain of the loss of your son, how did you feel upon hearing the other expressing the pain?

Wife: When I hear my husband's pain I worry about him, I fear that it is too much pain for him to bear. I didn't share with you my fear that something could happen to you.

Husband: I know you are worried and that's the reason that I refrain from talking to you about Ido, fearing that it will be an additional pain to what you are already experiencing.

Therapist: I think that you are trying to protect each other from what you think will increase the pain instead of relieving it, is it possible?

Husband: That's exactly it. I look at you and see the tears in your eyes, I hear you crying at night, and I don't know how to help you: that is the reason for my withdrawal.

Wife: (*crying*)

Therapist: What are some of your thoughts as you heard your husband's words that brought about tears?

Wife: I realize that we each delved in our pain and made efforts to help the other in a wrong way.

Therapist (*using a circular question*): Do you feel that by way of avoiding sharing your pain you become closer to each other or distanced from each other?

The wife answered that they were growing apart from each other and the husband agreed by nodding his head.

Reflections

1. Ido's parents are each absorbed in grief, and their wish to support and protect each other is important (rational).
2. Assessing the emotional consequence of avoidance is indicative of their thinking that they must protect each other from too much pain (irrational). They fear that each one's pain will become a burden for the other.
3. Both are concerned about the pain, the other experiences, that the outcome is they are too careful not to hurt each other. There is a silent agreement not to discuss their son Ido nor their pain.

The identification of the thinking errors with regard to protecting each other from additional, unnecessary pain resulted in avoidance and distancing from each other.

In the above case of acute grief, the major aim of the therapist was to facilitate an adaptive process both for each individual and at the joint spousal levels, by minimizing the tendency to avoid giving additional pain to each other, which they wrongly believed would increase the pain. It was therefore important to change their dysfunctional (irrational) evaluations into more functional (rational) ones, so that their support for each other would be more effective and enable sharing of thoughts and emotions as they talked about their beloved son. Between sessions assignments included practicing more functional statements such as, "I know it's painful to talk about Ido but avoiding the talking keeps us apart, so I am going to try to talk about him with you" (husband or wife), and being attuned to the emotions the thought elicits. Additional assignments were to include sharing with their daughter.

Therapy lasted for six once-a-week sessions in which information about grief, its processes and components was given, while stressing that though both of them had experienced a loss it was normal that each would grieve in unique ways. Sharing their grief, though painful, instead of avoiding it, would keep their relationship closer rather than increasing the distance between them.

A follow-up session three months later revealed that both were grieving their loss intensely. They looked very sad, but said that they were more open with each other and could share their pain and the memory each had of their son. In their own words: "Sharing the pain doesn't take it away but there is some solace in knowing that we are there for each other." Though they looked sad, their facial expressions were less tense, less rigid, and more than anything else open, with a feeling of closeness. It seemed to be a more appropriate process for both of them.

In this case illustration the individual experience of grief that followed the loss of the son was so intense and overwhelming for each spouse (an expected reaction following the traumatic circumstances of the death, which had occurred a few months earlier), who assumed that avoidance was appropriate. The couple came to realize that the pain was enduring and avoiding its discussion did not necessarily relieve the pain but increased the distance between them. Part of learning to live with the enduring pain was through building intimacy as "a secure base" and a source of solace for each. It involved overcoming the fear that added to an already intense pain.

Jo Will Always Remain His Mother's Son

Marital intimacy has many forms. Pre-loss intimacy that decreases as a result of the loss of the child was described in the case of Ido's parents. From the perspective of the family life cycle (Walsh & McGoldrick, 1991/2004), Ido's parents have reached the stage of launching their children, a stage that involves the children leaving home, and one that has also the potential of increasing marital intimacy, which seemed to occur between Ido's parents. But the death of their child was perceived as a threat to their intimacy. The parents mistakenly assumed that their wish to maintain intimacy would be best preserved by avoiding discussion of the pain and yearning for their son—only to realize that the opposite occurred. Avoidance as a way to protect each other increased distancing rather than promoting intimacy.

Mr. and Mrs. Jonas came to therapy a few months after their son Jo, aged nine, died of cancer. He was the oldest of their three children, the brother of Lea (age eight) and Hanna (age four).

Mrs. Jonas initiated therapy as she felt that family life after Jo's death had become too difficult. Over the phone she expressed her worries about the deterioration of her relationship with her husband, who reluctantly agreed to come to therapy and give it a chance.

Jo's parents described a low preloss level of intimacy. "Families with young children" was the developmental stage of Jo's family. During that stage couples are often absorbed in their parental roles and marital intimacy is kept at a minimal level. When a death of a child occurs during that stage the suddenness and untimeliness of the loss renders marital relationships particularly vulnerable.

TTMoB assessment revealed that Mr. Jonas's dominant axis was Track I, focusing on functioning issues as a way of "continuing with life." Mr. Jonas expressed his difficulties with his wife whose expressions of grief were so different from his own. His way of meaning construction was one of "moving on with life." He mentioned that work was a "helpful place to escape."

Mrs. Jonas's profile was a Track II dominance of relationship with the deceased. She expressed her grief by focusing on recollections of Jo and a need to share with her husband the details of Jo's death. She expressed positive feelings toward Jo in a manner that excluded from the story other family members, including her husband. This resulted in her thinking that she was not being understood, leading to feelings of loneliness on her part.

REBT-constructivist assessment disclosed that each of the Jonases held to a set of irrational beliefs: Mr. Jonas wanted to help his wife but believed that the way it could be done was by her giving up talking about their dead son Jo, and if not, "I can't help her, therefore I am avoiding being close to her." Mrs. Jonas on the other hand believed that the only way her husband could express his understanding of her was to listen to her talking about Jo, and if not she refused "his" help and withdrew from emotional and physical contact with him.

As was already mentioned, these actions were interpreted to be their distorted way of caring for each other. After identifying their distorted cognitions and explaining the connection between cognitions and emotions (B-C connection), a search for alternative cognitions was carried out. In order to increase intimacy, which both wanted to focus on in therapy, they were shown how each had the alternative choice of cognitively interpreting what the other was saying, in spite of differences they had regarding their expectations of each other. Therapy with Mr. and Mrs. Jonas lasted six months, once a week, during which time the first anniversary of Jo's death was commemorated.

Mr. Jonas's said that, "My wife wants to talk about the death of our son and I can't stand it as she goes over and over it." This became a focus of retelling their story as a way to turn the "silent presence" of their beloved son Jo into a constructive force to increase their intimacy.

The following occurred during the tenth session:

Therapist to Mr. Jonas: You said that you can't stand your wife's talking about Jo. How would you like it to be different?

Mr. Jonas (*angrily*): She shouldn't talk about Jo at all!

Mrs. Jonas (*crying*): No, no that is impossible.

Therapist to both: Let's imagine both alternatives: one is that things continue to be as they are now, which is Mrs. Jonas's way of remembering Jo, and Mr. Jonas's alternative that talk about Jo should stop so that life goes on.
Both listened silently.

After a pause, **Mr. Jonas:** I don't know what is the best way.

Therapist: You don't know what is the best way for what?

Mr. Jonas: The best way to go on with life after Jo died.

Therapist: Does that mean that you are thinking of another way?

Mr. Jonas: I have tried to immerse myself in work, thinking that going on with life will ease the pain, but alas it didn't.

Therapist to Mrs. Jonas: As you hear these words what goes on in your mind?

Mrs. Jonas: This is the first time I have heard about your pain, you never mentioned anything. You kept away from me and I thought that you were trying to forget Jo. Although it is not easy to hear about your pain it feels closer.

Therapist: It seems that Jo is in your hearts and you each have your way of handling the pain that evolves.

Mr. Jonas: It is hard for me to talk about it now, it feels so painful.

Therapist: You have tried to overcome pain by avoiding it and now that you experience the pain without avoiding it, perhaps the most important thing is the revelation that pain is part of life without Jo. Perhaps it is sufficient for today and you can talk about it sometime during the week, or perhaps you would rather continue it at the next session (the therapist provides the couple with a choice).

Mrs. Jonas turned to her husband and asked if it was OK to talk about it during the week, to which Mr. Jonas replied: "Let's give it a try."

The in between session assignment was to talk about Mr. Jonas's thoughts and feelings about experiencing pain, with Mrs. Jonas listening and supporting him.

Reflections

1. Both husband and wife experienced the pain of the loss but each one expressed it differently: Mrs. Jonas wanted to talk about Jo whereas Mr. Jonas thought that talking about it would increase the pain. Their beliefs resulted in an increased distancing from each other. Legitimizing their individual ways of grief facilitated listening emphatically to each other in a more rational way so that pain could be experienced more openly, in their search for meaning to a life without Jo.

Once pain was openly experienced and discussed, the "ownership" of the inner relationship with Jo was extended to include both spouses, with each becoming more sensitive to and patient with the other's needs to talk about him or the wish to refrain from it. Jo, the dead child, had found his place in both parents as well as between them.

Conclusion

Similar to cognitive therapy with individuals, couple cognitive grief intervention during the acute phase of grief under traumatic circumstances, as well as when anticipated, is aimed at identifying what thinking distortions block an open and flexible sharing between the couple, and changing their evaluations into more adaptive ones to facilitate a more adaptive process. Frequently, short term intervention based on a thorough assessment is sufficient, while a follow-up is recommended. At other times when intimacy is "wounded" as a result of the loss, or because it was minimal prior to the loss intervention, the focus will be on strengthening the relationship so that it becomes "a safe haven" for each partner.

Yearning and pain are woven into the parents' search for constructing a meaningful inner bond with the dead child. Similar to couple therapy, in couple grief therapy a triad (parents and child) can be identified as a source of marital conflict; but unlike couple therapy, the acceptance by both parents that the spirit of the dead child is theirs becomes a source for increasing intimacy between them, and provides support for the continuing bonds each maintains with the dead child. Once again, these cases illustrate that a shift to a more adaptive process of grief does not alleviate the pain of a loss, but enables the individuals to experience it openly while expressing emotions, without a fear of adding strain to oneself and to the other.

Chapter 10

Cognitive Grief Therapy with Families

"All happy families resemble one another, each unhappy family is unhappy in its own way."—Leo Tolstoy, *Anna Karenina*

A Death in the Family

There is a vast literature on individual processes, with their various dimensions, responses, and experiences. Their outcomes may be desirable or nondesirable, possibly because bereavement is viewed first and foremost as an intrapersonal experience. However, even though grief is an individual process of reorganizing the inner relationship with a person who is no longer alive, the bereaved are also social beings and part of a family. C.S. Lewis (1961) described the paradox of grief being an intrapersonal process, which cannot be experienced alone:

No one ever told me that grief felt so like fear. I am not afraid but the sensation is like being afraid. The same fluttering in the stomach, the same restlessness, the yawning. I keep on swallowing.

At other times it feels like being mildly drunk, or concussed.

There is a sort of invisible blanket between the world and me.

I find it hard to take in what anyone says. Or perhaps, hard to want to take in.

It is so uninteresting. Yet I want the others to be about me.

I dread the moments when the house is empty.

If only they would talk to one another and not to me. (p. 1)

When a loss is experienced by a family, its process of reorganization to continue as an entity begins in parallel, but is not necessarily in synchrony with the individual process. The family is also searching for ways to accommodate the multiple levels of the meaning of the loss.

We now examine grief following loss in families, which integrates individual grief with that of the family as a system, and will focus on the interplay and interconnection between the two. Each family member's grief is individually based on a unique relationship with the deceased, and though grief is an intrapersonal process, it nevertheless involves relationships between the bereaved and the deceased (Track II of the TTMoB) and between other grieving family members, each relationship that was held with the deceased being unique.

The loss of a family member changes the relationships among living survivors, and that change will be followed by a search for an alternative balance. The type and nature of the existing relationship will greatly affect the process as experienced by each bereaved family member. Both the degree of closeness as perceived and experienced by each family member, and the way each views others as part of the process, will in itself influence the process. Recognizing the importance of the family context in bereavement and how it affects the individual bereaved has become more widespread both as an issue to be explored empirically (Rosenblatt, 2005) and clinically (McBride & Simms, 2001).

A loss in the family is not only a loss of relationships (Bowen, 1991/2004). Deceased family members remain part of the family and in a unique way become part of the family history, story, tradition, or legacy. At the same time, each individual member constructs personal memories of the deceased that reflect the type of relationship (parent, child, sibling, spouse, grandchild, or cousin), the way the relationship was perceived in actuality, and as how they wished it had been.

1. A family is an organized system of relationships, interactions, roles, and rules, which may be present or not in other members of the family.
2. Family relationship patterns are understood in their context where the history and intergenerational relationships are presented as a central source of information.
3. Family interactions are conveyed through verbal and nonverbal communication, which is cognitive, emotional, and behavioral. Preloss relationships, as well as factors such as who died and the circumstances of the loss, the phase of the family life cycle, age, gender, financial, and

sociocultural factors will shape the rearrangements of relationships among living family members, and the way they remember the deceased. There seem to be two contradictions tasks that a family faces when the death of one of its members occurs, that of facing the loss and accommodating to the change within the family and the need to continue with life (Shapiro, 1996). Under such circumstances the families own resources to support its members are temporarily shaken and external help might be needed.

It is understandable why a loss *in* the family is many times perceived and experienced by families as a loss of the family; the death event conveys a sense of finality. Truly, in many ways something has been lost and changed forever, but not all is lost; memories and a legacy remain, and internal relationships with the deceased are transformed and reshaped.

In many ways grief in the family parallels the individual process. Inasmuch as individuals get stuck in the grief process, so do families; family therapy for families who experienced sudden untimely and traumatic loss are more likely to get stuck as the death event shakes the system, and may create what Bowen (1991/2004) termed "an emotional shock wave." Bowen noted:

> A family unit is in functional equilibrium when it is calm and each member is functioning at a reasonable efficiency for that period. The equilibrium of the unit is disturbed by either the addition of a new member or the loss of a member. The intensity of the emotional reaction is governed by the functioning level of emotional integration in the family at the time . . . . A well integrated family may show more overt creativeness at the moment of the change but adapt to it rather quickly. A less integrated family may show little reaction at the time and respond later with symptoms of physical illness, emotional illness or a social misbehavior. (pp. 91–92)

Cognitive Family Therapy Following a Loss

Similar to the individual process, adaptation to the new reality includes assimilation of the loss into the existing family belief system, and past experiences with losses, while accommodating the system to its outcomes through the adoption of new beliefs, roles, and relationships.

Cognitive grief family therapy combines individual and systemic strategies to help the system regain its sense of being a family without the deceased. The family grief process is a compound of individual responses to loss based on the family history, belief system, and intergenerational relationships that have evolved through the years.

From a cognitive, systemic perspective, family schemas are formed and transformed throughout the years and are combinations of family of origin schemas (family tradition) and the ones developed jointly by family members. Loss of a family member unbalances existing patterns of relationships and shatters the family's belief system. Family therapy from a cognitive-constructivist perspective views the individual or family as a system that construes meanings of events in their life through story-telling. A death event can sometimes disrupt the life story very abruptly and violently and a new meaning or "a new chapter" begins to be constructed in a variety of combinations, some of which may seem to be functional (enabling a more adaptive accommodation to the loss), while others are dysfunctional if they restrict the family from experiencing an open, flexible way of finding meaning or searching for meaning (Nadeau, 1998). Even though it is a restrictive or maladaptive process, it is nevertheless a way of meaning making.

The Therapeutic Alliance with the Family System

The therapeutic alliance when working with couples and families has two layers, one alliance is with the system (the couple or the family) and the concurrent alliance is with individual members who comprise the system. For example, the provision of information about grief, its components, courses, and outcomes will refer to both the collective and shared grief and the individual response to the loss. The same applies to normalizing the process and stressing the system's way of responding to the loss and the individual's idiosyncratic response; although all go through a similar process, each one experiences it differently. A therapeutic alliance with a couple or family system is very dynamic and related to the phase of the therapy. Listening attentively and continuously to the individual voices (verbal and nonverbal alike), along with those of the system (parents who speak for the family), are of utmost importance. Using circular questions as a way of giving voice to all family members can strengthen the dynamic therapeutic alliance as therapy progresses.

Assessment

In a cognitive-systemic assessment in addition to a demographic one, special attention will be paid to the following: family life cycle stage; relationships of each member with the deceased; relationships between family members; family's past experiences with losses; family beliefs and behavior systems concerning individual and family grief; family rituals; and time for requesting or referral to therapy.

REBT-based cognitive family grief therapy interventions have six aims to facilitate an adaptive individual and family system process:

1. Identify each family member's irrational beliefs (demands on self, others, and the world) and their emotional (e.g., anxiety), behavioral (e.g., avoidance), and physiological consequences (e.g., breathing difficulties, heart palpitations), and their effects on the individual and family members' relationships with each other.

2. Explain and teach the connections between beliefs (B) and consequences (C), and assess individual idiosyncratic consequences and their effect on relationships with other family members, and identify secondary symptoms.

3. Identify and assess the family system's idiosyncratic beliefs, myths, and consequences. Are loss and death discussed openly or avoided; were there past losses, and if so how were they shared among the family members? Ask family members to use specific language to describe emotions, behaviors, and specific physiological reactions, and change distorted thinking constructions into "rational" functional ones through practicing cognitive emotional, behavioral, and physiological strategies and openly sharing thoughts and emotions.

4. Assist in a search for alternative ways of retelling the shattered family's story through helping them to construct a shared one, as well as developing each individual's own changed narrative.

5. Assign homework between sessions to increase sharing thoughts and emotions among family members in a more adaptive way while normalizing and legitimizing idiosyncratic grieving styles and pace.

6. Explore with family members ways to continue bonds with the dead family member (in ways of remembering, memorabilia, commemoration, etc.).

A Case Illustration: When God Was Found Guilty: Family Therapy Following the Loss of a Child

Family G requested therapy a few months after their youngest daughter, aged 2, died suddenly. The parents were in their late 30s and said they needed help discussing the death of their daughter.with their older girls (aged 9 and 4).

The first two sessions with the parents included a demographic assessment: details about the family, families of origin, occupations, past history with losses. In response to the question as to what had happened, the parents told the tragic circumstances of their daughter's death:

> It was a Saturday morning, we were all at home. Saturday is a day of togetherness when we do things that during the week we are too busy to do. I (the father) was with the two older girls in the garden and my wife was busy with the house chores. The little girl was running in and out and everybody kept on sending her to the other. After a short while a scream was heard. The little girl had climbed on a trolley which stood unsteadily in the corner of the room, it tipped over, and she was fatally wounded in the neck. We were shocked and immediately called for an ambulance and drove to the hospital. We realized from the very beginning how fatal the accident was. This was confirmed by the physicians who tried to do all they could to save our daughter's life, but alas, she died. On the way back home from the hospital we talked between us about the chain of events leading to the fatal death of our little girl, and we agreed that one subject will not be discussed and that is the subject of guilt. We returned home and told the girls the terrible news of the death of their little sister. We were devastated, with difficulties in concentration and functioning with whatever we did at home, and with sleepless nights it became harder to function; we came to feel that if we wanted life to continue and if we cared about the girls, we had to pull ourselves together and so we did. We each returned to work and the girls went back to school. We are very anxious about the well-being of our girls and wonder what would be the right way to manage our life, what should we say and what not to the girls, what is the right way to talk about the pain, or perhaps it is preferable to refrain from too much talking about it?

From the TTMoB perspective, it is possible to determine from the way the story was told that Track I (the functioning track) is predominant, with functioning and concentration difficulties, sleeping difficulties, anxiety, and possible guilt feelings, which were avoided in a very decisive way. In the family domain efforts were made to protect and support family members, perhaps at the expense of the individual's response to the loss.

From the REBT perspective, the efforts made by the parents to protect and support the family seemed to be a central theme that needed to be assessed to determine whether they are functional or dysfunctional cognitions, the B-C. Along with the individual cognitive assessment, an assessment of the family belief system, family rules, and boundaries was carried out. The interconnection between the individual and the family belief system was also evaluated (Bowen, 1991/2004; Walsh & McGoldrick, 1991). The sudden and traumatic circumstances of the loss were also examined as an additional stressor to a family in the child-rearing stage of its life cycle, and whether or not they would have another child. In order to set goals for therapy, the importance of understanding both the family belief system and the individual members' cognitive map was essential.

The initial hypothesis concerned the guilt feelings connected with the tragic loss of their daughter and which threatened the wholeness of the family; through the parents the family chose to avoid the issue of guilt in order to protect itself from disintegrating. The parents disagreed with the hypothesis, saying that guilt was not the issue as they had already decided not to discuss it. In other words this issue had already been taken care of. An alternative hypothesis was formed by proposing that loyalty to the continuation of the family as a whole seemed a central belief for its members, hence the family's choice to carry on first and foremost with the task of continuing with life as a way to survive and protect itself. The hypothesis was accepted by the parents who further supported it when they talked about the importance they ascribed to keeping the family together as whole. From a systemic, intergenerational perspective, the theme of protecting the family at all costs and remaining loyal to the family as a system was strongly embedded in the family's belief system. It was probably related to an early experience of separation that the mother had experienced as a child when her parents divorced and her relationship with her father was severed. The memory of this event was too hard to be discussed, and possibly intensified the belief that "the family must not die" but must remain intact.

The time that had elapsed from the loss, its traumatic circumstances, and the family's decision not to discuss the issue of guilt, were considered in planning the intervention and setting the goal of facilitating an adaptive grief process. The second goal was to assist the family with what was most important, to protect its members and stay intact in a more functional way; in other words, to create a secure basis for family members.

Therapy lasted four months with one-hour weekly sessions alternating between joint family sessions and sessions with the parents alone. The rationale was to strengthen the parental spousal unit in addition to the family one, provide information about what the process entailed, and normalize differences in grieving styles and pace. Information regarding differences between adult and children's grieving was essential. Preparing the family for recurrent waves of pain and sadness, which may affect family members functionally in their relationships, was an issue discussed frequently during the sessions. Helping the family to carry on with routine activities such as joint meals, sharing thoughts and feelings, and initiating activities to spend time together, were topics raised and discussed during the sessions. Relationships with extended family and friends were good and provided ample support.

On terminating therapy a follow-up was carried out once every three months with the last one taking place close to the first anniversary of the death. The family seemed sad but less stressed; they expressed their concern over their reactions and spoke sadly with tears in their eyes about the preparations for the occasion. They told about the girls' active role in writing to their beloved sister telling her how much they missed her. Generally, they said, they were functioning well. In the last follow-up session the therapist summed up by emphasizing that the family's choice to invest in life, and how to continue it and not dwell on emotional issues, could be understood as either waiving or postponing those issues to a later point in time. An open door for future consultation was proposed and accepted by the parents.

The family's belief in protecting its members seemed to be channeled in an adaptive way in their own way they were beginning to attend to the second task of facing the loss and the consequent changes within the family. The family's way of making some meaning of the loss seemed at this phase to evolve around its survival, with less focus on the dead child. Therapy thus provided a secure basis as an element that enabled an adaptive course of bereavement.

As a therapist I was debating with myself whether long term outcomes of the parents' decision not to discuss the issue of guilt would prove to be right or not. What is therapeutically right or wrong in discussing an issue that with the passage of time may turn into one that blocks the family? This is what Bowen (1991/2004) referred to as the "emotional shock wave." According to him, this is a network of underground "aftershocks" of serious life events that can occur anywhere in the extended family system in the months or years following the serious emotional events in the family. It operates on an underground network of emotional dependence of family members on each other. The emotional dependence is denied, the serious life events appear to be unrelated, the family attempts to camouflage any connectedness between the events, and there is a vigorous, genial reaction when any one attempts to relate the events to each other (p. 83).

Reflections

1. The parents' decision to not discuss the subject of guilt presents the therapist with a dilemma. This desire to not discuss guilt may have some irrational elements, however, it had only been a few months since their daughter's death, and the family was experiencing acute grief. Therefore, their choice to avoid dealing with guilt as a way of protecting the family was appropriate and respected.
2. The therapist formulated an alternative hypothesis that focused on loyalty and the parents' commitment to protect their daughters so that life can continue.
3. Therapeutic goals were to facilitate an adaptive grief process and assist the family in what the parents regarded as most important in order to continue with life's tasks.

Guilt and Family Therapy

From the above description we can see the connection between the family legacy and the construction of meaning following the traumatic loss of a child. The family views the preoccupation with guilt as a threat to its existence, and in order to protect itself prefers to avoid touching on guilt. From an existential point of view, guilt feelings are associated with the threat to the self (Kubany & Menke, 1995) and experiencing it has a functional survival value.

Cognitive approaches view guilt as a feeling of discomfort created in response to the belief that "I should have thought, felt, or behaved differently from how I actually did." It is a multidimensional construct with an affective component and a set of beliefs about the role of the self in adverse events and how it functions. If the outcome of the event is evaluated as negative it is likely to find the emotional component of guilt as a source for stress. Kubany and Menke (1995) delineated four cognitive components that determine guilt: wrongdoing, acceptance of responsibility, perceived lack of justification, and false beliefs about preoutcome knowledge caused by hindsight bias ("I knew it was going to happen").

Guilt and shame are similar in that they both are related to the way we judge ourselves based on the construction of meaning patterns about ourselves, our life experiences, and the values that we are committed to. Guilt is related to our inner moral code, and if violated, we accept responsibility for that violation and guilt increases. Guilt and shame are both forms of anxiety;

whereas guilt is related to what we see as a violation of our value system, shame anxiety appears when we deviate from what we assume to be our "ideal self" (Kubany & Menke, 1995). Guilt feeling is the outcome of a perceived behavior as wrongdoing, and the fear that it will be discovered. Guilt is also context-related, and in many ways has a regulatory element to encourage favored social behaviors. There are a number of ways to deal with guilt. One can express guilt, apologize, and ask for forgiveness (e.g., the Day of Atonement as reparation) or one can avoid it and hope that it will disappear or be self-punishment. Avoidance and self-punishment are forms that are commonly identified in therapy.

In cognitive therapy, thinking errors eliciting guilt will be identified and corrected or changed into more functional ones. Irrational beliefs that increase feelings of guilt are phrased in a demanding way: "I must have known beforehand that this was going to happen"; or "I shouldn't have done it"; or "How could I respond in such a way"; and "I should have listened to her." These beliefs increase and intensify guilt. A rational phrasing will be less self-condemning, less self-criticizing, and the emotional consequence will be remorse rather than guilt. Remorse is more functional. In other words it is the meaning assigned to the event that increases or decreases guilt and guilt anxiety. Reevaluating the event less rigidly and more flexibly minimizes the guilt feeling and enables a more adaptive functioning (Dryden & Ellis, 1996).

The loss of a loved one, especially under sudden, unexpected, and traumatic circumstances, often increases both the individual and family system's sense of dysfunctional guilt. Such "collective" dysfunctional guilt patterns can take the following forms:

1. The guilt-provoking event is frozen, everything remains intact, nothing is being moved.
2. There is avoidance of the event as if trying to erase its occurrence, moving to another place, taking away all the deceased's belongings to avoid reminders, as if nothing had happened.
3. Involvement in daily routine and many times extending it, such as spending longer hours at work, which helps one to be immersed in the here and now and avoid "facing" the past.
4. Dichotomous thinking (automatic thoughts), black and white, all or nothing, generalizing as a way of avoiding guilt.

In cases of dysfunctional guilt, the family develops a set of ritualistic, repetitive behaviors as a way of protecting itself from facing the pain. In such cases a therapeutic ritual is an effective intervention (Bowen, 1991/2004; Van der Hart, 1983; and also see the previous chapter). Rituals can either be structured similarly to traditional mourning or those based on existing family rituals (meals, doing things together, etc.).

We return to our family: Who is guilty?

A Case Illustration (continued)

Five years later the family requested therapy for the second time. The reason for their request was that the second of the three daughters was suffering from unexplained psychosomatic symptoms and social problems at school. She was a good student and no academic problems were mentioned. Parents described her as a quiet and introverted person. The family was composed of father, mother, and three girls—the youngest was 4 years old, born after the 2-year-old's death. The older daughter was described as a mature, viable youngster and socially very active. The youngest girl as the parents describe her was "spoiled, very spoiled." All family members watched her every move, and she often heard the phrase: "It's very dangerous." The youngest daughter got along better with her mother than with her father, and sometimes when her mother had to leave earlier for work, she prepared the girl in advance that her father would take care of her so that her responses would be less stressful, because she refused to be cared for by the father. The mother reported that lately she had been tired, tense, nervous, and cried easily. Recently they marked the fifth anniversary of their daughter's death. To the question whether they talk about her, the answer was "no." The girls did not visit to the cemetary, as a way of protecting them from the pain involved. The father did not discuss with anyone the subject of the death of their daughter five years earlier, but was very active at work, a member of a number of committees. In the past he took antidepressants, but stopped taking them because they were not effective.

Cognitive-systemic family therapy maintains possible connections between losses in the past and acute life events (Baruth & Hubert, 1989; Cecchin, Lane, & Ray 1992), similar to Bowen's intergenerational approach and the "emotional shock wave which is an underground after shock." In line with these, and our past therapy experiences, a hypothesis was formulated about a possible connection between the "spirit of the dead" and acute life events (Gelcer, 1983), and the second daughter's unexplained symptoms (for which there was no medical basis). An assessment of the family functioning and communicating patterns, as well as the pattern of their sharing of thoughts and emotions was needed to move the family from being stuck, which could have been related to the former decision to avoid discussing the issue of guilt. Details provided by the family included their moving to another house, believing it was a way to have a new beginning, and the birth of the baby (4 years of age when referral took place), thinking that a new baby brings happiness and helps the older family members forget the painful past. These details support the hypothesis that adopting a new lifestyle and new behaviors is perceived by the family as a way to alleviate the pain and even help to forget the past. The mother's description of her symptoms was evidently proof that the past cannot be forgotten and continues to be a source of stress the more one's efforts are invested in forgetting it. There remained the question of the connection between the daughter's symptoms and the loss, which could be explained in a number of ways, but at that point was left to be further explored.

The therapeutic goals included:

1. Assisting the family to reorganize itself in a more adaptive way regarding issues of guilt and pain and unattended grief among family members ("There is not even one single day that I don't think of her" would be the words of the mother in the following session).
2. Reorganize in a more functional manner present relationships so that the family as a system could experience loss-related emotions that were avoided heretofore, and continue to be a source of support to its members but in a more effective way. This in turn would increase the family's sense of mastery over their lives, even though they had no control over the daughter's death.
3. Help the family re-create a story wherein the loss was woven and could become part of the family's narrative. The way the story was being told, loss was missing and its avoidance intensified the absent part. It was as though telling the story had stopped from the moment the death occurred (and was probably associated with the mother's past experience of her parents' painful divorce).

The dysfunctional collective guilt patterns identified included avoidance of discussing the event, moving house to start a new life, and being involved in the here and now, such as working long hours. All family members seemed anxious about the safety of the youngest child, born after the death.

By using circular questions, the therapist explored the pattern of relationships and how they were formed and organized. Who was closer to whom? If we were to ask the girls would they agree with the given description? What did they usually talk about and do together and when alone? What did the family refrain from doing or talking about? Who noticed when the father was sad? Who noticed when the mother cried? As a way to overcome avoidance, the questions were aimed at eliciting information, but also allowed "forbidden zones" to be entered, subjects to be discussed that had not been discussed in the past. Circular questions put the therapist in the position of the curious expert (Cecchin et al., 1992) who knew a lot about families but was a "stranger" (Minuchin, 1974) to this particular family, and in a joint collaboration learned about the family and guided its members through questioning to view things in different terms. In many ways it was a mutual journey of discovering an unspoken and hidden agenda. It was possible to get an idea about the "avoidance ritual" of sharing thoughts and emotions concerning the death of their daughter. To that point in time, the youngest daughter hadn't been told about the death in the family, any reminder of the dead child had been taken away, including family albums from that period. Time had frozen. Besides, the family was very active in everyday life, hiking and traveling together, and greatly enjoying being together. All efforts were made to avoid the pain for fear of dissolving the family, but paradoxically, pain was indirectly expressed by the second daughter in a symptomatic form.

The first therapy sessions were held with the parents only because the girls at that stage didn't want to join them; it was assumed that working with the parents alone at that stage would be more effective in planning a family joint session. During the sessions the parents talked more openly, though not without difficulty, about the profound sadness each felt. The therapist, together with the parents, was planning to reconnect the missing part of the story, the death of their daughter, with the family narrative.

The following were between-sessions assignments:

1. A recommendation to read a book on the subject of loss and bereavement to which the father commented: "I could never read a book on the subject, even today it is hard for me to read. I don't discuss it with anybody. To me it is a closed issue."
2. The parents were asked to gather together during a meal or any other suitable time and share with the girls memories of the deceased child. They were encouraged to invite the older daughters to join in.
3. They were asked to take the albums out and together with all family members to look at the photographs. (The father revealed that from time to time when nobody was there he would take the albums out and peek at the photos.)
4. They were to plan a visit to the cemetery with the children, suggesting that they come, but not forcing them.

In the following session the parents described how difficult it was for them to carry out the assignments of sharing memories about their daughter, but how relieved they felt afterwards. Talking openly with the girls about the pain and sorrow was a moving experience for all. After that the girls sent a message with the parents: "We want to come to therapy with Mom and Dad, we have questions to ask and we want to say a few things, too."

Planning the joint family sessions proceeded and we discussed how each person felt, what were their worries and concerns regarding the session, what did they want the session to be like, and who would experience the most difficulties.

In the next session the parents said they had continued to share memories and took out the photo albums and looked at them. They were all very moved, with tears in their eyes, they talked about their pain and yearning for their beloved daughter. A recurrent motif was that each one continued to think almost every day about their lost sister and daughter, and was preoccupied with the circumstances of the death.

The parents told about the two older girls: the eldest had read with much curiousity the book that her father had bought about bereavement and she had a lot to say about it; the second daughter was talking more openly about the deceased sister. There was a sense of relief and less avoidance. The next session was to be with all family members.

The Joint Family Session

The parents and the three daughters arrived with the little girl holding a plastic bag with a photo album. They took their seats with the parents each sitting on one side and the children between them. The little girl turned to me and said she wanted to show the album and tell me who is in the pictures. She said: "This is my sister, she is dead and now I know her. She fell off her trolley." I listened intensely to the story told by the little girl. There was silence and sadness in the room, though the girl told the story in a cheerful way. When she finished I turned to the older daughters asking them to tell their stories and ask the questions they said they wanted to ask me or their parents. Their reply was: "We never talked about it; we never asked questions about what had happened, and you never told us what really happened." The second daughter agreed that they should talk about the death of their sister in spite of it being so painful. Mother and father reminded them that they were told about what happened but probably forgot it. The daughters requested that the story be retold with all the details and said how important they thought it was to talk openly about the event and tell at least parts of the story to the little girl. Not too much they said, but some of it was OK so as not to cause her too much pain. Father retold the story with all the details, and then asked each one of the girls to tell her story. The second daughter told how shortly after she took care of the baby she was standing next to her older sister explaining to her about the plants they were planting. "It all happened when I went to explain about the plants. Maybe I am guilty," she said. The older daughter commented that if one feels guilty one needs to talk about it and not suppress it, just as she does. "Talking about it eases the pain," she said. "Did you have guilt feelings?" asked the second daughter. She recalled that when mother and father went to the hospital she tried to talk to her sister, but her older sister asked her to leave her alone because she said she was praying to God. She believed in God and if one believes in God and prays for help he helps. Therefore she said "It is important to know who is guilty." The oldest daughter agreed and said she never knew what had really happened and who was to blame. Then father told in as many details as he could what had happened and added that he felt guilty for not having prevented the sequence of events. Mother listened attentively to father and said she never realized that father was still so much preoccupied with the event, and she shared with the family how hard it had been for her to get over her feeling of guilt because she "must have known that something terrible might happen if there wasn't anyone there to watch the baby."

Then the oldest daughter turned to the father and asked: "But what did she die of?" The father replied: "I don't know." To this the daughter commented, "That's why we need to find who is guilty!" "Who do you think is guilty?" the father asked, to which she instantly said: "God! Because if there was God he wouldn't have let it happened, so he is guilty and since then I don't believe in God." The daughter was very shaken and all other family members including myself were moved, surprised, and relieved. The feeling of relief was then followed by an open sharing about the missing daughter, the yearning each felt for her, and how each one was continuing to think of her without knowing that the others experienced the same feelings.

I concluded the session by saying that they had the courage to talk about the sister that died and what each thought and felt about it, believing until now that keeping it to themselves would have kept them together, but today they realized that the opposite, talking and sharing, was a better way to feel closer to each other in spite of the difficulty in doing so. With regard to the guilt and the demand to find who is guilty, I added that it was my belief that it is not always so crucial to find who is guilty, because many times it is not possible to find who is guilty, and not less significant, as the second sister said: "What for, what will you gain?" Sometimes the search itself is too tiresome without necessarily finding the "true answer." I thought that leaving the question open would let each member construct his or her own "right" answer.

Finally, the family was asked to discuss at home the photo album, what were some of their ideas about how and where it should be kept (in response to their telling that none of the daughters' friends knew anything about the loss; because of the family moving to another home, and they did not talk about it). They were to decide whether the albums should be put away or kept open and visible.

The following session was devoted to a discussion of how family members felt and whether or not things were different now in comparison to the way they were before. The atmosphere in the room was as if a heavy burden had been taken away and left them exhausted but relieved and at peace. The father spoke and said that going through the experience had been most difficult and painful for each one of them but they all felt how important it was to break the "wall of silence." We discussed ways to continue the sharing, knowing that it would always be painful and sad.

At a follow-up session four weeks later, the parents came without the children and said that the daughter's symptoms had disappeared, she was still very reserved, but much more attentive to her surroundings, and took an active part in the decision to leave the photo album on display. Father described the inner journey he had made and the most significant outcome of it had been that he could talk about the dead daughter. There were still inner barriers to letting the thoughts run freely, but step by step was his pace. Mother reported that she felt a lot better, especially when she saw that they were all less withdrawn and more open with each other; their being together was a lot more fun. "We broke the silence barrier!" At this point therapy was terminated with once a year follow-up at the request of the family.

Reflections

There are several ways to reflect on the second phase of therapy with family G.

1. From a systemic perspective the loss of their daughter five years earlier created "an emotional shock wave" which was furthered when their third daughter (fourth counting the deceased child) was born. Their loyalty to the family led them to invest their efforts in routine life tasks and avoid anything related to the loss. That was their way of protecting the girls, especially the younger one, who was born after the loss and wasn't told about it. Once the dead child regained her place within the family legacy they could tell the younger girl about the loss and take the photo album out from its hidden place. Attending to life tasks was then carried out in a more balanced way.

2. Reflecting from the TTMoB we can see that five years after the death of their daughter and first referral to therapy the family was still preoccupied with the death and it was seen as a bodily sign (Track I), hinting at difficulties with the relationship with the deceased (Track II). Therapy at that stage provided an opportunity for family members to talk openly about the dead child.

3. From the REBT perspective the parents' decision not to discuss the issue of guilt was irrational, but was understood by the therapist as the family's way of protecting itself. Therapist's respect for the parents' choice and her decision to facilitate an adaptive grief strengthened the family, and when they were ready to talk about the guilt issue, in spite of the painful memories it elicited, the family members felt relieved.

A central issue in the therapy with the family described evolved around the family's belief system of what was the right thing to do in order to protect itself when a danger to its survival was felt to be so real. The family made a choice based on what they believed to be the right choice, and probably it was right for the acute phase of the bereavement process, but it proved dysfunctional with the passage of time. Their choice to avoid the issue of guilt reflected their belief that it was necessary to keep the family "alive" following the death of their little girl. That choice also reflected their way of "keeping things under control" in an uncontrollable situation that had shattered their lines.

The Loss of a Grandchild: Grief and Despair

Bowen's (1991/2004) metaphor that a death in the family is like "an emotional shock wave," captures the effect of the loss on both immediate and extended family members. The emotional shock wave has a ripple effect, and when a child dies the parents are considered to be in the first wave, followed by other siblings, while the third wave involves grandparents, with extended family members at a further distance.

The voice of the grandparents' grief is beginning to be heard with the realization that they too grieve, while less attention has been given so far to their specific needs (Lou Reed, 2003). Grandparents' grief is in many ways unrecognized and unacknowledged—the disenfranchised grief referred to by Doka (1989)—but fully experienced. Though unrecognized, their experience is nevertheless most intense. The death of a grandchild involves not

only grieving over his or her death but also caring for their own child's grieving. If the death of a child is the death of a future for the parents, a death of
a grandchild is in many ways an injury to the family's legacy. The grandchild who was expected to represent the family's continuing lifeline has
died. The natural course of life has been shattered since grandparents are
expected to predecease their children and grandchildren (Lou Reed, 2000,
2003;Rando,1986). Lou Reed called grandparents' grief "a dual loss": "mourning the death of their grandchild and grieving their adult child's suffering"
(2003, p. 1).

Moreover, grandparents' grief is frequently a hidden one, because they
believe they cannot openly express their own sorrow and pain or their helplessness, and because they think they must be strong when their own child is
grieving the loss. There is a hidden assumption that for the sake of their son
or daughter whose life is shattered, it is their responsibility to care for the
bereaved parents, or at least refrain from becoming a burden with their grief.
On the one hand they resign their role as grievers by remaining first and foremost parents to their bereaved child, while on the other hand they feel helpless as parents who cannot protect their own child and feel their role as
protector of their own child has failed. Grieving then becomes synonymous
with weakness, and the issue becomes an intergenerational one.

The following is an intervention with grandparents who sought help after
their granddaughter (their son's daughter) was killed in a terrorist attack.

The Silent Broken Heart

Mr. and Mrs. Oldman, in their late 60s, consulted the therapist and requested
therapy. In an apologetic manner they explained that the reason for requesting help was their worry over their son who lost his daughter in a terrorist
attack. They wanted to know how to help him and his family. In the first session, Joseph and Miriam looked devastated as they described the circumstances of their granddaughter's death. "We feel that life has become a long
dark night. Our beloved grandchild was killed by a suicide bomber who
entered the restaurant where they were sitting. Our daughter-in-law was
wounded and our granddaughter was killed. In one second our life has
changed from a happy family to one that has crashed. How do we pick the
pieces? What can we do? We feel devastated and helpless. We want to help
and don't know how. All seems so confusing and painful."

Dorit was 10 years of age when she died. She was their oldest grandchild, with a younger brother aged 8 and a sister aged 6. Their son who
was Dorit's father is their younger son. Their pain was complicated by

their previous experiences with losses. Joseph and Miriam had both lost their families in the Holocaust and their dream of having a family of their own was shattered along with their feelings that as parents they had failed to protect their son and his daughter. They felt that it was their responsibility to support their son and his family but were hesitant in offering any help for fear of being rejected.

Both Miriam and Joseph felt that what they needed most as parents and grandparents was to find ways to help their son's family. They cried during the session and said that this was the only place where they "could afford" to be weak and express their grief. It was agreed that this grief would be the focus of therapy. TTMoB assessment revealed a combination of Track I (How can we be "helpful parents?") and Track II ("The pain of the loss of our beloved granddaughter will never disappear").

Therapy was focused and short-term, and consisted of five weekly one hour sessions with a follow-up three months later. Cognitively, the most prominent theme was the sense of their shattered dream: A happy family.

In the first two sessions, in line with the general goals of grief therapy or intervention, normalization, legitimization, and provision of information about grief, its process components, and possible outcomes were discussed in order to facilitate a more adaptive process. Miriam and Joseph felt a sense of relief on receiving the information about grief, its process, and especially its legitimacy.

In the third and fourth sessions, Joseph and Miriam both looked very sad but said they felt somewhat more encouraged and were thinking of ways to help and "be useful" rather then "useless." It turned out that they had a very close relationship with the siblings (Dorit's brother and sister), they spent time together and had a "lot of fun." This was also something that would be appreciated by their son and his wife who were too immersed in their own grief. They discussed possible ways of doing things together. Miriam came up with the idea that perhaps they could write and draw something about Dorit with their grandchildren. Joseph was hesitant but was willing to give it a try.

In the fifth session, Joseph was very satisfied with the "project" with their grandchildren. There was a feeling of sadness and intimacy when the four wrote and drew what each felt about Dorit and how much each missed her and how painful it was. Miriam and Joseph said that the children were sad but could remember with laughter moments of fun with their sister. Miriam commented that it was the most difficult thing to do but it she was glad they did it.

As the end of the fifth and last session was approaching, Miriam and Joseph said they felt more confident as grandparents, which also helped them as parents, but most of all they would be more tolerant of experiencing pain as they remembered Dorit.

Three months later in a follow-up session Miriam and Joseph's grief was apparent but in a more contained manner. The first anniversary of the grand-daughter's death had taken place a few weeks earlier. It was difficult, painful, they all cried as they approached the grave, and missed little Dorit so much. They felt a sense of togetherness.

Reflections

1. Joseph and Miriam's request for therapy was somewhat hesitant as if they doubted their right to grieve and ask for help. Their grief follow-ing their beloved grandchild's death under violent circumstances was mixed with their anxiety about their roles as parents to the bereaved father, their son.
2. Their past experiences as Holocaust survivors was discussed indirectly. Their hope of raising a happy family after they lost their own families was shattered and necessitated searching for ways to save the family rather than become immersed in their past.
3. In therapy the focus was on showing them the difference between nor-mal grief, and being absorbed in what they called "historical losses." Legitimizing and normalizing grief enabled them to openly experi-ence their sadness and pain, and to search for additional ways to func-tion as parents of their grieving son, without ignoring their roles as grandparents to the living grandchildren.

Conclusion

The loss of a family member has many voices. The experience of each mem-ber affects the family no less than the family as a whole: the two are con-nected and interrelated. The echoes of continuing bonds with the deceased when heard from a family perspective have many sounds that may change in intensity and volume with the passage of time but will never disappear. They are there and will remain so as each member of the family and the family as a unit continue to maintain bonds with the deceased.

Bowen's emotional wave shock (1991/2004) has a ripple effect and one wave is the grandparents' grief for their grandchild, for their child's grief, and the pain of their "parental failure" to protect their child and his or her family.

Helping grandparents retain their roles as parents as well as grandparents can help them restore a sense of meaning and function as caregivers for their family, specifically when being involved with other siblings. In cases of the family and family members being "stuck" in their grief process, family therapy could help the system by weaving into their life story the meaning of the loss in a more adaptive form.

Part III

Difficulties and Challenges
for Therapists

Chapter 11

Cognitive Models for Therapists Working with Grief: When Helpers Think "Irrationally"

"All men are mortal."—Tolstoy, *The Death of Ivan Illich*

Unlike other types of therapy, therapy with the bereaved confronts therapists with issues of their own mortality and the loss of their own loved ones, issues that need to be dealt with in order to attain understanding of and contain clients' pain (Rubin, 2000). It is therefore not surprising that working with the bereaved is recognized as a strenuous and demanding type of intervention that involves an exceptional emotional load (Malkinson, 2006).

Incorporating REBT principles that distinguish between functional and dysfunctional thinking on those occasions when therapists identify their own personal blocks can endorse more "rational" and efficient work with bereaved clients and in therapists' own lives, and also enable therapists to become more resilient and even experience spiritual growth.

Therapists as Human Beings

Although helping families with a dying patient and families or individuals who have experienced a loss through death are among professionals' routine concerns, this type of work is nevertheless recognized as a "loaded" subject that challenges professionals. Unlike many other psychological problems, death is one issue that professionals are likely to encounter. Death is an inevitable event in human lives, one that professionals have to deal with in relation to themselves as well as with their clients. The medical revolution has placed death in the backyard, and its avoidance has become common in contemporary society (Fieffel, 1987). However, its "irrational" avoidance has not replaced the inevitability of its occurrence. Not only did death not disappear, the number of losses and casualties resulting from wars, terror attacks, traffic accidents, suicide, homicide, and natural disasters is ever increasing, and so is the need to provide help to victims of traumatic losses.

Inasmuch as grief therapy is about death and dying, it involves issues such as fear of death in general, fear of one's own death, and fear of death of loved ones that cannot be avoided. Working with bereaved or dying patients confronts therapists with these issues, whether the fear of dying or the fear of being dead (Neimeyer, 1994; Tomer,1994).

The REBT approach distinguishes between adaptive and maladaptive thinking and emoting. It offers a way which involves neither complete avoidance of the fear of death nor its other extreme, of immersing oneself in it. It involves a search for a balanced attitude within which one is aware of death-related issues and has fears and concerns about death and dying, instead of death anxiety, which prevents self-actualization and hinders professional functioning. From the ABC frame of reference, death is the A (activating event) about which the person has some thoughts (B), and emotional consequences (C) that facilitate resilience and even growth ("I can't prevent death—my own or those of my dear ones—but that does not have to prevent me from living life to its fullest even though it may be difficult at times"). Irrational thoughts (irBs) and their related emotional responses (C), however, may increase distress and impede functioning ("If death is inevitable, life is pointless and worthless"). As Ellis (2002) pointed out, "therapists are members of the human race and prone to various disturbances" (p. 204) or stressors, as in the case of bereavement, which must be dealt with.

A Personal Account

The first time I learned about my own irrational belief, (and it was hard for me to admit its irrationality) was when I did my fellowship training at the Albert Ellis Institute in 1988. By then I was already an experienced therapist who wanted to train in REBT. I was impressed with the model's concept of the ABC connection over an event, which seemed most pertinent to working with bereaved individuals and families to help them experience an adaptive grief process and minimize a maladaptive one. The training involved clinical work, which was supervised by the Institute supervisors, one of whom was

Albert Ellis. I played a taped session with a woman who suffered from depression. After presenting the problem, along with some details about the client and what went on in the session, I played the tape. Sooner than I expected, Dr. Ellis, in his usual roaring voice, said: "Speak up, your voice is so quiet, and this is unhelpful to a depressed client, your soft voice reinforces the woman's way of emoting! Speaking softly is wrong! If you want to help her get out of her depression use a much louder voice." I was very offended because I thought that my way of talking and my quiet voice communicated empathy and warmth to the client; nonetheless, as much as I felt embarrassed, I listened to Ellis's criticism, thought over, and searched for an irrational belief that Ellis was referring to. I came to realize that my way of speaking was related to my wanting to help the woman and empathize with her, and the way to convey it, as I believed, was by talking quietly. I identified my erroneous thinking that empathy and a quiet voice are synonymous. But there was the additional irrational belief that was related to my being criticized: "I, an experienced therapist, must not be criticized!" That is in fact one of the comments made by Ellis (1985): "You may be resistant to surrendering them [irrational beliefs] . . . because first, you may be reluctant to admit that you as a psychotherapist have deep-seated emotional difficulties" (p. 167). An irrational belief, indeed! I looked back at my work with individuals who had suffered a loss and experienced so much pain, and could identify a pattern in my interpretations regarding grief and pain. My tendency was to handle the conversation in a very gentle way, being careful not to impose additional pain; a soft voice, I thought, would be appropriate. Dr. Ellis's comment made me aware of my irrational thinking: "I must be gentle and must not hurt somebody in pain." The outcome was that my listening and responding to people's idiosyncratic experience of pain and grief has changed. I learned that some people benefit more when I speak in a loud and clear voice, whereas others need a quiet and clear voice. I learned that at times a loud voice can convey a message of energy, which the bereaved lacks at a specific moment; sometimes a quiet voice is needed to comfort and support a stormy mood. Identifying the bereaved's needs in a differentiated manner means focusing on their idiosyncratic needs at any given moment in therapy instead of interpreting empathy as a set of reactions that fits all situations.

Working with the Bereaved: Can I Be of Any Help?

In therapy, "help" typically refers to a process aimed at a change, usually for the better or at least signifying some improvement as a result of the therapeutic relationship. In contrast, therapy with the bereaved begins when a change in the client's life has already occurred. Thus help involves assisting the bereaved in their search for ways to adapt to the change and its consequences, and to learn to live with the pain and yearning for the dead person. Helping people at the moment of their devastation also involves caring for them, containing their pain, and cocreating new paths to a life that has changed. At the same time, the right balance must be found between an adaptive and maladaptive grief process, as well as maintaining a balance between the helper's personal and professional needs. A belief that these are possible therapeutic tasks is essential for providing help.

It is not uncommon for therapists to think that people who have suffered a loss through death are so devastated that helping them is difficult and at times almost impossible, a thought that many times leads to experiencing helplessness and questioning one's competence to be professionally helpful. In cognitive models, the distinction between the event and its interpretation is very explicit: the ABC of REBT postulates that the loss is an irreversible event, one over which the bereaved had no control, but in contrast, inner control over one's life from the moment of the death onward is not lost and can be more controllable. Such a distinction provides new paths for additional meaning constructions.

"Irrational blocks" that May Hinder the Therapist

Therapists working with bereaved clients may experience stress related to the challenge they face in helping a client in crisis, and are at times confronted with self-doubts about their ability to do so. Losses under traumatic circumstances expose therapists to an additional source of stress of being vulnerable to their own death or the death of their loved ones. Situations where therapists and clients are "in the same boat," and its impact on each party, have been discussed elsewhere (Geron, Malkinson, & Shamai, 2005).

From a cognitive perspective, the therapist's desire (a rational belief) to help the bereaved may become an obstacle whenever it turns into a dire need (an irrational belief). The therapist's grief-related irrational beliefs can be directed toward the self, others, and the world, and take the form of guilt feelings, feelings of incompetence, countertransference, and overidentification with the client's suffering.

Ellis (1985) identified a number of irrational beliefs (irBs) that often lead to "therapeutic inefficiency." Some of the more common ones are the demanding from me as a therapist that "I have to be successful with all my clients practically at all times"; "I have to be respected and loved by my clients"; and "my clients should feel better as a result of therapy" (1985, pp. 165–166). Thoughts such as: "I must be helpful, I must understand the person who experienced a loss, and I must express my empathy. My client is going through so much pain and I must help him or her to suffer less. I must ease the pain" are examples of irrational blocks.

Although pain is unavoidable in grief, nevertheless it is a source for creating irrational beliefs related to the expectation that successful therapy has taken place only when the bereaved is healed of his or her pain. Failure to do so is interpreted by therapists as, "I failed in healing pain therefore I am a failure." Two erroneous cognitions are evident. One concerns the therapist as a failure and the other is about the demand that grief must be painless. It is an irrational evaluation about the bereaved's experience of discomfort. We as therapists wish to relieve the pain and suffering because seeing people in pain is painful, hence our efforts to try and "cure" it. Seeing an individual in pain and suffering makes one feel uneasy and uncomfortable, and our immediate reaction is to try to help reduce the pain. In the case of grief this is not possible because pain is embedded within it and will remain part of it. This issue of helplessness was addressed by Bowlby (1980): "The loss of a loved person is one of the most intensely painful experiences a human being can suffer, and not only is it painful to experience, but also painful to witness, if only because we are so impotent to help" (p. 7).

Below are some examples that illustrate common erroneous evaluations frequently made by professionals, which reveal their cognitive and emotional responses to working with bereaved clients.

Feelings of Helplessness

"When the mother described in detail how her son was killed I felt helpless and the thought that I could not help her persisted."

"When I listened to the family telling the circumstances of their loss the pain was so overwhelming and there was nothing that I could do."

Inability and Frustration about Themselves

"We started the group and the parents each told their story, and I felt like I will never be able to be of any help."

"I wanted to do something to help but there was nothing I could do, so I sat quietly and said absolutely nothing and felt like I was a worthless professional."

Feelings of Exhaustion and Loss of Control

"I found myself exhausted from listening to the stories about loss and grief."

"The moment I heard there was a suicide bomb I knew I had to go and support the families but couldn't move."

Putting the Self Down

"I must do something to help and if not I am a pretty bad therapist."

"I must not enjoy life when my client is suffering so much."

These statements reflect the difficulties that therapists encounter when working with bereaved clients and reveal that therapists often feel sad and anxious, feel that their belief in themselves as helpers has been shaken, and doubt their skills. These are beliefs that paradoxically increase feelings of helplessness, incompetence, and inadequacy—the helplessness loop.

Another stressful situation for therapists is when bereaved clients, especially those referred to therapy, ask: "How can you help? Can you bring my child back?" Such a question challenges the therapist and often leads to an irrational belief: "If I can't bring the dead child back I can't help." Such a belief expresses feelings of helplessness.

Some irrational beliefs may focus on the circumstances of the loss, in particular when the loss has been a traumatic one. Therapists may think: "The loss is awful and it is really the end of the world; I don't think I could withstand such a horrible death, let alone be of any help." It is an evaluation of the event and the therapist's fear of becoming a victim.

Irrational thinking, especially when the circumstances of the death are violent, can also be directed toward the world's injustices and unfairness: "A therapist may find him or herself experiencing feelings of helplessness, depression, or despair about the uncontrollable forces of nature or human violence" (McCann & Pearlman, 1990, p. 139). In REBT terms, stated as a desire or preference ("The world is unfair and I wish there would be more justice in the world") does not harm therapist's functioning and may even be protective and constructive (McCann & Pearlman, 1990) as opposed to the dire demand about fairness and justice in the world ("There shouldn't be injustices in the world") which is dysfunctional.

Yet another common belief among therapists is the one that they should not enjoy life if their clients undergo so much suffering and pain and they refrain from any activity that involves any such feelings: "I must not do anything I enjoy because my client suffers so much."

Thinking errors can also be expressed in all-or-none or black-and-white forms of errors that increase helplessness and exhaustion.

In the statements cited we can identify the wish that things be different (rational belief) and demanding that because this is one's wish things shouldn't be the way they are (irrational belief). Let us consider the following vignette: A therapist who had experienced the loss of her mother a few months earlier brought her dilemma to supervision, asking how she should respond to a client whose mother had died two weeks earlier. This is what she said:

> My mother was ill but we never suspected that she was so seriously ill. Her death was sudden in that we didn't think that her state would deteriorate so fast. I try to understand, and go over and over again about the details of the last few weeks of her life. This happened a few months after my cousin died of cancer, and I was very much involved with supporting his family. So last week when my client came for therapy I wasn't aware that she was going to discuss the loss of her mother. I hadn't seen her for a number of weeks because I was away. She looked at me and said she knew about my mother's death, and then she started telling me about her mother. The moment she described her experience and relationship with her mother I felt dizzy and couldn't say a word for a moment but then I revived and said something stupid to her. I felt awful. I didn't help her at all. What am I going to do with her in the next session?

Personal and professional elements are intertwined, therefore the identification of personal grief is necessary so that it does not interfere with professional considerations, and vice versa, that professional considerations do not interrupt the personal grieving process. Grieving the loss of her mother a month earlier, as well as the loss of her cousin a few months before, was accepted by the therapist as human and normal. Having to deal with the loss of her client's mother, however, aroused an additional stress, which was explored to reveal the following thinking errors: "I must be helpful to my client;" "I must not think about my personal grief;" "I am an experienced therapist therefore I must not fail;" "She knows about my personal grief and perhaps she will find out that I am weak." These experiences have also been identified among therapists working with traumatized patients.

How can the ABC of REBT be applied by professionals as a way to balance rational and irrational thinking in a more functional way, and construct a resourceful meaning to a strenuous interventions?

Accumulated Effects of Traumatic Events on Therapists

Over the years there has been a growing body of knowledge on the accumulated effects of traumatic events—of which death is one—on caregivers and therapists. With the growing number of mass losses, such as terrorist attacks, earthquakes, tsunamis, and automobile accidents, the probability increases that therapists working with the bereaved will encounter situations where their personal experience interfaces with that of their clients.

Whereas some of the potential hazards are related to the nature of the event, and to the level of direct or indirect exposure, there are situations where therapists themselves may become victims of the traumatic event. For example, working with families who suffered a loss of their dear one as a result of an auto accident is an event where stress is created for the therapist if he or she has been or would have been hurt in similar circumstances. Vulnerability to being exposed to a horrendous event with a high level of threat creates additional stress (Malkinson & Geron, 2006).

Studies suggest that caregivers supporting individuals who have suffered traumatic events are also prone to risks that require attention (Figley, 1995; 2002). A number of terms have been coined to describe this phenomenon: *secondary traumatic stress, compassion fatigue,* and *vicarious traumatization* signify a combination of the therapist's direct and indirect exposure to traumatic events that increase vulnerability to intense stress. Compassion fatigue occurs when therapists themselves are directly exposed to traumatic events. Of interest is the concept of vicarious traumatization proposed by McCann and Pearlman (1990). According to them it refers to "the psychological effects, effects that can be disruptive and painful for the helper and can persist for months or years after work with traumatized persons, . . . these are long-term alterations in the therapists' own cognitive schema, or beliefs, expectations, and assumptions about self and others" (pp. 132–133). It is the prolonged exposure to traumatic experiences of clients that has a profound effect on therapists' belief system about themselves, others, and the world. Although there is a potential for negative accumulated outcome from a cognitive perspective, these changes can be constructively channeled. Therapists need to become aware of the hazards they are exposed to, and identify and assess their dysfunctional beliefs in order to adopt a more realistic worldview of their clients' traumatic activating events. In REBT these are understood as an interaction between the traumatic, horrendous event, its cognitive processing, the emotional consequences (ABC model), and the meaning attributed to it. The application of coping strategies is apparent.

Ways to Protect Therapists and to Increase their Competence

Group counseling for bereaved parents is one of the interventions with the potential to increase therapists' anxiety and self-doubts about their professional competence. The death of a child is considered to be particularly difficult to adapt to because it represents a disruption in the normal course of the life cycle, where parents care for their children and children are expected to die after, not before, their parents (Rubin & Malkinson, 2001). When a group for parents who had lost their children to cancer was planned in a children's hospital, the professional team expressed mixed feelings. On the one hand, this was an innovative move that recognized the parents' needs, but at the same time it aroused many doubts about the professionals' competence to assist parents: "We have seen the parents with their sick children and we know how they feel. How can we help them when we failed to save their child?" They experienced guilt in addition to anxiety. Contacting the parents and offering them a support group was received very positively by the parents. The therapists were pleased with the response, but it also increased their doubts about their ability to alleviate the parents' pain and grief. Preparing for the group included reading relevant literature on parental grief and support groups, sharing and discussing their feelings, normalizing them, and normalizing possible failures in intervention during the group meetings.

A short-term group intervention was provided for the parents. The therapists kept a written record of the group meetings, including a description of their experiences. The first meetings were the most difficult ones because each parent told the group the story of his or her loss. The encounter with a group of parents who had met in the hospital as individual parents fighting for their child's life, and now were grieving that child's death, meant that the therapists had to shift gears from supporting the parents in their efforts to save the child to meeting them when the battle was lost. There was a feeling of failure ("After all we have done to save the child's life, we failed") which needed to be dealt with. Listening to the parents' pain and grief when they were telling who the child was, the stories mixed with a sense of loss of faith in justice and fairness, was difficult for the therapists to grasp. In supervision, both the therapists expressed the loss of their belief in the world as a safe and fair place. At that stage the therapists felt the group was superfluous. They were very skeptical about their professional competence to bring solace to the parents. In many ways there were parallel processes of pain and grief.

Normalizing their own feelings, along with normalizing the parents' feelings, was important. Although it did not stop the pain, it alleviated the pain. From believing that they could not help as they thought they should, therapists changed their belief, saying: "Perhaps allowing the parents to express their difficult pain is helpful. Losing a child is painful."

As the sessions progressed, it was apparent that parents perceived the group as an important social support source where they could share their thoughts, feelings, and questions about family, marital relationships, and relationship with their other children; they felt that the group was a safe place to grieve and talk about the pain without being judged. On the contrary, in the group they were understood as feeling "normal" when crying and laughing at the same time.

As group cohesion and trust developed, the therapists' competence in their ability to lead the group increased. Likewise, their sensitivity to the importance of members' expression of pain enabled them to attend to these issues by feeling more confident without having to avoid or defend themselves when the subjects were brought up. Their level of tolerance to pain was significantly higher. A sense of empowerment was experienced by both therapists and group members.

Listening empathically and nonjudgmentally, providing support and information, and searching for alternative ways to experience life with memories of the dead child were a source of self-worth for the parents and the therapists believed that professionally they had helped the parents. Initiating another group was the best way to describe their confidence in their competence. Providing the parents with the opportunity to form a safe haven was a source for self-growth for them as therapists.

The above description illustrates a number of issues relevant to therapists working with bereaved individuals: (1) Challenges and risks are intertwined and they are not either-or. (2) Vacillation between the two along the intervention is apparent. (3) Frustration directed toward the self or toward the bereaved, avoidance of "loaded" subjects like pain, is mixed with feelings of accomplishment and competence. Arnold, Calhoun, Tedeschi, and Cann (2005) report that working with bereaved families who suffered a traumatic loss is strenuous and risky but also has the potential to facilitate clients' posttraumatic growth.

Posttraumatic growth in clients is described by Neimeyer (2005) as positive changes resulting from the struggle with life crises. Similarly, therapists working with bereaved clients can experience positive changes as well (Malkinson & Geron, 2006). Calhoun and Tedeschi (1999) observed that positive changes experienced as a result of a major life crisis can be organized into three categories: Changes in self-perception; interpersonal relationships; and philosophy of life. Additional themes characteristic of posttraumatic growth include feelings of mission, experiencing the client's posttraumatic growth, a sense of satisfaction in helping clients overcome their trauma, developing empathy, growing professionally through acquiring additional ability in therapeutic interventions, and adopting a more realistic and proportionate life philosophy that life is not either-or, but that good and bad coexist. Also identified was the ability to develop feelings of resilience that increased a sense of self-empowerment.

It was noted that bereavement as a result of death under violent, traumatic circumstances is horrendous. Moreover, therapists who work under a constant threat of potentially being hurt may experience increased compassion fatigue and burnout, as well as increased resilience, self-empowerment, improved professional performance, and personal growth.

From the REBT perspective, irrational negative evaluation increases the likelihood of professionals developing secondary traumatization, whereas rational negative evaluation will moderate it. It can be followed potentially by alternative evaluations, some of which may even be positive. On the other hand, positive evaluations would probably result in posttraumatic growth.

How to Help the Helper

How do we take care of ourselves as therapists who work with bereaved and traumatized individuals? As is postulated by cognitive therapies for clients with impaired thinking, by identifying our emotional distress and the associated irrational belief, a B-C connection is established. This can then be followed with a thought restructuring or self-talk to change the belief into a rational one. Ellis suggested the following: "Consider these irBs as hypotheses—not facts—that you can dispute and surrender" (1985, p. 168). It is important to change our philosophy of demandingness to one of preference and recognizing our limitations and weaknesses in helping, and our capabilities as human beings and therapists. Truly, working with those who have experienced a loss and are grieving is a reminder of our own and our loved ones' mortality.

Furthermore, experiencing helplessness, which is automatically avoided for fear it will prevent us from effectively helping the bereaved, followed with an evaluation that it is a sign of weakness and failure, may increase the likelihood of developing vicarious traumatization. Viewing it totally negatively and fighting helplessness ("I must not feel helpless, otherwise I will feel like a failure") is what blocks us. If on the other hand, we allow ourselves to reexamine our evaluations of helplessness not as a weakness or professional incompetence, but rather as a normal response, then we will rediscover the humanity of helplessness. This will enable us to view it not as a *cause* of compassion or fatigue but as a human response to a traumatic event and as a *source* of compassion and part of our professional canon, as well as part of our human experience.

Evidently, there is no single right way for therapists to enhance their effectiveness in doing grief therapy. We have elaborated on the cognitive perspective that focuses on correcting thinking errors and creating a meaning for the work with "wounded clients," realizing that we too as therapists are sometimes "wounded healers" (Alexander & Lavie, 2000). The Hasidim quote Rabbi Menachem Mendel of Kutz as saying: "There is nothing more complete than a broken heart."

References

Alexander, A., & Lavie, Y. (2000). The "wounded healer": Group co-therapy with bereaved parents. In R. Malkinson, S. Rubin, & E. Witztum (Eds.), *Traumatic and nontraumatic loss and bereavement: Clinical theory and practice.* (pp. 231–254). Madison, CT: Psychosocial Press.

American Psychiatric Association. (1994). *Diagnostic and statistical manual of mental disorders* (4th ed.). Washington, DC: Author.

American Psychiatric Association. (2000). *Diagnostic and statistical manual of mental disorders* (text rev.). Washington, DC: Author.

Aponte, H. J., & Van Deusen, J. M. (1981). Structural family therapy. In A. S. Gurman & D. P. Kniskern (Eds.), *Handbook of family therapy* (pp. 310–360). New York: Brunner/Mazel.

Archer, J. (1999). *The nature of grief: The evolution and psychology of reactions to loss.* New York: Routledge.

Ariel-Henig, L. (1998). *Listening to bereavement: Analysis of parents' interviews regarding relationship to the deceased and living children.* Unpublished MA thesis, University of Haifa.

Arnold, D., Calhoun, G. L., Tedeschi, R., & Cann, A. (2005). Vicarious posttraumatic growth in psychotherapy. *Journal of Humanistic Psychology, 45* (2), 239–263.

Artlet, T. A., & Thyer, B. A. (1998). Treating chronic grief. In J. S. Wodarsky & B. A. Thyer (Eds.), *Handbook of empirical social work practice* (Vol. 2, pp. 341–356). New York: Wiley.

Asmar-Kawar, N. (2001). *Perceptions of loss among Jews and Arabs: Culture, gender and the two-track model of bereavement.* Unpublished MA thesis, Tel Aviv University.

Attig, T. (1996). *How we grieve: Relearning the world.* New York: Oxford University Press.

Attig, T. (2000). *The heart if grief: Death and the search for lasting love.* New York: Oxford University Press.

Aviad, Y. (2001). *The social construction of children's responses to the loss of a parent: Evaluating the contributions of the two-track model of bereavement and relationship to the surviving parent.* Unpublished MA thesis, University of Haifa.

Baruth, L. G., & Huber, C. H. (1989). *Rational emotive family therapy.* New York: Springer Publishing Company.

Beck, T. A. (1963). Thinking and depression. *The Archives of General Psychiatry, 9,* 324–333.

Beck, T. A. (1964). Thinking and depression: Theory and therapy. *Archives of General Psychiatry, 10,* 561–571.

Beck, T. A. (1967). *Depression: Clinical, experimental and theoretical disorders.* New York: Harper & Row.

Beck, A. T. (1976). *Cognitive therapy and the emotional disorders.* New York: International Universities Press.

Beck, A. T. (1989). Cognitive therapy. In A. Freeman, K. M. Simon, L. E. Beutler, & H. Arkowitz (Eds.), *Comprehensive handbook of cognitive therapy* (pp. 21–36). New York: Plenum Press.

Beck, T. A. (1993). Cognitive therapy: Past, present and future. *Journal of Consulting and Clinical Psychology, 61* (2), 194–198.

Beck, A. T. (1996). Beyond belief: A theory of modes, personality, and psychopathology. In P. M. Salkovskis (Ed.), *Frontiers of cognitive therapy* (pp. 1–25). New York: Guilford.

Beck, A. T. (2006). How an anomalous finding led to a new system of psychotherapy. *Nature Medicine, 12* (10), 1139–1141.

Beck, A. T., Emery, G., & Greenberg, R. L. (1985). *Anxiety disorders and phobias: A cognitive perspective.* New York: Basic Books.

Beck, A. T., Rush, A. J., Shaw, B. F., & Emery, G. (1979). *Cognitive therapy for depression.* New York: Guilford.

Beck, A. T., Wright, F. W., Newman, C. F., & Liese, B. (1993). *Cognitive therapy in substance abuse.* New York: Guilford.

Black, D., Newman, M., Harris-Hendriks, J., & Mezey, G. (Eds.). (1997). *Psychological trauma.* London: Gaskel.

Blanco, C., Lipsitz, J., & Caligor, E. (2001). Treatment of chronic depression with a 12-week program of interpersonal psychotherpay. *American Journal of Psychiatry, 153* (3), 371–375.

Boelen, P. A., Van den Bout, J., De Keijser, J. (2003). Traumatic grief as a disorder distinct from bereavement-related depression and anxiety: A replication study with bereaved mental health care patients. *American Journal of Psychiatry, 160,* 1229–1241.

Boelen, P. A., Van den Bout, J., Van den Hout, M. A. (2003). The role of cognitive variables in psychological functioning after the death of a first degree relation. *Behaviour Research and Therapy, 41,* 1123–1136.

Bonanno, G. A. (2001). Grief and emotion: A social functioning perspective. In M. S. Stroebe, W. Stroebe, & R. O. Hansson (Eds.), *Handbook of bereavement research: Consequences of coping and care* (pp. 493–516). Cambridge, U.K.: Cambridge University Press.

Bonanno, G. A. (2004). Loss, trauma and the human resilience. *American Psychologist, 59,* 20–28.

Bonanno, G. A., & Field, N. P. (2001). Evaluating the delayed grief hypothesis across 5 years of bereavement. *American Behavioral Scientist, 44,* 798–816.

Bonanno, G. A., & Kaltman, S. (2001). The varieties of grief experience. *Clinical Psychology Review, 20,* 1–30.

Bonanno, G. A., Wortman, C. B., Lehaman, D. R., Tweed, R. G., Haring, M., Sonnega, J., et al. (2002). Resilience to loss and chronic grief: A prospective study from preloss to 18 months postloss. *Journal of Personality and Social Psychology, 83* (5), 1150–1164.

Bonanno, G. A., Wortman, C. B., & Nesse, R. M. (2004). Prospective patterns of resilience and maladjustment during widowhood. *Psychology of Aging, 19,* 260–271.

Bowen, M. (2004). Family reaction to loss. In F. Walsh & M. McGoldrick (Eds.), *Death in the family* (2nd ed.) (pp. 47–60). New York: W.W. Norton. (Original work published 1991).

Bowlby, J. (1960). Grief and mourning in infancy and early childhood. *The Psychoanalytic Study of the Child, 15,* 9–52.

Bowlby, J. (1963). Pathological mourning and childhood mourning. *Journal of American Psychoanalytic Association, 11,* 500–541.

Bowlby, J. (1969). *Attachment and loss: Vol. 1. Attachment.* London: Hogarth.

Bowlby, J. (1973). *Attachment and loss: Vol. 2. Separation, anxiety and anger.* New York: Basic Books.

Bowlby, J. (1980). *Attachment and loss: Volume 3: Loss, sadness and depression.* London: Hogarth.

Bowlby, J. (1988).Developmental psychiatry comes of age. *American Journal of Psychiatry, 145,* 1–10.

Breuer, J., & Freud, S. (1955). Studies on hysteria. In J. Strachey (Ed. & Trans.), *The standard edition of the complete psychological works of Sigmund Freud*, (Vol. 2) (pp. 1–311). London: Hogarth Press. (Original work published 1883–1895).

Brom, D., & Kleber, R. (2000). Coping with trauma and coping with grief: Similarities and differences. In R. Malkinson, S. Rubin, & E. Witztum (Eds.), *Traumatic and Nontraumatic Loss and Bereavement: Clinical Theory and Practice* (pp. 41–66). Madison, CT: Psychosocial Press.

Burns, D. (1989).*The feeling good handbook: Using the new mood therapy in everyday life.* New York: Morrow.

Calhoun, L. G., & Tedeschi, R. T. (1999). *Facilitating posttraumatic growth: A clinician's guide.* Mahawah, NJ: Earlbaum.

Caplan, G. (1964). *Principles of preventive psychiatry.* New York: Basic Books.

Cecchin, G., Lane, G., & Ray, W. A. (1992). *Irreverence: A strategy for therapists' survival.* London: Karnac Books.

Christ, G. H., Bonanno, G. A., Malkinson, R., Rubin, S. S. (2003). Bereavement experiences after the death of a child. In M. J. Field, and R. E. Behrman (Eds.), *When children die: Improving palliative and end-of-life care for children and their families.* Washington, DC: National Academy Press.

Clark, D. (1986). A cognitive approach to panic. *Journal of Behavior Research & Therapy,* 24 (4), 461–470.

Cudmore, L., & Judd, D. (2001). Traumatic loss and the couple. In C. Clulow (Ed.), *Adult attachment and couple psychotherapy* (pp. 152–170). New York: Brunner-Routledge.

Cutler, J. L., Goldyne, A., Markowitz, J. C., Devlin, M. J., & Glick, R. A. (2004). Comparing cognitive-behavior therapy, interpersonal psychotherapy, and psychodynamic psychotherapy. *American Journal of Psychotherapy,* 161 (9), 11567–1573.

Dattilio, F. M., & Padesky, C. A. (1990). *Cognitive therapy with couples: A practitioner's guide.* Sarasota, FL: Professional Resource Exchange.

DiClemente, C. C., & Prochaska, J. O. (1982). Self-change and therapy change of smoking behavior: A comparison of cessation and maintenance. *Addictive Behaviors,* 7, 133–142.

DiGiuseppe, R. (1991). Rational-emotive model of assessment. In M. Bernard (Ed.), *Using rational emotive therapy effectively: A practitioner's guide* (pp. 151–170). New York: Plenum.

Doka, K. J. (1989). Disenfranchised grief. In K. J. Doka (Ed.), *Disenfranchised grief: Recognizing hidden sorrow* (pp. 3–11). Lexington, MA: Lexington Books.

Dryden, W. (1991). *Reason and therapeutic change.* London: Whurr.

Dryden, W. (2002). *Fundamentals of rational emotive behavior therapy: A training handbook.* London: Whurr.

Dunmore, E., Clark, D. M., & Ehlers, A. (2001). A prospective investigation of cognitive factors in persistent posttraumatic stress disorder (PTSD) after physical or sexual assault. *Behaviour Research and Therapy,* 39, 1063–1084.

Edelstein, L. (1984). *Mental bereavement.* New York: Praeger.

Ellis, A. (1962). *Reason and emotion in psychotherapy.* Secaucus, NJ: Lyle Stewart.

Ellis, A. (1976). The biological basis of human irrationality. *Journal of Individual Psychology,* 32, 145–168.

Ellis, A. (1985). *Overcoming resistance: Rational-emotive therapy with difficult clients.* New York: Springer.

Ellis, A. (1986). Discomfort anxiety: A new cognitive behavioral construct. In A. Ellis & R. Griager (Eds.), *RET handbook of rational emotive therapy* (Vol. 2) (pp. 105–120). New York: Springer.

Ellis, A. (1991). The revised ABC's of rational-emotive therapy (RET). *Journal of Rational Emotive and Cognitive Behavior Therapy,* 9 (3), 139–172.

Ellis, A. (1993). Rational-emotive imagery: RET version. In M. E. Bernard & J. L. Wolfe (Eds.), *The RET resource book for practitioners* (pp. II.8–II.10). New York: Institute for Rational-Emotive Therapy.

Ellis, A. (1994a). *Reason and emotion in psychotherapy. A comprehensive method of treating human disturbances* (Rev. ed.). New York: Birch Lane.

Ellis, A. (1994b). General semantic and rational emotive behavioral therapy. In P. P. Johnson, D. D. Burland, & U. Klien (Eds.), *More e-prime* (pp. 213–240). Concord, CA: International Society for General Semantic.

Ellis, A. (1994c). Post-traumatic stress disorder (PTSD): A rational emotive behavioral theory. *Journal of Rational Emotive and Cognitive Therapy, 12* (1), 3–26.

Ellis, A. (1995). Rational emotive behavior therapy. In R. J. Corsini & D. Wedding (Eds.), *Current psychotherapies* (5th ed.) (pp. 162–196). Itasca, IL: Peacock.

Ellis, A. (1998). Rational emotive behavior therapy belongs in the constructivist camp. In M. F. Hoyt (Ed.), *The handbook of constructivist therapies* (pp. 83–99). San Francisco: Jossey-Bass.

Ellis, A. (2002). *Overcoming resistance: A rational emotive behavior therapy integrated approach.* New York: Springer.

Ellis, A., & Bernard, M. E. (Eds.). (1985). *Clinical application of rational-emotive therapy.* New York: Plenum.

Ellis, A., & Dryden, W. (1997). *The practice of rational emotive behavior therapy.* New York: Springer.

Epictetus. (1890). *The collected works of Epictetus.* New York: Longmans, Green.

Epstein, S. (1993). Bereavement from the perspective of cognitive-experiential self-theory. In M. S. Stroebe, W. Stroebe, & R. O. Hansson (Eds.), *Handbook of bereavement: Theory, research and intervention* (pp. 112–125). Cambridge, U.K.: Cambridge University Press.

Eysenck, H. J. (1967). Single-trial conditioning, neurosis and the Napalkov phenomenon. *Behavior Research and Therapy, 5,* 63–65.

Exline, J. J., Dority, K., & Wortman, C. B. (1996). Coping with bereavement: A research review for clinicians. *In Session: Psychotherapy in Practice, 2* (4), 3–19.

Faschingbauer, T. R. (1981). *Texas revised inventory of grief manual.* Houston: Honeycomb.

Fiefel, H. (1987). Grief and bereavement: An overview and perspective. *Society and Welfare, 7* (3), 203–209 (in Hebrew).

Field, N. P., Gao, B., & Paderna, L. (2005). Continuing bonds in bereavement: An attachment theory based perspective. *Death Studies, 29,* 1–23.

Figley, C. R. (1995). *Compassion fatigue: Secondary traumatic stress.* New York: Brunner/Mazel.

Figley, C. R. (2002). Compassion fatigue: Psychotherapists' chronic lack of self-care. *Psychotherapy in Practice, 58* (11), 1433–1441.

Fleming, S., & Robinson, P. (2001). Grief and cognitive-behavioral therapy: The reconstruction of meaning. In M. S. Stroebe, W. Stroebe, & R. O. Hansson (Eds.), *Handbook of bereavement* (pp. 647–669). Cambridge, U.K.: Cambridge University Press.

Foa, E., & Rothbaum, B. (1998). *Treating the trauma of rape: Cognitive-behavioral therapy for PTSD.* New York: Guilford.

Foa, E. B., Dabcu, C.V., Hembree, E.A., et al. (1999). The efficacy of exposure therapy, stress inoculation training and their combination in ameliorating PTSD for female victims of assault. *Journal for Consulting and Clinical Psychology, 67,* 194–200.

Freeman, A., & White, D. M. (1989). The treatment of suicidal behavior. In A. Freeman, K. M. Simon, L. E. Beutker, & H. Arkowitz (Eds.), *Comprehensive handbook of cognitive therapy* (pp. 231–346). New York: Plenum.

Freud, E. L. (Ed.). (1961). *Letters of Sigmund Freud.* New York: Basic. *346* (13), 982–987.

Freud, S. (1957). Mourning and Melancholia. In J. Strachey (Ed. and Trans.), The standard edition of the complete psychological works of Sigmund Freud (Vol. 14, pp. 239–58). London: Hogarth. (Original work published 1917).

Gauthier, Y., & Marshall, W. L. (1977). Grief: A cognitive-behavioral analysis. *Cognitive Therapy Research, 1,* 39–44.

Gelcer, E. (1983). Mourning is a family affair. *Family Process, 22,* 501–516.

Geron, Y., Malkinson, R., & Shamai, M. (2005). Families in war zone: Narratives of the "me" and the "other" in the course of therapy. In J. Kliman (Ed.), *Touched by war zones, near and far: Oscillations of despair and hope* (pp. 17–28). AFTA Monographs Series, 1 (1). Washington, DC: American Family Association Academy.

Gluhosky, V. L. (1995). A cognitive perspective on bereavement: Mechanisms and treatment. *Journal of Cognitive Psychotherapy: An International Quarterly, 9* (2), 75–80.

Goffer-Shnarch, M. (2006). *A comparison of bereaved and non-bereaved adults from the perspective of the Two-Track Model of Bereavement: On functioning and relationship to the parent.* Unpublished MA thesis, University of Haifa.

Goldfried, M. R. (1995). *From cognitive-behavior therapy to psychotherapy integrated.* New York: Springer.

Green, B. L., Grace, M. C., Lindy, J., Gleser, G., & Goldine, C. (1990). Risk factors and PTSD and other diagnoses in Vietnam veterans. *Journal of Anxiety Disorders, 4* (1), 31–39.

Green, B. L., Krupnick, J. L., Stockton, P., Corcoran, C., & Petty, R. (2001). Psychological outcome of traumatic loss in young women. *American Behavioral Scientist, 44* (5), 265–266.

Hackman, A. (1993). Behavioral and cognitive psychotherapies: Past history, current application and future registration issues. *Behavioral and Cognitive Psychotherapy, 21* (suppl.1), 1–75.

Hansson, R. O., & Stroebe, M.S. (2003). Grief, older adulthood. In T. Gullota & M. Bloom (Eds.), *Encyclopedia of primary prevention and health promotion* (pp. 515–521), New York: Kluwer Academic/Plenum.

Harvey, J. H. (2002). *Perspective on loss and trauma assaults on the self.* London: Sage Publications.

Hensley, P.A. (2006). A review of bereavement-related depression and complicated grief. *Psychiatric Annals, 36(9),* 619–626.

Hogan, N., & DeSantis, L. (1996). Basic constructs of a theory of adolescent sibling bereavement. In D. Klass, P. R. Silverman & L. Nickman (Eds.), *Continuing bonds* (pp. 113–124). Washington, DC: Taylor & Francis.

Hogan, N., Worden, J. W., & Schmidt, L. A. (2004). An empirical study of the proposed complicated grief disorder criteria. *Omega, 48* (3), 263–277.

Horowitz, M. (1979). *States of minds.* New York: Plenum.

Horowitz, M. J. (1986). *Stress response syndrome* (2nd ed.). Northvale, NJ: Jason Aronson. (Original work published 1976).

Horowitz, M. J. (1990). A model of mourning: Change in schemas in self and other. *Journal of American Psychoanalytic Association, 38,* 297–324.

Horowitz, M. J. (2001). *Stress response syndromes.* (4th ed.). Northvale, NJ: Jason Aronson.

Horowitz, M. J. (2003). *Treatment of stress response syndromes.* Washington, DC: American Psychiatric Association.

Horowitz, M. J. (2006). Meditating on complicated grief disorder as a diagnosis. *Omega, 51* (1), 87–89.

Horowitz, M. J., Bonanno, G. A., & Holen, A. (1993). Pathological grief: Diagnosis and explanation. *Psychosomatic Medicine, 55,* 260–273.

Horowitz, M. J., Field, N., & Classen, C. C. (1993). Stress response syndromes and their treatment. In L. Goldberg & S. Breznitz (Eds.). *Handbook of stress: Theoretical and clinical aspects* (pp. 757–773). New York: The Free Press.

Horowitz, M. J., Siegel, B., Holen, A., Bonnano, G. A., Milbrath, C., & Stinton, C. H. (1997). Diagnostic criteria for complicated grief. *American Journal of Psychiatry, 154* (7), 904–910.

Horowitz, M., Marmar, C., Weiss, D., De Witt, K., & Rosenbaum, R. (1984). Brief psychotherapy of bereavement reactions. *Archives General Psychiatry, 41,* 437–448.

Horowitz, M., Weiss, D., Kaltreider, N., Krupnick, J., Wilner, N., Marmar, C., & De Witt, K. (1984). Reactions to the death of a parent: Results from patients and the field subjects. *Journal of Nervous and Mental Disease, 172,* 383–392.

Horowitz, M. J., Wilner, N., & Alvarez, W. (1979). Impact of event scale: A measure of subjective stress. *Psychosomatic Medicine, 41,* 209–218.

Horowitz, M., Wilner, N., Marmar, C., & Krupnick, J. (1980). Pathological grief and the activation of latent self-images. *American Journal of Psychiatry, 137,* 1157–1162.

Huber, C. H., & Baruth, L. G. (1989). *Rational emotive family therapy.* New York: Springer.

Jacobs, S. (1999). *Traumatic Grief: Diagnosis, Treatment and Prevention.* Philadelphia: Brunner/Mazel.

Jacobs, S., & Prigerson, H. G. (2000). Psychotherapy of traumatic grief: A review of evidence for psychotherapeutic treatment. *Death Studies, 24*(6), 479–495.

Jacobs, S., & Prigerson, H. (2000). Psychotherapy of traumatic grief: A review of evidence for psychotherapeutic treatments. *Death Studies, 24,* 479–495.

Jacobson, E. (1938). *Progressive relaxation.* Chicago: University of Chicago Press.

Janoff-Bulman, R. (1992). *Shattered assumption: Towards a new psychology of trauma.* New York: Free Press.

Johnson, S. M. (2002). *Emotionally focused couple therapy with trauma survivors.* New York: The Guilford Press.

Jones, E. (1957). *The life and work of Sigmund Freud* (Vol. 3). New York: Basic Books.

Jordan, J. R., & Neimeyer, R. A. (2003). Does grief counseling work? *Death Studies, 27* (9) 765–786.

Kaltman, S., & Bonanno, G. A. (2003). Trauma and bereavement: Examining the impact of sudden and violent deaths. *Journal of Anxiety Disorders, 17,* 131–147.

Karniel-Lauer, E. (2003). *Post Traumatic Stress Disorder and Grief Response: Their Inter-Relationship, and the Contribution of Damage to "World Assumption" and "Self Perception."* Unpublished doctoral dissertation, Tel Aviv University, Tel Aviv, Israel.

Kato, P. M., & Mann, T. (1999). A synthesis of psychological intervention for the bereaved. *Clinical Psychology Review, 19* (3), 275–296.

Kauffman, J. (2001). Mourning. In G. Howarth & O. Leaman (Eds.), *Encyclopedia of death and dying* (pp. 311–314). New York: Routledge.

Kauffmann, J. (2002). (Ed.). *Loss of the assumptive world: A theory of traumatic loss.* New York: Brunner-Routledge.

Kavanagh, D. J. (1990). Towards a cognitive-behavioral intervention for adult grief reactions. *British Journal of Psychology, 157,* 373–383.

Kelly, G. A. (1991). *The psychology of personality constructs.* New York: W.W. Norton. (Original work published 1955).

Kelly, G. A. (1963). *A theory of personality: The psychology of personal constructs.* New York: W.W. Norton.

Kissane, D. W., & Bloch, S. (1994). Family grief. *British Journal of Psychiatry, 164,* 728–740.

Klass, D., Silverman, P. S., & Nickman, L. (Eds.). (1996). *Continuing bonds.* Washington, DC: Taylor & Francis.

Kleber, R. J., Brom, D., & Defares, P. B. (1992). *Coping with trauma: Theory, prevention and treatment.* Amsterdam: Sweft & Zeitlinger Publishers.

Klerman, G. L., Weissman, N. M., Rounsaville, B. J., & Chevron, E. S. (1984). *Interpersonal psychotherapy for depression.* New York: Basic Books.

Kubany, S. E., & Manke, F. P. (1995). Cognitive therapy for trauma-related guilt: Conceptual bases and treatment outlines. *Cognitive and Behavioral Practice, 2,* 27–61.

Kübler-Ross, E. (1969). *On death and dying.* New York: Macmillan.

Kuhn, T. (1970). *The structure of scientific resolution* (2nd ed.). Chicago University of Chicago Press.

Lehaman, D. R., Wortman, C. B. & Williams, A. F. (1987). Long-term effect of losing a spouse or a child in a motor vehicle crash. *Journal of Personality and Social Psychology, 52,* 218–231.

Lewis, C. S. (1961). *Grief observed.* New York: Bantam Books.

Lieberman, E., Compton, N. C., Van Horn, P., & Gosh Ippen, C. (2003). *Losing a parent to death in the early years: Guidelines for the treatment of traumatic bereavement in infancy and early childhood.* Washington, DC: Zero to Three Press.

Lindemann, E. (1944). Symptomatology and management of acute grief. *American Journal of Psychotherapy, 101,* 141–148.

Lindemann, E. (1979). *Beyond grief: Studies in crisis intervention.* New York: Jason Aronson.

Liese, B. S., & Franz, R. A. (1996). Treating substance use disorder with cognitive therapy: Lessons learned and implications for the future. In P. Salkovskis (Ed.), *Frontiers of cognitive therapy* (pp. 470–508). New York: Guilford.

Litterer Allumbaugh, D., & Hoyt, W. T. (1999). Effectiveness of grief therapy: A meta-analysis. *Journal of Counseling Psychology, 46,* 370–380.

Lou Reed, M. (2000). *Grandparents cry twice.* Amityville, NY: Baywood.

Lou Reed, M. (2003). Grandparents' grief—who listens. *The Forum, Association for Death Education and Counseling, 29* (1), 1–4.

Lund, D. A. (1989). Conclusions about bereavement in later life and implications for interventions and future research. In D. A. Lund (Ed.), *Old bereaved spouses* (pp. 217–231). New York: Hemisphere.

Lund, D. A., Castera, M. S., & Dimond, M. F. (1993). The course of spousal bereavement in later life. In M. S. Stroebe, W. Stroebe, & R. O. Hansson (Eds.), *Handbook of bereavement: Theory, research and intervention* (pp. 240–254). Cambridge, U.K.: Cambridge University Press.

Mahoney, M. J. (1991). *Human change processes.* New York: Basic Books.

Mahoney, M. J. (1993). Introduction to special section: Theoretical developments in cognitive psychotherapies. *Journal of Consulting and Clinical Psychology, 61,* (2), 187–193.

Mahoney, M. J. (2004). *Constructive Psychotherapy: Practice and Theory.* New York: The Guilford Press.

Mahoney, M. J. (2004a). *Scientist as subject: The psychological imperative.* Clinton Corner, NY: Eliot Werner.

Malkinson, R. (1993). Rational emotive therapy in bereavement. In R. Malkinson, S. Rubin, & E. Witztum (Eds.), *Loss and bereavement in Jewish society in Israel* (pp. 95–116). Jerusalem: Cana Ministry of Defense (in Hebrew).

Malkinson, R. (1996). Cognitive behavioral grief therapy. *Journal of Rational-Emotive and Cognitive-Behavioral Therapy, 14* (4), 156–165.

Malkinson, R. (2001). Cognitive behavioral therapy of grief: A review and application. *Research on Social Work Practice, 11* (6), 671–698.

Malkinson, R.,& Bar-Tur, L. (2004–2005). Long-term bereavement processes of older parents: The three phases of grief. *Omega, 50* (2), 103–129.

Malkinson, R., & Ellis, A. (2000). The application of rational-emotive behavior therapy (REBT) in traumatic and non-traumatic grief. In R. Malkinson, S. Rubin, & E. Witztum (Eds.), *Traumatic and non-traumatic loss and bereavement: Clinical theory and practice* (pp.173–196). Madison, CT: Psychosocial Press.

Malkinson, R., & Geron, Y. (2006). Intervention continuity in post traffic fatality: From notifying families of the loss to establishing a self-help group. In E. K. Rynearson (Ed.), *Violent death: Resilience and intervention beyond the crises.* New York: Routledge.

Malkinson, R., Rubin, S., & Witztum, E. (Eds.). (2000). *Traumatic and non-traumatic loss and bereavement: Clinical theory and practice.* Madison, CT: Psychosocial Press.

Malkinson, R., Rubin, S., & Witztum, E. (2005). Terror, trauma and bereavement: Implications for theory and therapy. In Y. Danieli, D. Brom, & J. Sills (Eds.), *The trauma of terrorism: Sharing knowledge and shared care, An international handbook,* (pp. 467–477). New York: Haworth Press.

Malkinson, R., Rubin, S., & Witztum, E. (2006). Therapeutic issues and the relationship to the deceased: Connecting and reworking with "whom" and "what" were lost. *Death Studies,* 30 (9), 797–815.

Malkinson, R., & Witztum, E. (2000). Collective bereavement and commemoration: Cultural aspects of collective myth and the creation of national identity. In R. Malkinson, S. Rubin, & E. Witztum (Eds.), *Traumatic and non traumatic loss and bereavement: Clinical theory and practice* (pp. 295–320). Madison, CT: Psychosocial Press.

Mandell, S. (2003). *The blessing of a broken heart.* New Milford, CT: Toby Press.

Marmar, C. R., Horowitz, M. J., Weiss, D. S., Wilner, N. R., & Kaltreider, N. B. (1988). A controlled trial of brief psychotherapy and mutual-help group treatment of conjugal bereavement. *American Journal of Psychiatry,* 145 (2), 203–209.

Matthews, L. T., & Marwitt, S. J. (2004). Complicated grief and the trend toward cognitive-behavioral therapy. *Death Studies,* 28, 849–863.

Maultsby, M. J., Jr. (1971). Rational emotive imagery. *Rational Living,* 6 (1), 24–27.

Maultsby, M. C., & Ellis, A. (1974). *Techniques for using rational emotive imagery (RETC).* New York: The Institute for Rational Living.

Mawson, D., Marks, I. M., Ramm, L., & Stern, R. S. (1981). Guided mourning for morbid grief: A controlled study. *British Journal of Psychiatry,* 138, 185–193.

McBride, J., Simms, S. (2001). Death in the family: Adapting family systems framework to the grief process. *The American Journal of Family Therapy,* 29, 59–73.

McCann, L., & Pearlman, L. A. (1990). Viacarious traumatization: A framework for understanding the psychological effects of working with victims. *Journal of Traumatic Distress,* 3(1), 131–149.

Meichenbaum, D. (1986). Cognitive-behavior modification. In F. H. Kanfer & A. P. Goldstein(Eds.), *Helping people change* (pp. 60–72). New York: Pergamon.

Melges, F. T., & Demaso, D. R. (1988). Grief-resolution therapy: Reliving, revising and revisiting. *American Journal of Psychotherapy,* 34, 51–61.

Mikulincer, M., & Florian, V. (1996). Emotional reactions to interpersonal loss over the life span: An attachment theoretical perspective. In C. Magai & S. H. McFadden (Eds.), *Handbook of Emotions, Adult Development and Aging* (pp. 269–285). New York: Academic Press.

Mikulincer, M., & Shaver, P. R. (in press). Attachment bases emotion regulation and Posttraumatic adjustment. In D. K. Snyder, J. A. Simpson, & J. N. Hughes (Eds.), *Emotions regulations in families: Pathways to dysfunction and health.* Washington, DC: American Psychological Association.

Miller, L. (2002). Psychological interventions for terroristic trauma: Symptoms, syndromes and treatment strategies. *Psychotherapy:Theory/Research/Practice/Training,* 39(4), 283–296.

Minuchin, S. (1974). *Families and families therapy.* Cambridge, MA: Harvard University Press.

Moore, R. H. (1991). *Traumatic incident reduction: A cognitive emotive resolution of post-traumatic stress disorder (PTSD).* Clearwater, FL: Moore.

Moorey, S. (1996). When bad things happen to rational people: Cognitive therapy in adverse life events. In P. M. Salkovskis (Ed.), *Frontiers of cognitive therapy* (pp. 450–469). New York: Guilford.

Moss, M. S., Moss, S. Z., & Hansson, R. A. (2001). Bereavement and old age. In M. S. Stroebe, W. Stroebe, & R. O. Hansson (Eds.), *Handbook of bereavement* (pp. 241–260). Cambridge, U.K: Cambridge University Press.

Nadeau, J. W. (1998). *Families Making Sense of Death.* Thousands Oaks, CA: Sage.

Neimeyer, R. A. (Ed.). (1994). *Death and Anxiety Handbook: Research, instrumentation and Application.* Washington, DC: Taylor & Francis.

Neimeyer, R. A. (1996). Process interventions for the constructivist psychotherapist. In H. Rosen & K. Kuehlwein (Eds.), *Constructing realities* (pp. 371–411). San Francisco: Jossey-Bass.

Neimeyer, R. A. (1998). Can there be a psychology of loss? In J. Harvey (Ed.), *Perspective on loss: A sourcebook* (pp. 331–341). Philadelphia: Bruner/Mazel.

Neimeyer, R. A. (1999). *Lessons of loss: A guide to coping.* New York: McGraw-Hill.

Neimeyer, R. A. (2002). The language of loss: Grief therapy as a process of meaning making. In R. A. Neimeyer (Ed.), *Meaning reconstruction and the experience of loss* (pp. 261–292). Washington, DC: American Psychological Association.

Neimeyer, R. A. (2004). Research on grief and bereavement: Evaluation and revolution. *Death Studies, 28,* 489–490.

Neimeyer, R. A. (2005a). Re-storying loss: Fostering growth in posttraumatic narrative. In L. Callhoun & R. T. Tedeschi (Eds.), *Handbook of postraumatic growth: Research and practice.* Mahwah, NJ: Earlbaum.

Neimeyer, R. A. (2005b). Widowhood, grief and the quest for meaning: A narrative perspective on resilience. In D. Carr, R. M. Nesse, & C. B. Wortman (Eds.), *Late life widowhood in the United States.* New York: Springer.

Neimeyer, R. A. (2006). Complicated grief and the quest for meaning: A constructivist contribution. *Omega, 52* (1), 37–52.

Neimeyer, R. A., & Hogan, N. (2001). Quantitative or qualitative: Measurement issues in the study of grief. In M. S. Stroebe, R. O. Hansson, W. Stroebe, & H. Schut (Eds.), *Handbook of bereavement and research: Consequences coping and caring* (pp. 89–118). Washington, DC: American Association of Psychology.

Neimeyer, R. A., & Jordan, J. R. (2002). In K. Doka (Ed.), *Disenfranchised grief* (pp. 95–117). Champaign, IL: Research Press.

Neimeyer, R. A. & Jordan, J. R. (2002). Disenfranchisement as empathic failure: Grief-therapy and the co-construction of meaning. In K. Doka (Ed.). *Disenfranchised Grief* (pp. 95–117). Champaign, IL: Research Press.

Neimeyer, R. A., Keese, N. J., & Fortner, B. V. (2000). Loss and meaning recontruction: Proposition and procedures. In R. Malkinson, S. Rubin, & E. Witztum (Eds.), *Traumatic and nontraumatic loss and bereavement* (pp. 197–230). Madison, CT: Psychosocial Press.

Neimeyer, R. A., Prigerson, H. G., & Davies, B. (2002). Mourning and meaning. *American Behavioral Scientist, 46* (2), 235–251.

NFO Research. (1999, June). When a child dies: A survey of bereaved parents. *Forum Newsletter, 25*(6), 1, 10–11. (Survey undertaken on behalf of The Compassionate Friends)

O'Connor, M., Nikoletti, S., Kristjanson, L. J., Faaaai, R. L., & Willcock, B. (2003). Writing therapy for the bereaved: Evaluation of an intervention. *Journal of Palliative Medicine, 6*, (2), 195–205.

Palzzoli, M. S., Boscolo, L., Checcin, G. & Prata, G. (1980). Hypothesizing-circularity-neutrality: Three guidelines for the conductor of the session. *Family Process, 19*(1), 3–12.

Parad, H. J. (1965). *Crisis interventions: Selected readings.* New York: McGraw-Hill.

Parkes, C. M. (1965). Bereavement and mental illness. Part I. A clinical study of the grief of bereaved psychiatric patients. Part II. A classification of bereavement reactions. *British Journal of Psychology, 38*, 1–36.

Parkes, C. M. (1970). The first year of bereavement: A longitudinal study of the reaction to loss of London widows to the death of their husbands. *Psychiatry, 33*, 442–467.

Parkes, C. M. (1975). Determinants of outcomes following bereavement. *Omega, 6*, 303–323.

Parkes, C. M. (1985). Bereavement. *British Journal of Psychiatry, 146*, 11–17.

Parkes, C. M. (1988). Bereavement as a psychosocial transition: Processes of adaptation to change. *Journal of Social Issues, 44*, 53–65.

Parkes, C. M. (1993). Bereavement as a psychosocial transition: Processes of adaptation to change. In M. S. Stroebe, W. Stroebe, & R. O. Hansson (Eds.), *Handbook of bereavement: Theory, research and intervention* (pp. 91–102). Cambridge, U.K.: Cambridge University Press.

Parkes, C. M., & Weiss, R. S. (1983). *Recovery from bereavement.* New York: Basic Books.

Penn, P. (1985). Feed-forward: Future questions, future maps. *Family Process, 24*,(3), 299–310.

Pennebaker, J. (1993). Putting stress into words. *Behavior Research and Therapy, 131*, 539–548.

Pennebaker, J. W. (1997). Writing about emotional experiences as a therapeutic process. *American Psychological Society, 8*, 162–166.

Pennebaker, J. W., & Beall, S. K. (1986). Confronting a traumatic event: Towards an understanding of inhibition and disease. *Journal of Abnormal Psychology, 95*, 274–281.

Piaget, J. (1950). *The psychology of intelligence.* New York: Harcourt, Brace.

Piaget, J. (1952). *The Origins of Intelligence in Children.* New York: International Universities Press.

Phill, C., & Zabin, J. L. (1997). Lifelong legacy of early maternal loss: A women's group. *Clinical Social Work Journal, 25*, (2), 179–195.

Pivar, I., & Field, N. G. (2004). Unresolved grief in combat veterans with PTSD. *Journal of Anxiety Disorder, 18*, 745–755.

Pivar, I., & Prigerson, H. (2005). Traumatic loss, complicated grief and terrorism. In Y. Danieli, D. Brom, & J. Sills (Eds.), *The trauma of terrorism. Sharing knowledge and shared care, an international handbook* (pp. 277–288). New York: Haworth.

Polak, P. R., Egan, D., Vandenbergh, R., & Williams, W. V. (1975). Prevention in mental health: A controlled study. *American Journal of Psychiatry, 132* (2), 146–149.

Pollock, G. H. (1989). *The Mourning-Liberation Process.* (Vol. 1.) Madison, CT: International University Press.

Potocky, M. (1993). Effective services for bereaved spouses: A content analysis of the empirical literature. *Health and Social Work, 18*, 288–301.

Prigerson, H. G. (2004). Complicated grief: When the path to adjustment leads to a dead-end. *Bereavement care, 23*, 38–40.

Prigerson, H., Ahmed, I., & Silverman, G. (2002). Rates and risks of complicated grief among psychiatric clinic patients in Karachi, Pakistan. *Death Studies, 26*, 781–792.

Prigerson, H. G., Bierhals, A. J., Kasl, S. V., Reynolds, C. F., Shear, M. K., Day, N., et al. (1997). Traumatic grief as a risk factor for mental and physical morbidity. *American Journal of Psychiatry, 154,* 616–623.

Prigerson, H. G., Frank, E., Kasl, S. V., Reynolds III, C. F., Anderson, B., Zubenko, G. S. et al. (1995). Complicated grief and bereavement-related depression as distinct disorders: Preliminary empirical validation in elderly bereaved spouses. *American Journal of Psychiatry, 152,* 22–30.

Prigerson, H. G., Maciejewski, P. K., Reynolds, C. F., et al. (1995a). Inventory of complicated grief: A scale to measure maladaptive symptoms to loss. *Psychiatry Research, 59,* 65–79.

Prigerson, H., & Jacobs, S. (2001a). Traumatic grief as a distinct disorder: A rationale. Consensus criteria and a preliminary empirical test. In M. S. Stroebe, W. Stroebe, & R. O. Hansson (Eds.), *Handbook of bereavement* (pp. 613–646). Cambridge, U.K.: Cambridge University Press.

Prigerson, H., & Jacobs, S. (2001b). Caring for bereaved patients. *Journal of American Medical Association, 286,* (11), 1369–1376.

Prigerson, H. G., & Maciejewski, P. K. (2006). A call for a sound empirical testing and evaluation of criteria for complicated grief proposed for DSM-V. *Omega, 52* (1), 9–19.

Prigerson, H. G., Maciejewski, P. K., Reynolds III, C. F., Bierhals, A. J., Newsom, J. T., Fasiczka, A., et al. (1995). A scale to measure maladptive symptoms of loss. *Psychiatry Research, 59,* 65–79.

Prigerson, H. G., Shear, M. K., Jacobs, S. C., Reynolds III, C. F., Maciejewski, P. K., Davidson, J. R. T., et al. (1999). Consensus criteria for traumatic grief: A preliminary test. *British Journal of Psychiatry, 174,* 67–73.

Pynoos, R. S., Nader, K., Frederick, C., Gonda, L. & Stuber, M. (1987). Grief reactions in school children following a sniper attack in school. *Israel Journal of Psychiatry, 24,* 53–63.

Ramsay, R. W. (1979). Bereavement: A behavioral treatment of pathological grief. In P. O. Sjodeh, S. Bates, & W. S. Dochens (Eds.), *Trends in behavior therapy* (pp. 217–247). New York: Academic Press.

Rando, T. A. (1984). *Grief, dying and death: Clinical interventions for caregivers.* Champaign, IL: Research Press.

Raphael, B. (1977). Preventive intervention with recently bereaved. *Archives of General Psychiatry, 34,* 1450–1454.

Raphael, B. (1983). *Anatomy of bereavement.* New York: Basic Books.

Raphael, B., & Martinek, M. (1997). Assessing traumatic bereavement and post-traumatic stress disorder. In J. P. Wilson, & T. M. Keane (Eds.), *Assessing psychological trauma and PTSD.* New York: Guilford.

Raphael, B., Middelton, W., Martinek, N., & Misso, V. (1993). Counseling and therapy for the bereaved. In M. S. Stroebe, W. Stroebe, & R. O. Hansson (Eds.), *Handbook of bereavement: Theory, research and intervention* (pp. 427–456). Cambridge, U.K.: Cambridge University Press.

Resick, P. A., & Schnicke, M. K. (1995). *Cognitive processing therapy for rape victims: A treatment manual.* Thousand Oaks, CA: Sage.

Reuveni Ben–Israel, O. (1999). *The effects of time on the adjustment of war-bereaved parents: Functioning, relationship to the deceased son, and influences on the marital relationship.* Unpublished MA thesis, University of Haifa.

Reynolds III, C. F., Miller, M. D., Paternak, R. E., Frank, E., Perel, J. M., Cornes, I. C., et al. (1999). Treatment of bereavement-related major depressive episodes in later life: A controlled study of acute and continuation treatment with nortriptyline and interpersonal psychotherapy. *American Journal of Psychiatry, 156* (2), 202–208.

Random House Dictionary of the English Language (2nd ed.). (1987). New York: Random House.

Richards, D., & Lovell, K. (1997). Behavioral and cognitive approaches. In D. Black, M. Newman, J. Harris-Hendriks, & G. Mezey (Eds.), *Psychological trauma* (pp. 264–274). London: Gaskel.

Rosenblatt, P. (2005). Intimate relationship in bereavement. *Grief Matters, Summer* 50–53.

Rubin, S. S. (1981). A two-track model of bereavement: Theory and application in research. *American Journal of Orthopsychiatry, 51,* 101–109.

Rubin, S. S. (1984a). Mourning distinct from melancholia. *British Journal of Medical Psychology, 57,* 339–345.

Rubin, S. S. (1984b). Maternal attachment and child death. On adjustment, relationship and resolution. *Omega, 15,* 347–352.

Rubin, S. S. (1985).The resolution of bereavement: A clinical focus on relationship to the deceased. *Psychotherapy: Theory, research, training and practice, 22,* 231–235.

Rubin, S. S. (1986). Child death and the family: Parents and children confronting loss. *International Journal of Family Therapy, 7,* 377–388.

Rubin, S. S. (1992). Adult child loss and the Two-Track Model of Bereavement. *Omega, 24* (3), 183–202.

Rubin, S. S. (1993). The death of a child is forever: The life course impact of child loss. In M. S. Stroebe, W. Stroebe, & R. O. Hansson (Eds.), *Handbook of bereavement* (pp. 285–299). Cambridge, U.K.: Cambridge University Press.

Rubin, S. S. (1995). The resolution of bereavement: A clinical focus on the relationship to the deceased. *Psychotherapy, 22,* 231–235.

Rubin, S. S. (1996). The wounded family: Bereaved parents and the impact of adult child loss. In D. Klass, P. R. Silverman, & L. Nickman (Eds.), *Continuing bonds: Understanding the resolution of grief* (pp. 217–232). Washington, DC: Taylor & Francis.

Rubin, S. S. (1999). The Two-Track Model of Bereavement: Prospects and retrospect. *Death Studies, 23,* 681–714.

Rubin, S. S. (2000). Psychodynamic perspective on treatment with bereaved: Modification of the psychotherapeutic-transference paradigm. In R. Malkinson, S. S. Rubin, & E. Witztum (Eds.), *Traumatic and non-traumatic loss and bereavement: Clinical theory and practice* (pp. 117–141). Madison, CT: Psychosocial Press.

Rubin, S. S., & Malkinson, R. (2001). Parental response of child loss across the life cycle: Clinical and research perspective. In M. S. Stroebe, W. Stroebe, & R. O. Hansson (Eds.), *Handbook of bereavement* (pp. 219–240). Cambridge, U.K.: Cambridge University Press.

Rubin, S. S., Malkinson, R., & Ben Nadav, K. (2004). Two Track Bereavement Questionnaire. Unpublished manuscript, University of Haifa.

Rubin, S. S., Malkinson, R., & Witztum, E. (2000). An overview of the field of loss. In R. Malkinson, S. S. Rubin, & E. Witztum (Eds.), *Traumatic and non-traumatic loss and bereavement: Clinical theory and practice* (pp. 5–40). Madison, CT: Psychosocial Press.

Rubin, S. S., Malkinson, R., & Witztum, E. (2003). Trauma and bereavement: Conceptual and clinical issues revolving around relationship. *Death Studies, 27,* 1–23.

Rubin, S. S., Malkinson, R., & Witztum, E. (2005). The sacred and the secular: The changing face of death, loss and bereavement in Israel. In J. D. Morgan & P. Lainngani (Eds.), *Death and bereavement around the world: Vol. 4. Asia, Australia, and New Zealand* (pp. 65–80). New York: Baywood.

Rubin, S. S., & Schechter, N. (1997). Exploring the social construction of bereavement: Perceptions of adjustment and recovery for bereaved men. *American Journal of Orthopsychiatry, 67* (2), 279–289.

Rynearson, E. K. (2001). *Retelling violent death.* New York: Brunner-Routledge.

Sabatiani, L. (1988). Evaluating a treatment program for newly widowed people. *Omega, 19,* 229–236.

Salkovskis, P. (1996). Cognitive therapy and Aaron Beck. In P. Salkovskis, (Ed.), *Frontiers of cognitive therapy* (pp. 531–540). New York: Guilford.

Sanders, C. M. (1980). A comparison of adult bereavement in the death of a spouse, child and a parent. *Omega 10,*303–322.

Sanders, C. M. (1989). *Grief: The mourning after.* New York: Wiley.

Sanders, C. M. (1993). Risk factors in bereavement outcome. In M. S. Stroebe, S. Stroebe, & R.O. Hansson (Eds.), *Handbook of bereavement: Theory, research and intervention* (pp. 255–270). Cambridge, U.K: Cambridge University Press.

Sanders, C. M., Mauger, P. A., & Strong, P. A. (1991). *A manual for the grief experience inventory.* Palo Alto, CA: Consulting Psychologists Press/ Charlotte, NC: Center for the Study of Separation and Loss. (Original work published 1985)

Schefer, R. (1992). Retelling a life: Narrative and dialogue in psychoanalysis. New York: Basic Books.

Schut, H. A.W., de Keijser, J., Van den Bout, J., & Stroebe, M.S. (1996). Cross-modality grief therapy: Description and assessment of a new program. *Journal of Clinical Psychology, 52* (3), 357–365.

Schut, H., Stroebe, M. S., Van den Bout, J., & Terheggen, M. (2001). The efficacy of bereavement interventions: Determining who benefits. In M. S. Stroebe, W. Stroebe, R. O. Hansson, & H. Schut (Eds.), *Handbook of bereavement research: Consequences, coping and caring* (pp. 705–737). Washington, DC: American Psychological Association.

Selvini, P. M., Boscolo, L., Cechin, G., & Prata, G. (1980). Hypothesizing-circularity-neutrality: Three guidelines for the conductor of the session. *Family Process, 19* (1), 3–12.

Shapiro, E. R. (1996). Family bereavement and cultural diversity. A social developmental perspective. *Family Process, 35,* 313–332.

Shaver, P. R., & Tancredy, C. A. (2001). Emotions, attachment and bereavement. In M. S. Stroebe, S. Stroebe, & R. O. Hansson (Eds.), *Handbook of bereavement: Theory, research and intervention* (pp. 63–88). Cambridge, U.K.: Cambridge University Press.

Shear, K., Frank, E., Foa, E., Reynolds III, C. F., Vander Bilt, J., & Masters, S. (2001). Traumatic grief treatment: A pilot study. *American Journal of Psychiatry, 158* (9), 1056–1508.

Shear, K., Frank, E., Houck, P. R., & Reynolds III, C. F. (2005). Treatment of complicated grief: A randomized controlled study. *Journal of American Medical Association, 293,* (21), 2601–2608.

Shear, K., & Smith-Caroff, K. (2000). Traumatic loss and the syndrome of complicated grief. *PTSD Research Quarterly, 13* (2), 2–7.

Shechory, S. (2003). *The subjective experience and the objective assessment of bereaved parents: A longitudinal narrative analysis of bereaved parents.* Unpublished MA thesis, University of Haifa.

Shuchter, S. R, & Zissok, S. (1993). The course of normal grief. In M. Stroebe, W. Stroebe, & R. O. Hansson (Eds.), *Handbook of bereavement: Theory, research and intervention,* (pp. 23–43). New York: Cambridge University Press.

Silverman, P. R. (1981). *Helping women cope with grief.* Beverly Hill, CA: Sage.

Silverman, P. R. (2004). *Widow to Widow* (2nd ed.). New York: Brunner-Routledge.

Silverman, P., Klass, D., & Nickman, S. L. (1996). Introduction: What's the problem? In D. Klass, P. Silverman, & S. L. Nickman (Eds.), *Continuing bonds* (pp. 3–27). Washington, DC: Taylor & Francis.

Silverman, P. R., & Nickman, S. L. (1996). Bereaved children's changing relationship with the deceased. In D. Klass, P. Silverman, & S. L. Nickman (Eds.), *Continuing bonds* (pp. 87–112). Washington, DC: Taylor & Francis.

Sireling, L., Cohen, D., & Marks, I. (1988). Guided mourning for morbid grief: A replication. *Behavior therapy*, 29, 121–132.

Smyth, J. M., Stone, A. A., Hurewitz, A. & Kael, A. (1999). Effects of writing about stressful experiences on symptom reduction in patients with asthma or rheumatoid arthritis. *Journal of American Medical Association*, 281 (14), 1304–1309.

Spence, D. P. (1982). *Narrative truth and historical truth: Meaning and interpretation in psychoanalysis*. New York: W.W. Norton.

Stein, D. J. (1992). Schemas in cognitive and clinical science. *Journal of Psychotherapy Integration*, 2, 45–63.

Stroebe, M. S., & Schut, H. (1999). The dual process model of coping with loss. *Death Studies*, 23, 1–28.

Stroebe, M. S., & Schut, H. (2001). Models of coping with bereavement: A review. In M. S. Stroebe, W. Stroebe, R. O. Hansson, & H. Schut (Eds.), *Handbook of bereavement: research consequences of coping and care* (pp. 375–404). Cambridge, UK: Cambridge University Press.

Stroebe, M., & Schut, H. (2006). Complicated grief: A conceptual analysis of the field. *Omega*, 52 (1), 53–70.

Stroebe, M. S., Schut, H., & Finkenauer, K. (2000). The traumatization of grief? A conceptual framework for understanding the trauma-bereavement interface. *Israel Journal of Psychiatry*, 38, 185–201.

Stroebe, M., Van Son, M., Stroebe, W., Kleber, R., Schut, H., & Van den Bout, J. (2000). On the classification and diagnosis of complicated grief. *Clinical Psychology Review*, 20, 57–75.

Stroebe, W. & Stroebe, M. (1987). *Bereavement and health: The psychological and physical consequences of partner loss*. Cambridge, U.K.: Cambridge University Press.

Stroebe, W., Stroebe, M., Abakoumkin, G., & Schut, H. (1996). The role of loneliness and social support in adjustment to loss: A test of attachment versus stress theory. *Journal of Personality and Social Psychology*, 70, 1241–1249.

Tomer, A. (1994). Death anxiety in adult life—A theoretical perspective. In R. A. Neimeyer (Ed.), *Death anxiety handbook: Research, instrumentation and application* (pp. 3–30). Washington, DC: Francis & Taylor.

Van der Hart, O. (1983). *Rituals in psychotherapy*. New York: Irvington.

Van der Hart, O. (1986). (Ed.). *Coping with loss*. New York: Irvington.

Van der Hart, O. (1987). Leave taking rituals in mourning therapy. [Special issue] *Society & Welfare*, 7 (3), 266–279 (in Hebrew).

Volkan, V. D. (1981). *Linking object and linking phenomena*. New York: International Universities Press.

Walen, S., DiGiuseppe, R., & Dryden, W. (1992). *A practitioner's guide to rational-emotive therapy*. New York: Oxford University Press.

Walen, S., DiGiuseppe, R., & Wessler, R. L. (1980). *A practitioner's guide to rational-emotive therapy*. New York: Oxford University Press.

Walls, N., & Meyers, A. W. (1985). Outcomes in group treatment for bereavement: Experimental results in recommendations for clinical practice. *International Journal of Mental Health*, 13, 349–357.

Walsh, F., & McGoldrick, M. (1991). *Living beyond loss: Death in the family*. New York: W. W. Norton.

Warren, R., & Zgourides, G. D. (1991). Anxiety disorders: A rational emotive perspective. New York: Pergamon Press.

Wiener-Kaufman, E. (2001). *Attitudes of physicians, clinical psychologists and the public towards grief reactions and intervention methods in situations of loss and bereavement: The effect of the bereaved's personality functioning, self-experience and the relationship to the deceased on the evaluation of the bereavement response after loss of a spouse.* Unpublished MA thesis, University of Haifa.

Wijngaards-deMeij, L., Stroebe, M., Schut, H., Stroebe, F., Van de Bout, J., Van der Heijden, P. et al. (2005). Couples at risk following the death of their child: Predictors of grief versus depression. *Journal of Consulting and Clinical Psychology, 73,* 617–623.

Witztum, E. (2005). *Mind, loss and bereavement.* Tel Aviv: The Ministry of Defence publishing House, Israel (in Hebrew).

Witztum, E., Malkinson, R., & Rubin, S. (2005). Traumatic grief and bereavement resulting from terrorism: Israeli and American perspectives. In S. C. Heilaman (Ed.), *Death, bereavement and mourning: What we have learned after 9/11* (pp. 105–120), New Brunswick, NJ: Transaction.

Witztum, E., & Roman, I. (1993). Psychotherapeutic intervention with complicated grief: Metaphor and leave-taking ritual with the bereaved. In R. Malkinson, S. Rubin, & E. Witztum (Eds.), *Loss and bereavement in Jewish society in Israel* (pp.143–172). Jerusalem: Cana Ministry of Defense (in Hebrew).

Worden, J. W. (1982). *Grief counseling and grief therapy:* New York: Springer.

Worden, J. W. (1991). *Grief counseling and grief therapy: A handbook for the mental health practitioner.* New York: Springer (2nd ed).

Worden, J. W. (2003). *Grief counseling and grief therapy: A handbook for the mental health practitioner.* (3rd ed.). New York: Brunner-Routledge. (Original work published 1982).

Wortman, C. M., & Silver, R. (1989). The myth of coping with loss. *Journal of Consulting & Clinical Psychology, 57,* 349–359.

Wortman, C. M., & Silver, R. (1993). The meaning of loss and adjustment to bereavement. In M. Stroebe, W. Stroebe, & R. O. Hansson, (Eds.), *Handbook of bereavement: Theory, research and intervention* (pp. 349–366). Cambridge, U.K.: Cambridge University Press.

Zilberg, N. J., Weiss, D. S., & Horowitz, M. J. (1982). The impact of event scale: A cross validation study and some empirical evidence supporting a conceptual model of stress response syndromes. *Journal of Consulting and Clinical Psychology, 50,* 407–414.

Zisook, S., & Shuchter, S. R. (2001). Treatment of the depression of bereavement. *American Behavioral Scientist, 44* (5), 782–797.

Index

Note: Figures are indicated by *f* following the page number.